# MAKING
# TELEVISION

# Media and Society Series

J. Fred MacDonald, General Editor

# MAKING TELEVISION

## Authorship and the Production Process

*Edited by*
## Robert J. Thompson
*and*
## Gary Burns

**Media and Society Series**

PRAEGER

New York
Westport, Connecticut
London

**Library of Congress Cataloging-in-Publication Data**

Making television : authorship and the production process / edited by
  Robert J. Thompson, Gary Burns.
        p.    cm.—(Media and society series)
    Includes bibliographical references.
    ISBN 0-275-92746-6 (alk. paper)
    1. Television—Production and direction.   2. Television
authorship.   I. Thompson, Robert J., 1959-   .  II. Burns, Gary,
1952-   .  III. Series.
PN1992.75.E9     1990
791.45′0232—dc20        89-48746

Library of Congress Catalog Card Number: 89-48746
ISBN: 0-275-92746-6

First published in 1990

Praeger Publishers, One Madison Avenue, New York, NY 10010
An imprint of Greenwood Publishing Group, Inc.

Printed in the United States of America

The paper used in this book complies with the
Permanent Paper Standard issued by the National
Information Standards Organization (Z39.48-1984).

10 9 8 7 6 5 4 3 2 1

# Contents

# Introduction

The Author is dead and contemporary criticism has written the obituary. Once we recognize that every text—whether it be a novel, a painting, a poem, a symphony, or a TV show—is generated in and by a complex web of cultural, social, political, and formal conventions and expectations, it is irresponsible to continue to look at those texts in the simplistic way they used to be looked at. The old idea that the lone artist-genius is the exclusive source of meaning in a text, and that the role of the critic is to find and explicate this meaning, is no longer tenable in light of the critical theory developed in the past twenty years. To the extent that we cling to the notion of one work/one artist, we become blind to the complexities of how meaning is generated in works of art, and we confine our attention too readily to a specific canon.

While contemporary criticism required a complete retooling of traditional academic industries (such as literary studies), it also assisted in the development of new industries (like TV studies) where the identity of the author had never been clear in the first place. Textual analysis of TV could never be accommodated by traditional criticism partly because TV appeared authorless (or, to be more precise, so confusingly polyauthorial). Questions like "Who is the author of this TV show?" were very hard to answer and contemporary criticism has to some extent let us off the hook.

Nonetheless, the study of TV is suffering because it has announced the death of an author that it never acknowledged in the first place. While we—as readers, users, and teachers of contemporary criticism—certainly do not suggest that the study of TV should regress back to the one work/one artist approach, we do think it is worthwhile to study the human agents who work in the production of television as part of a complex system of communication. It is not our goal to be able to say "*The Love Boat*, by Aaron Spelling," but to explain how *The Love Boat* was produced within the complex structures of the American television system, by a powerful corporation dominated by Aaron Spelling, whose control over the show was significant.

When a helicopter stunt went awry during the filming of *The Twilight Zone: The Movie* in 1983 and left three actors dead, the courts needed someone to summon. John Landis conveniently pointed out in questioning and court testimony that he, as director of the film, was just another employee. If the auteur theory did nothing else, it at least placed a degree of responsibility for a text onto an individual agent. Just as indirect verbs hide the origin of decisions ("your services will no longer be needed"), authorless approaches to art can obfuscate rather than clarify. In an extreme case such as *The Twilight Zone: The Movie*, one might almost say that the "death of the author" provides a handy legal defense reminiscent of the missing corpus delicti.

Legal issues aside, the critic also often needs someone to summon. The essays in this volume suggest numerous candidates for authorial accountability—producers, network and studio executives, directors, and others. The purpose of these chapters is not to assign one author to each text, but to examine how various authors work within the institutional, cultural, and economic settings that characterize the television industry.

# MAKING
# TELEVISION

# Part I
## Authorship Case Study: Hugh Wilson

# 1

# Television Authors: The Case of Hugh Wilson

## *Richard Campbell and Jimmie L. Reeves*

In November 1988, we acted as coleaders of a day-long seminar on *Frank's Place* at the national convention of the Speech Communication Association. Fittingly enough, the host city for the convention was New Orleans (which is the setting for *Frank's Place*). We conceived of the seminar as a critical forum challenging scholars operating from diverse interpretive traditions to make sense of this highly acclaimed series. Television researchers from Louisiana State, Northeastern, Northwestern, Rutgers, Texas Christian, the University of Michigan, the University of Texas, the University of Wisconsin, and other institutions prepared papers for the forum that were based on close textual analyses of five representative episodes of the series.

Three of these papers appear as chapters in this section. All three analyze the aesthetic dimension of the series: one considers the program's authentic sense of place; the second, its provocative use of music; and the third, its cinematic style. In setting the stage for these analytic papers, this chapter will not deal directly with appraising the many achievements of *Frank's Place*. Instead, we hope to render a report on the seminar that condenses and organizes what amounted to a six hour interview session with Hugh Wilson.

Wilson, the creator and executive coproducer of *Frank's Place*, accepted our invitation to attend the seminar in New Orleans. Because of our previous experience with prime-time TV producers (who shall remain nameless), we expected Wilson to be a fast-talking mercenary—brusque and aloof—with an ego the size of Alaska. When he turned out to be a chivalrous southerner who wears his humor and humanity on the sleeve where some people wear their religion, we were, quite frankly, caught off guard. A down-home raconteur in the tradition of Mark Twain and Will Rogers, Wilson seemed to treat the seminar as an opportunity to get a lot of things off his chest. By the end of the day we were left with the feeling that Wilson genuinely relished this encounter with a live audience who appreciated the artistry of *Frank's Place*. As he put it, "making a television show is like sending out a message in a bottle. You never know if anybody ever gets your message."

*Frank's Place* featured the tragicomical experiences of Frank Parrish (played by Tim Reid), a professor of Italian Renaissance history. Parrish is forced to give up his affluent life in Boston when his estranged father dies and Parrish inherits a New Orleans restaurant. The program was one of the most highly acclaimed series of the 1987–88 television season. For example, Michael Pollan, writing for *Channels* magazine, declared *Frank's Place* "revolutionary," "a sitcom of uncommon freshness and a 'black' show of uncommon dignity." And, in an interview with *Newsweek*, Alvin Poussaint (the Harvard psychiatrist who consults for *The Cosby Show*) went so far as to describe *Frank's Place* as a "breakthrough," "the first black show since *Roots* to take black culture seriously." This enthusiasm was shared by many other critics. *Electronic Media*'s semi-annual poll of newspaper reviewers rated *Frank's Place* among the top three shows of the year; only *L.A. Law* and *The Wonder Years* ranked higher.

Unfortunately, after winning three Emmys, *Frank's Place* was cancelled because of low ratings just as the show was set to produce 13 new episodes as a mid-season replacement during the 1988–89 season. Although *Frank's Place* premiered well in fall 1987 (14.9 rating/25 share), its final airing on October 1, 1988, garnered dismal numbers that ranked it among the week's lowest rated network shows (5.6 rating/10 share). As any viewer who tried to follow the show knows, the chief reason for its failure was inept scheduling and promotion on the part of Kim LeMasters, head of CBS's entertainment division. In twelve months, LeMasters moved the show into six different time slots on four different nights. Both Wilson and Reid claim that, eventually, even their own mothers could no longer find the show on the schedule.

Since the forum took place only about a month after CBS finally cancelled the series, Wilson was still hurting from the experience. However, Wilson was not at all reticent about discussing the tragedy of errors that resulted in the demise of the program.

As to why *Frank's Place* failed, I don't think I've got what would be considered a clean test here. When it was run on Saturday night in reruns, we were only on in 82 percent of the markets. Even in Atlanta they weren't running it—they were running a game show. I was really surprised. We were the lowest rated show on television one week. And we were cancelled the next week. My reaction by the time we got cancelled was: "Please. Do it. This is embarrassing. And I'm mad." I like Kim LeMasters a lot, personally. And so does Tim [Reid]. And that's one of the reasons we haven't just raised holy hell over this thing.

Wilson predicts that the failure of *Frank's Place* will have long-term consequences on the future of both television comedy and "black" shows.

Most of the letters I got were from people in the business saying, "My God. How did you do this? How did you pull this off? How did you get the network to go along with this?" If *Frank's Place* had succeeded, it would have had enormous impact. As it turned out, the cancellation was a real blow. The day it got cancelled, every schlockmeister in town used *Frank's Place* as a prime example of what not to do: "You see what happens when you do that?" When a bad shows fails, nobody says, "Let's learn our lesson." When a good show goes down, everybody goes, "Ya see?"

Although we certainly don't have the space to provide a complete transcript of his words, Wilson addressed many issues directly relevant to the theme of this volume. Consequently, in editing the transcript, we have tried to emphasize the following four areas of special interest to media scholars concerned with questions of authorship: the making of a television producer; achieving creative control; the Wilson imprint; and orchestrating a collaboration.

## THE MAKING OF A TELEVISION PRODUCER

Wilson, who is white, earned a journalism degree from the University of Florida in the 1960s. And his journey to *Frank's Place* began at the Armstrong Cork Company in Lancaster, Pennsylvania, where he went to work writing linoleum brochures. Strangely enough, at this job in the heart of Amish country, Wilson met Jay Tarses (who most recently produced *The Days and Nights of Molly Dodd* and *The "Slap" Maxwell Story*) and Tom Patchett (who now produces *Alf*). During their time at Armstrong Cork, Wilson assisted Tarses and Patchett in the staging of an amateur stand-up comedy routine. "Just as a hobby," Wilson remembers, "we'd go out on the weekends and I would sort of work the lights. They did a Nichols and May type thing—but it was not very good. I had to signal the pay-off. You know, if I didn't turn out the lights at the end, the audience didn't know when Tom and Jay delivered the big joke."

Wilson characterizes this early connection with Tarses and Patchett as "a great stroke of luck." Later, both of the future television producers would play decisive roles in aiding and promoting Wilson's early career in Hollywood.

After the Armstrong Cork episode, Wilson went back down south. Settling in Atlanta, he joined an ad agency and became a specialist in radio advertising. Inspired by Stan Freberg's work, Wilson wrote funny radio commercials that won several national awards. Significantly, he stayed in contact with Tarses and Patchett during this period, and earned their gratitude by using them as voice-over talent on some of the radio spots. He lived in Atlanta for ten years, becoming the copy chief and then creative head of the ad agency.

But then Wilson made an audacious career move. In his words:

I became very bored with the advertising business—and I grew not to like it. By this time, Tom and Jay had gone out to Hollywood and their stand-up career was finished, as it rightfully deserved to be. They had gotten jobs on Carol Burnett's writing staff, which was a great place to be. So, I went out to L.A. to shoot a television commercial, and I stayed with Jay.

Tarses helped Wilson set up a meeting with Grant Tinker, who was then the head of MTM Productions. At that meeting, Tinker told Wilson that the only job opening was as student-trainee, a position normally filled by fresh-faced kids from USC or UCLA.

Wilson took the student-trainee position and was a quick study: "Because all the other trainees were 21 and I was 32, they never asked me to get sandwiches or coffee. I would just sit up there in the stands and watch them make the *Mary Tyler Moore Show*. And I realized that the writer-producer was really the key guy. At that time on *Mary Tyler Moore* there were two: Allan Burns and Jim Brooks." Allan Burns went on to be the writer-producer of *Rhoda* and *Lou Grant*, while James Brooks has moved into filmmaking, receiving writer-producer-director Oscars for *Terms of Endearment*. Of the two, Brooks left the deepest impression on Wilson. In Wilson's words: "I would have to say watching Jim Brooks work was a real education."

After this crash course in producing comedy television, Wilson wrote scripts for several MTM Productions, specializing in the original *Bob Newhart Show*. Then, when Patchett and Tarses created *The Tony Randall Show* in 1976, they hired Wilson as a staff writer. Although the Randall sitcom was cancelled after only two years, Wilson still managed to improve his lot:

One day, Grant Tinker came around and said, "Ah, the leaves are falling. It must be pilot time. Think of something." We all did. I used to frequent a bar in Atlanta where what passed for our glitterati gathered—media people from local radio and television stations. I always enjoyed the radio guys. I had a friend who was a morning man. So, I started thinking about developing what would turn out to be *WKRP in Cincinnati*.

## ACHIEVING CREATIVE CONTROL

*WKRP* ran for four seasons. Although it did not score great ratings during its initial run, it has earned the MTM company over $100 million in syndication. For Wilson, producing *WKRP* was a frustrating and exhausting experience. Perhaps his greatest frustrations involved network scheduling. *WKRP* was developed when Robert A. Daly was head of CBS Entertainment. Daly scheduled *WKRP* right after *M\*A\*S\*H*, which, according to Wilson, was "the most wonderful place to be." Unfortunately, Daly moved on to Warner Brothers in 1980 and Harvey Shepherd became the CBS executive in charge of programming. Wilson believes Shepherd is responsible for killing *WKRP*:

Harvey Shepherd didn't like me, and didn't like the show. He had nothing personal at stake with the show. And he moved us all over. That show was a hit and he just wore it out. He just killed it off trying to promote his other stuff. I'd always maintained to Harvey and to Bud Grant [former president of CBS Entertainment] that *WKRP* was not an eight o'clock show—and that they had to get me out of there because I was beating my brains out against *Happy Days* and *Little House on the Prairie*. I knew *WKRP* was a nine o'clock show. But they thought with the rock-and-roll music it had kid appeal.

Wilson confesses that the creative, intellectual and physical demands of television's assembly-line storytelling had also taken their toll:

I told everybody involved in *WKRP*, all the actors, that I would never do another television series again because of the unrelenting nature of this thing. I'm a writer. It's easy to act in a series, once you get a handle on the character. But the writing is like Sisyphus rolling the rock up, and every Friday night, it rolls back down again. And you start all over. It's just eating up material. In essence, you're asked to write twelve hours of comedy in a matter of twenty-five weeks, and then turn around and do it again.

Despite these bad memories, Wilson is very proud of his work on *WKRP*.

However, he gives the impression of being ashamed of the next stage in his career. In his words, "I wanted very much to get involved in movies, having the mistaken conception that you could do better work in movies. Of course, this was completely ludicrous. By this time the *Animal House* thing had taken over movie comedy, and the sixteen-year-old male was king in terms of the audience they were going for. I helped perpetuate this ugly trend."

Leaving television, he began working as a "script doctor" hired to punch up film comedies for money and no screen credit. When he was given the script of the original *Police Academy* to rewrite, Wilson says he initially refused the assignment:

They couldn't find anyone in town to direct it. It was such a mess. But, by then, I was determined that I wanted to direct movies. So, I said I would rewrite it for free, if they would let me direct it. After I did my rewrite, I told my wife, "These people are going to be so impressed." They saw it, and they said, "O.K. Time out. Five on the play." And they sat me down and I watched, in one afternoon, *Porky's*, *Fast Times at Ridgemont High*, *Stripes*, and *Animal House*—four movies I'd never seen before. And then we started again. They used some of my script and some of the old script. We shot it in Toronto, for what Hollywood would call cab fare, thinking it was a drive-in movie— which it was—for teenage boys. I cut this thing and I told my wife, "I'm finished. I'm dying. We're moving back to Georgia." And we took it out and tested it. They brought in a young audience, 15 to 23, emphasis on males. And they went crazy. Just crazy.

*Police Academy* grossed $132 million. But although Wilson would direct other features, he remained frustrated by the limitations of film comedy. As he puts it: "I became very disappointed in myself for getting involved in the machine, in the packages, and whatnot. And I began to realize that I could have more creative freedom and do more interesting work on television than I could in the movies—because I was the *Police Academy* guy. It was a coat I couldn't take off."

In returning to network television production as the *"Police Academy* guy," Wilson achieved the creative control and relative autonomy necessary for television authorship. The first project of his second career in television was the *Easy Street* pilot for Loni Anderson (who played Jennifer Marlow on *WKRP*). Tim Reid (who played *WKRP*'s Venus Flytrap) then talked Wilson into doing a pilot with him. As Wilson recalls it:

William Morris, who represented both of us, saw *Package*, which is what their life is all about. Packages. And they went to CBS. And CBS had an idea. We went in and sat down with two gentlemen, Kim LeMasters and Gregg Maday [former CBS vice-president for comedy program development]. They said, "We've always heard you'd like to do something about the South." I've always been pretty vocal about Hollywood's inability to deal with the South in any sort of believable fashion. So they said, "How about New Orleans? And how about Tim inherits a restaurant down there?" So, CBS had the bones of the idea. I liked that because I always felt—and I've been proven wrong here—that if they thought of it as their baby, they'd nurture it and look after it and take care of it.

It's worth noting in passing that there are several interesting parallels between the Wilson-CBS arrangement that resulted in *Frank's Place*, and the Welles-RKO arrangement that resulted in *Citizen Kane*. Most importantly, both *Frank's Place* and *Citizen Kane* fit into a pattern of invention and innovation connected to inferior market positions. A desperate company is more likely to seek out new ideas and new talent, more likely to sponsor experimentation, more likely to take risks—and less likely to interfere in the creative process. In the case of *Citizen Kane*, the financially troubled RKO lured Orson Welles away from his spectacular radio and stage career with an unprecedented six-film contract that promised the "boy genius" complete creative control over his projects. In the case of *Frank's Place*, CBS was not holding its own with the other networks and so desperately wanted the Wilson/Reid package that Wilson was able to negotiate a "complete hands-off deal."

In fact, Wilson readily acknowledges that ABC and NBC would not have given him such creative freedom:

CBS, they were desperate. They were struggling. They weren't [number] three—yet. Consequently, they were the best people to work for from a creative standpoint. NBC behaves just like ABC did when they were number one. They are sure they have it all figured out, and that it's not just dumb luck. But if Bill Cosby hadn't walked in there, they would be in as much trouble as they were before. Since they are absolutely sure they have it all figured out, they want to get into your stuff. They think they can fix shows by changing scripts, by changing attitudes, by adding characters.

## THE WILSON IMPRINT

Of course, it's a mistake to think of television authorship solely in terms of the expression of an individual's artistic vision. *Frank's Place* is clearly not

Wilson's private property. Instead, Wilson worked in dialogue with the network, who provided the basic premise, with Tim Reid, who shared executive production duties and was active in the early stages of series development, and with other creative personnel who would play decisive roles in shaping the look and feel of the program.

Even so, Wilson's was still the strongest voice in the creative collaboration—and he definitely left his imprint on the series. We suggest that this imprint is apparent in three areas of the show: the cultural orientation; the cinematic look; and the writing philosophy.

## The Cultural Orientation

Here, Wilson's imprint is apparent along two symbolic planes: region and profession. These planes intersect in the very setting for *Frank's Place*: the Chez Louisianne, a Creole restaurant located in a black neighborhood in New Orleans.

Offended by TV's *Dukes of Hazzard* treatment of things southern, Wilson was determined to create a more authentic vision of his native region. According to Wilson, CBS had originally intended the restaurant to be located on Bourbon Street: "They were hoping to cash in on the Cajun-cooking craze that was sweeping the nation, and they were thinking a French Quarter, straw hat, showboat-type ambience."

However, Wilson and Reid had other ideas. "We decided that it would be more interesting to put it in a black community," Wilson remembers. "So, when we came down here, we just skipped Bourbon Street and went into the black community. And we did some good research down here. In fact, we worked just like oral historians. We'd just go around with tape recorders."

In our telephone interview with Tim Reid, he referred to this crucial research stage as "venturing into history"—something that Reid feels is sorely lacking in most network programming. Indeed, the quest for authenticity during this research stage is at the heart of what Michael Pollan celebrates as the show's "painstakingly evoked locale" and what Horace Newcomb describes as the show's profound "sense of place."

Interestingly, Wilson says this crucial research stage was heavily informed by both his experience as a civil rights worker and his experience as a TV writer.

I had done a little bit of civil rights when I was at the University of Florida. When we would go into these little towns in northern Florida, there would be the minister and the funeral home director and, usually, a restauranteur. But it was always the minister and the funeral home director that seemed like the key guys. We were thinking he [Reid's character, Frank Parrish] would inherit a funeral home and restaurant and some apartments. Because I'm a writer, I always look for lots of venues, you know. Otherwise, I'm going to be stuck after eight shows. On *WKRP*, we did four shows and we said, "Well, that's all we know about radio. What now!?" So, I wanted funerals and restaurants and tenants and all that.

Perhaps the most important person Wilson and Reid encountered during their time in New Orleans was Austin Leslie, who runs a Creole restaurant named the Chez Helene. In fact, the Chez Helene would be the inspiration for the Chez Louisianne and Leslie would be the model for Big Author, the head cook on the series. As further evidence of Wilson's commitment to authenticity, Leslie would even come to Los Angeles to talk to the writers about running a restaurant.

Which brings us to the second dimension of the cultural orientation of *Frank's Place*—profession. One of the hallmarks of Wilson's oeuvre is his exploration of the world of work. Even *Police Academy* is about occupation and profession. And Wilson's passion for the world of work is evident in his valuation of other comedy series.

He is particularly outspoken about his admiration for *M\*A\*S\*H* and *Barney Miller*. In Wilson's words:

*M\*A\*S\*H* made bad writers good. I'm not talking about Gene Reynolds and Larry Gelbart. I mean outside writers. They'd write for *M\*A\*S\*H* and be wonderful—and then they'd get stuck on something like *The Montefuscos*, which is really hard to write. *M\*A\*S\*H* was easy to write because it was the ideal setup. [I would think of *M\*A\*S\*H*] when we were sitting around at three o'clock in the morning in a writers' meeting at *WKRP* trying to figure out how to blow the show off. [I'd think,] "How do we end this sucker? How do we end it? How do we end it?" And I would have given anything in the world if radio stations had in-coming wounded. Because, at *M\*A\*S\*H*, they always had this wonderful device of saying, "Hey, we've all kidded; we've all laughed; jokes are over; in-coming wounded; music up; people running out the door." It had devices—and I don't mean that in a pejorative sense. It had wonderful devices. I like to write about people at work, obviously, and these were people at work, but it was their home as well.

Given Wilson's preoccupation with the world of work, it's not at all surprising that he also admires *Barney Miller*. In fact, as a writer, he sees certain similarities between what he calls the "setup" for *Barney Miller* and the "setup" for *Frank's Place*:

In *Frank's Place*, the stories were coming pretty easy to us. I always thought that the reason for this was that it [the restaurant] was a public place. A story could walk in the door. I wrote something called "The Bum Out Front" which was one of these episodes. It was about Frank, but it was also about this [homeless] guy who wouldn't go away. You know, he was singing for spare change, and hanging around. But that's a *Barney Miller* setup. A story can come in the door. *Barney Miller*'s wonderful. You have three stories and they walk in every week. One of the reasons I have never wanted to do a family show is that I don't know what the hell to do with this [setup]: [You've got] mom and dad; and you've got a dining room set and a kitchen. [In L.A.] you walk through one sound stage after another full of dining rooms and kitchens. I think that it is really hard to write for that setup.

## The Cinematic Look

According to Wilson, the quest for authenticity—or as he puts it, "getting it right"—also motivated the cinematic look of the show. After "venturing into history" in the research stage, Wilson reports that he then

went to CBS and said, "You know, I'm one of the few guys working on television that has also directed features. I could make this thing look like a feature. And I think that might be key, because I can't do this three-camera/live-audience and capture what I want of New Orleans. I think I'm going to need steam, and smoke, and music, and food." And I got everybody real excited about that. And they forgot that these things cost money.

In initially creating the look of the series, Wilson enlisted the talents of William A. Fraker, a veteran cinematographer. Fraker, whose screen credits include *Rosemary's Baby*, *Bullitt*, and *Close Encounters of the Third Kind*, has been nominated for six Academy Awards. Wilson remembers approaching Fraker about shooting the pilot for *Frank's Place*: "We had done this movie together— a very bad movie, I must say—and become great friends. I so admired him. So, he agreed to lower his price, or whatever. He was waiting around to shoot *Baby Boom*, the movie, and they were being delayed. So, he shot the pilot."

Although Fraker returned to filmmaking after shooting the pilot, Wilson says Fraker's look was perpetuated by his replacement, Marvin Rush:

We couldn't keep Fraker on because he really doesn't do television. We got a young guy who Tim and I knew from *WKRP*. He was the B Camera. The B Camera is the one in the middle [in three-camera sitcoms] that carries the master shot. And it's the hardest to shoot. As a matter of fact, he had done a couple of things that Tim had produced—low budget, nonunion projects. He was moving into film. And he knew a lot about lights. So, he came in and looked at Fraker's work and he copied it. His name was Marvin Rush. And he was the glue as far as the look because he lit all of the shows. He was the continuing force down there.

In fact, according to Wilson, Fraker's look (as copied by Rush) imposed limits on what the show's directors could do on *Frank's Place*:

The various directors would come in. Each person would have a slightly different approach. But it was incumbent upon all of them—as it is in all television—to continue the look. If you're going to do *L.A. Law*, you're going to sit down and look at a bunch of *L.A. Laws*. You can't impose something that is inappropriate on what they are doing. So, the directors, they had Marvin there. And he was going to light it the way he was going to light it. Sometimes camera movements would be different. Directors, traditionally, are not involved in lighting too much. They just want it to be real good. But they will decide where to put the camera. Each one is a little different. Some direct the camera. It's called that, you know. And the actors will get hardly any input. Others, particularly if they have a stage background, will concentrate on the Stanislavski stuff with the actors—and they will say to the cameraman, "Where should I put the camera?" So, it varies. But on

*Frank's Place*, they all had to copy the [Fraker] look. And most of them were delighted to do it. So, that's how there is continuity there.

The look that Wilson and Fraker devised for the series had other important consequences. As Welles discovered after *Citizen Kane* failed at the box office, hands-off deals are ephemeral creatures that often perish in the heat of competition. But, interestingly, the cinematic look of *Frank's Place* enabled Wilson to sustain creative control throughout the season.

The hands-off agreement stuck because of the way we shot it. If you do a three-camera sitcom, you rehearse it much like a stage play. And the networks send people down to look at run-throughs. You turn around, and they've all got their scripts out saying, "I feel like on page so-and-so. . . . " And some of them have amazing nerve. But we started shooting film style at seven o'clock in the morning. Bing! The lights were on. We rehearse it, shoot it, and shoot it out of order. There was no run-through to see. Consequently, we were left totally free. CBS people would look at the dailies—but they didn't know how to look at dailies because they weren't movie people. They'd just kind of look at them and say 'OK?' Or they would call and say, "Gee, that scene . . . " and I'd say, "Well, when we cut it all together, it'll be good."

According to Wilson, in addition to sustaining his creative control over the series, the cinematic look also caused him to abandon the laugh track. Where Wilson thinks the laugh track is appropriate in standard TV comedies using three-camera/live-audience production techniques, he discovered that the laugh track was extremely awkward using a one-camera/filmic approach. As he puts it:

As far as the laugh track goes, Jay Tarses—this is the *Molly Dodd* man—he carries the cross about the laugh track. He's out to get it. But I have no problem with laugh tracks. I like a live audience. I think that's good. I think in [situation] comedy, the track is very appropriate. Laughter is a form of agreement. I know that if you screen a movie comedy in front of three people and a couple of critics, you might as well blow your brains out. But if you watch a comedy with a crowd, it changes everything. So, I don't have any problem with the laugh track. But, because of the look, we just couldn't get the laugh track to work on *Frank's Place*. For some reason, because of the sound track, the [laugh track] audience had to be in the room. But they couldn't be in the room, because gradually, we were shooting all the way around. You got a strong feeling of "Where the hell are these [laughing] people?"

Unfortunately, a new programming category was invented by newspaper reviewers as a device for describing the appearance of several new shows that did not conform to the laugh track or three-camera conventions of situation comedy. *Frank's Place*, *The "Slap" Maxwell Story*, *The Days and Nights of Molly Dodd*, and *Hooperman*—all got tagged with the label of "dramedy." And Wilson believes that because this label became associated with low ratings, "guilt by association" with these shows helped doom *Frank's Place*. Like the *Police Academy* coat, the dramedy albatross was something that Wilson couldn't shed.

## The Writing Philosophy

The cultural orientation and cinematic look of *Frank's Place* were reflected in the philosophy that governed the writing of the series. Wilson hired four writers, including African-American playwright Samm-Art Williams, to join him in the creative process. And, according to Wilson:

We, or I should say I, decided right off that we would go for it—that we would not do the sitcom number on this thing because the look was already beginning to dictate the writing. And I had it in mind that we should try to—I mean, I would never say this to a network—but we should try to take the great American dead art form, the short story, and think of ourselves as short story writers. Although, of course, obeying the rules of drama—climax, resolution, building action, and whatnot.

With the short story as a model, Wilson also asked his writers to "regionalize" their thinking: "[I felt] we should bone up on southern authors to see what we could steal. Or to at least let some of that rub off on us."

A corollary of Wilson's short story philosophy was the avoidance of any storyline that faintly resembled the machinations of the conventional situation comedy. Because most sitcoms are primarily vehicles for showcasing comedic star performances, the individual episodes often become highly predictable and painfully contrived variations on a well-established theme. This theme, in fact, is the very "situation" that gives the formula its name and it is embedded in the ongoing relationships between the regular characters. Wilson and his ink-stained comrades essentially tried to write the "situation" out of television comedy. In Wilson's words:

People, myself included, would yell, "No, that's *Laverne and Shirley*. That's just right out." Laverne and Shirley, for some reason, became the shorthand for any kind of setup, setup, punch, setup, setup, punch. Also, actors saying things that were out of character—or interrupting the dramatic flow of something to get a joke out of it. Also, I decided that these stories didn't necessarily have to be funny. Our main thrust was story, story, story! What I was after was good stories. Let's do good stories.

## ORCHESTRATING A COLLABORATION

Where better to observe the circumscribed role of the author in contemporary cultural production than in commercial television? Because of the technological complexity of the medium and as a result of the application, to television production, of the principles of modern industrial organization (mass production, detailed division of labor, etc.), it is very difficult to locate the "author" of a television program—if we mean by that term the single individual who provides the unifying vision behind the program.

—Robert C. Allen.
*Channels of Discourse*, p. 4.

Because of what Allen terms "the circumscribed role of the author in contemporary cultural production," television authorship always takes place in the context of collaborative storytelling. In this context, television authorship does not in any way conform to the romanticized literary model of an individual artist writing in isolation. Instead, television authorship is more like coaching a championship football team or conducting a superb symphony orchestra. Like the coach and the conductor, the television author must coordinate and facilitate the concerted efforts of a large and complex team.

We have already addressed certain aspects of Wilson's orchestration of the *Frank's Place* collaboration: how Wilson's regional background and artistic commitment transformed CBS's basic premise; how Wilson's institutionalization of the "Fraker look" guided not only Marvin Rush's work, but also informed the performances of the various directors who worked on the show; how Wilson's writing philosophy encouraged his writing staff to subvert the conventionality of the typical situation comedy. As the coach and orchestrator of *Frank's Place*, Wilson was involved in everything from hiring cast and crew to supervising post-production editing.

In fact, Wilson tells an interesting story about locating the amateur actor who played the role of Shorty, a cook on the show. We include this story because it lends insight into both Wilson's commitment to authenticity and the importance attached to casting in the television industry. He first met Don Yesso during the research stage of the project:

I was flying to New Orleans and I had stopped smoking. But the plane started bouncing all over the place and there was lightning outside the window, so I said, "I'm getting out of here." I went back to the smoking section and Donny was sitting there. I bummed a cigarette and started talking to him. And he had the accent I wanted. There's that strange New Orleans accent that first sounds like it's coming from Brooklyn and then it's from Jackson, Mississippi, or Biloxi. I had it in the back of my mind that I would have to find a New Orleans actor. I was scared to death of accents because American actors don't do good Southern accents. British actors do, for some reason I don't understand. But I wanted to use that accent. So I started talking to him and I was mainly picking his brains about New Orleans. I was just a sponge. And it occurred to me in the conversation that this guy had a certain aliveness about him that I liked very much. I ordered a couple of drinks and said to him, "You ever act?" And I think he thought right there, "This guy's gay and trying to hit on me." So there was a long pause there.

Wilson couldn't prove on the plane that he was a genuine television producer who was only interested in Yesso as an actor because he doesn't carry business cards. According to Wilson, in the television business, "by the time you get the business cards printed, you get cancelled." However, once the plane landed in New Orleans, Yesso began to believe Wilson's professed occupation and motives: "We got to the airport and they had, per Hollywood style, arranged for a limousine to pick us up. So then Donny decided that maybe I was legit."

Even with Wilson's "hands-off deal," however, the network still retained final approval of casting decisions. But, ironically, because Wilson and Reid were lagging so far behind in putting the show together, they were able to push through unconventional talent like Yesso. As Wilson explains:

The way you do casting with the networks is that you cast the show with your casting director and then they're all sent to the networks for approval. And there are God-awful, terrible, terrible things that they do when these actors have to go in to read for the network people. It's usually in somebody's office. Or sometimes they have this big room where they do it. At NBC they had this idiotic setup where they forced so much light on the actor that you can't see who's watching. So, it's like a line up. They're just put in the most uncomfortable situations. And then they read—and you hope so much that they like who you picked.

So we cast the show very, very quickly. And I used the great excuse of "I'm so busy getting the sets ready and everything that I can't come." So Tim [Reid] went to read with the cast, and even he hadn't met a lot of them [the actors]. They got over there and the network was really surprised when Donny came in. Donny was so nervous that he went completely nuts. He had never read for me. I had just hired him. And he overacted terribly. It scared everybody, including myself. But they let me have him because I said, "Well, I can't make your delivery date unless you give me these actors."

As this story illustrates, Wilson's relationship with Reid was central to the vitality of the collaboration. And as with most of Wilson's working relationships, his association with Reid was cemented by friendship.

Reid and I are very close personal friends. He and his wife [Daphne Maxwell Reid, who plays mortician Hanna Griffin on *Frank's Place*] are godparents of my middle daughter. After *WKRP* we stayed in close touch and we like one another very much. But I would have never, ever, in my wildest dreams have given an actor any kind of responsibility— including president of the United States, I might add. Even so, I did that with Reid. Reid and I sat down. We said, "We've got to have a united front here. This is a biracial effort." And also . . . this is a show about black people and there's this one white guy running it with a Southern accent!? [I felt] this was inappropriate and Reid agreed. So we decided that we would be the coexecutive producers and that would be how we'd represent ourselves to the public. But in addition to that, what we would do within the show was kind of break things in two. I would, in essence, run the office, and he would run the stage. That's how we did it. I had control of the editing and writing and he ran the stage. I never had any problems with directors because most of those things were straightened out by Reid down there. So, I didn't have to run back and forth.

As a matter of strict policy, Wilson and Reid set about hiring a racially mixed crew. According to Wilson:

We made a commitment [to hire black crew members]. And I was more aggressive about this, in a way, than Tim was, although it was more appropriate that I be aggressive about it. When you came down on the stage, the camera operator was black and the first assistant director was black and second assistant director was black and the guys watching the trailer were black and it went on and on. It was an absolutely concerted effort on our part to do that. Everywhere we had equal talent, we would hire blacks. And one of the reasons we did was because it was only fair. Because white males run the show out there, they [black crew members] really have trouble. Nobody, when you're doing *Dynasty*, nobody says, "Uh, just get a black gaffer."

Tim Reid is also proud of this hiring policy, estimating that, of the just over 100 members of the cast and crew, 45 to 50 percent were black—and of that percentage, half were black women. Most significantly, as Reid is quick to point out, two of the show's directors were black women. That kind of hiring, according to Reid, "is almost unheard of today in network television."

Wilson contends that the mixed crew was a key ingredient in the *Frank's Place* collaboration. Because there was no live audience, Wilson says crew members became a surrogate audience and their reactions to the script and set provided a crucial "read" on whether "we were getting it right": "If you had a whole bunch of white people making that show, you couldn't read anything from the crew. They wouldn't know any more than *I* do." Reid agrees, adding, "If the crew didn't get into it, we knew we were in trouble."

Of course, the mixed crew also provided unusual challenges to Wilson and Reid. These challenges are perhaps best illustrated by an anecdote related by Wilson that concerned the name of a cat that appears in the series:

The disagreements—of a racial nature—that came up while we were making the show were few, but funny. [For example] we had this cat that we used for a while, which I often refer to as "that goddam cat." Anyhow, we named him, or I named him, Jesse Jackson. That was the cat's name—Jesse Jackson. Well, Frances Williams, who played Miss Marie, said, "I object to that. I think that is demeaning to Jesse Jackson." So, I talked to Reid. Reid said, "Aww, that's nuts. But I don't want to make Frances angry." So, what do we call the cat? The only thing I can come up with is Hank Aaron. But that's not alliteration. Jesse Jackson is an alliteration. It's funny. It's topical. I think Frances is really wrong. So, everybody talked to Frances. And then we were all going around talking—white people were pairing up with black people. You would see a white writer with a black makeup lady saying, "Uh, I want to talk to you about this cat." The vote, finally, was 50–50. Then Tim got into one of the most embarrassing experiences in his life. He goes to Chicago to make a speech and he's heard that Jesse's gonna be there. He's met Jesse before, so he says to me, "You know what? I'm just going to ask him about the cat." He goes there, and Jesse doesn't show up, but some friends of Jesse's are there. Reid says, "Is Jesse coming?" And they say, "No." And he said, "Oh darn. I wanted to ask him something." And they said, "Well, he's not going to be here." And that was the end of it. Now, Jesse Jackson is running for president of the United States. Reid, sitting at home minding his own business, gets a phone call. "Tim, this Jesse Jackson." Tim says, "Yeah, bullshit. Yeah. Who is this?" He says, "I'm not kidding you. This is Jesse Jackson. I was told to call you. You had a question?" [Reid thought,] Oh, no. He had just watched him [Jackson] on the *MacNeil-Lehrer Report*, you know, talking about foreign policy, and he's got Jesse Jackson on the phone. And he's got to say, "Well, Jesse, see, we got this cat on a television show. . . ." Oh, he was just dying. And Jesse gave him, I think, a politically smart answer. He says, "It doesn't offend me, but it may offend others."

The cat's name was, ultimately, changed to Hank Aaron. But, according to Wilson, Reid was so flustered by the incident that he called a meeting with the entire cast and crew that "saved us a lot of pushing and shoving and a lot of nonsense":

After the first and second show with the cat, Tim had a meeting with everyone. He said, "We're not going to get into this. This is nonsense. There'll be no politics. There'll be no power plays. We're going to do this about a bunch of people in New Orleans who happen to be black. It'll be about their experience and I don't want any [pause] I'm just cutting it off right here."

Of course, everything is political. And seminar participant Herman Gray, an African-American sociologist at Northeastern University, has characterized this Wilson/Reid collaboration as disturbingly similar to the old plantation system where a white man "ran the office" and his black overseer controlled the field hands. But, in fairness to Wilson and Reid, the politics and division of labor at the producer level made sense, given Wilson's background as a writer and Reid's as an actor. It's also worth emphasizing that Wilson deserves credit for his extraordinary sensitivity regarding racial issues. In the struggle for racial equality in the television industry, Wilson is clearly part of the solution, not part of the problem.

Wilson's personal and professional identities are anchored in his status as a writer. Over and over again during the seminar, Wilson said, "I'm a writer." For Wilson, everything else—producing, directing, editing, managing resources, cutting deals—is secondary. Not surprisingly, Wilson took the highest profile in the collaboration in the area of scripting the series:

The way this [the writing process] worked was, we would discuss the stories in a group. And we would talk these stories down. And we would talk and talk. And sometimes we would talk about a story for days and then decide to abandon it. Now, I don't want to mislead you. We did some unique things [on *Frank's Place*]. But, basically, it was a typical setup in terms of the writing. The reason there's so much discussion is—this is the best analogy I've ever heard for the type of writing I do—is that we're all safe crackers. And we're just sitting there going, "Twenty left. Nope. Twenty-two left. Ah!" It's like we're all detectives working on a nonexistent show. You sit in these meetings and somebody says, "Well, I don't know. Bob loses his briefcase? Who knows?" Somebody else: "Well, you know . . . what's in the briefcase?" And it goes from there. And it either goes somewhere and begins to track, and people begin to get excited, and they stand up and all that—or, you just sit there. And, oh, it's so terrible. Nobody will speak for twenty minutes.

According to Wilson, the episode called "The Bridge" (which won him the Best Writing Emmy in 1988) started as a food poisoning premise and then "got talked into" a poignant tale of a terminally ill man who commits suicide by driving off a bridge so that his family can sue the Chez Louisianne for serving him his final drink.

Although the writing process was intensely collaborative, Wilson still had the final word. According to Wilson, after "talking the story down," the staff writer who had the assignment would then write an outline:

We would all read the outline and then talk that to death. Then, the writer would write a draft, and sometimes a second draft. Then, he would give it to me, and I would write a third draft. This is egotistical of me to say, but that's why the shows sort of have a singularity of point of view. With the exception of one show, they all came through my final filter.

Now, this is typical. I mean, there were many writers on *Barney Miller*—but in the end, it all came through Danny Arnold. There were many writers on *Soap*, but in the end it all came through Susan Harris. There were many writers on *Taxi*, but in the end it all came through Jim Brooks.

Wilson's "final filter" metaphor, though not entirely original, is still perhaps the best way of conceptualizing the circumscribed role of the television author.

The Wilson filter was particularly evident during one moment in a *Frank's Place* episode which explored the fall and rise of a New York business tycoon named Mitchell Torrance. Near the end of the episode, Torrance shares a "great piece of information" with Shorty, the cook: "Whether we're talking cooks, piano players, or hit men in the Mafia, none of the really A-plus people are doing it for the money. They're doing it 'cause . . . they're in love." Raconteur, creator, producer, director, the *Police Academy* guy, coach, orchestrator, writer, final filter, TV author—Hugh Wilson is clearly a man who is in love with his work. Although he admittedly gets by with a lot of help from his many friends— Jay Tarses, Tom Patchett, the morning radio man in Atlanta, Tim Reid, Bill Fraker, Austin Leslie, even Kim LeMasters—his passion for writing, for telling "good stories," for "getting it right," is ultimately what transformed this network of friendships into the artistry of *Frank's Place*.

## NOTE

The authors are especially indebted to Christopher Campbell, Herman Gray, Horace Newcomb, and Mimi White for their support and encouragement during the early stages of this project. The authors also express appreciation to David Barker, Lawrence M. Bernabo, Chad Dell, Jackie Byars, Christy Greene, Joe Moorehouse, Dann L. Pierce, Mark Poindexter, Alan D. Stewart, and Bernard M. Timberg for lending their support to the project by participating in the SCA seminar. Finally, the authors thank Carolyn Moses for volunteering to assist in transcribing the interview tapes.

# 2

# Interpreting Television: A Closer Look at the Cinematic Codes in *Frank's Place*

*Bernard Timberg and David Barker*

We have been charged with examining five episodes of *Frank's Place* in terms of formal criticism that explores the audiovisual codes these episodes employ. Since televisual and cinematic codes tend to have meaning only to the degree that they articulate the narrative, and the narrative tends to make sense only in the context of the cultural or ideological issues it explores, the formal criticism in which we engage will be intimately connected to narrative and thematic critique.

To some extent we are making a distinction between *cinematic* codes of representation and *televisual* codes. Although they have cross-bred and inter-mingled, especially when production of television programming became more or less institutionalized within the Hollywood studio system in the mid–1950s, creating since then a veritable pallate of "hybrid" codes of representation, overtly cinematic visual structures have been the exception on American commercial television rather than the rule. After being pursued aggressively on *M\*A\*S\*H*, these structures seemed particularly appropriate for communicating the narrative and ideological complexities of *Hill Street Blues* and *St. Elsewhere*. By and large, their use within the genre of situation comedy, where the codes of multiple-camera proscenium shooting have firmly entrenched themselves, has been short-lived and sporadic. Perhaps, then, we should ultimately not be surprised that a series like *Frank's Place*, whose narrative and ideological complexities often rival those of a *St. Elsewhere*, has chosen to communicate these complexities through some of the most aggressively cinematic—and memorable—visual structures on commercial television in some time.

The visual structure of *Frank's Place* is therefore best discussed in terms of cinematic (as opposed to more typical televisual) codes. To establish the distinct role played by the artful execution of such codes, we will first look at the narrative formula of the series and the central ideological project to which the narrative returns repeatedly. Narrative structure and a central ideological project remain relatively constant, we will argue, throughout the series. By contrast, the codes of representation, while always firmly rooted in the cinema, vary considerably in texture and application, and give specific episodes in the series a sense of individuality rare for network television.

## THE NARRATIVE FORMULA

The narrative content of *Frank's Place* invariably raises issues of great complexity. The narrative formula of the series, however, is remarkably similar to many of the episodes. A representative of the outer world comes to the inner world of *Frank's Place*, the Chez Louisianne Restaurant in New Orleans. He, she, or they bring a problem with them. He, she, or they are affected, and in turn affect, the people in the restaurant. The denizens of *Frank's Place*—cooks, waiters, waitresses, and regular customers—characteristically become onlookers to the main action of each episode, which centers on the problem or crisis brought in from the outside world. The inhabitants of the Chez react in a variety of ways to the action that unfolds, with varying degrees of surprise, shock, envy, pity, or simple curiosity. Their reactions echo some of the responses that we as viewers may have to these outsiders and their problems, whether the outsiders be businessmen, basketball recruiters, visiting musicians from Africa, or the character of Frank himself, when he places himself under the influence of an efficiency expert in his desire to expand the restaurant's profits. The people of *Frank's Place* provide a collective point of view, a vantage point from which we, as viewers at home, can also respond to the drama that unfolds. In a very real sense, they are a chorus that responds antiphonally to the dramatic crisis of each episode, that questions the social and cultural meanings of the conflict. The characteristic narrative structure of *Frank's Place* is a play within a play, which we, as viewers, witness along with the more immediate audience in the restaurant.

Frank himself is a central figure in the chorus. His responses, like those of Mary Richards in *The Mary Tyler Moore Show*, or *Barney Miller*, or Alex in *Taxi*, center the show's organizing sensibility. We often see literally (through the use of subjective camera or Murnauian-motivated point of view shots) what he sees, and his narrative sensibility—detached, ironic, bemused, flustered, curious, dubious, or amazed—directly or indirectly anchors each episode. Though he may seem to flit through an episode quite peripheral to its central drama or conflict, he maintains an invisible, overarching presence.

As an individual episode proceeds, the central characters of the play within the play reach a decision. This resolves, at least in part, their dilemma. The decision is often only minimally affected by the responses of the *Frank's Place* family. But by the end of the show the home viewers have been encouraged to feel, like the staff of the restaurant, that they have witnessed something important—a lesson of some sort—and what they have learned is still being sorted out at one level or another at the end of the show.

The show does not conclude with a simple crowd-pleasing ending. The rousing moral fantasies that attend the denouement of much popular narrative fare, so-called "Hollywood endings," are not handed out at the end of *Frank's Place*. Justice is never accomplished in a clear, uncomplicated way. Frank generally does *not* achieve what he sets out to do. Most often, the show ends on a pause, a moment of reflection. What we hear and see at the end is not a closing out or neat tying-up of the issues the plot raises. Rather, what we experience at the end of *Frank's Place* is overtone and echo, a series of not quite submerged dissonances raised by the conflicts within the plot—personal and social values set at odds with each other. The tragedy of life, said filmmaker Jean Renoir, is that everyone has his (or her) reasons. *Frank's Place* often ends on exactly that note.

## THE IDEOLOGICAL ARENA OF CONTESTED VALUES

In each of the episodes of *Frank's Place*, social and cultural values are placed in sharp relief, and issues of class, race, and gender are engaged. One need only remember Frank's talk with the basketball recruiter from the small Mississippi college, or his first encounter with Miss Marie upon returning to the restaurant, or the high school basketball player's message to Frank, sitting beside him on the couch, about what *he* wanted out of life. In almost every episode, the restaurant chorus and the outside characters who bring a dilemma to the restaurant look at each other through opposite ends of a cultural telescope. The chorus often argues silently, through the raising of a collective eyebrow perhaps. But each week on *Frank's Place* a cultural pas de deux takes place: of North and South, of traditional working-class values and middle-class aspirations, of world-views that eye each other warily, if respectfully.

In narrative terms, the same thing occurs each time. The show proceeds on a relatively predictable path from stasis (a normal day in relative peace and harmony) to conflict introduced from outside (hostile takeovers, basketball re-cruitment pressures, external pressures to make money and succeed) to resolution (always, in some important sense, partial) to a moment of pause or reflection in which Frank or the chorus look back over the events of the day or week without completely digesting or understanding them. The narrative ends characteristically on a note of ambivalence or irony.

The sequence of cultural conflict within this narrative structure also follows an identifiable pattern. An individual goal of some sort is posed as the key problem of the episode. The dilemma always centers on a strongly held personal goal of one of the characters. One of Frank's own recurrent goals is to become a business and social success in his new hometown. In another episode, however, his goal is to help give a young high school basketball star an orientation toward what he, Frank, feels is the most important thing the boy could gain from college: a foundation in academics that would enable him to succeed off the basketball court. Another of Frank's goals is a more existential one: to inherit his father's restaurant and succeed while remaining entirely his own man with his own sense of purpose and value, free from the dead hand of the past. In the episode with the businessman, at a profound moment of personal crisis, the businessman questions the worth of his work building a paper empire with no social product. He raises, powerfully, a new ethic of what work should and could be. In every episode it looks as if the ideal or goal espoused may indeed be achieved, but social reality reasserts itself. The dream of the individual recedes or is dashed. Frank wakes up, literally, from his dream of social success in the first episode; the basketball star chooses along predictable lines of peer and recruiter pressure and opts for basketball over academic success; the businessman returns to the fray of business power politics he had moments before abandoned as meaningless. The balance of social and economic power determines how things actually work in the world, and the people of *Frank's Place* fall back, comfortable for the most part, into the niche of milieu, social class, and economic position they inhabit.

To summarize, as viewers we are encouraged to identify each week with a character who has a goal, ideal, or vision. There is a distinct gap between the individual's goal or ideal and the possibility of its realization in the social world, what Stuart Hall calls the "real world" of social relations. The gap appears to narrow. There is a build in the narrative in which it appears that the goal actually may be realized or, at least, there is the strong possibility that it will. Then comes the twist, a movement in which the goal or ideal is rolled back in the face of social reality. The conclusion, the final action or decision, is squarely within the forms of dominant social and economic powers. The CEO goes back to his job at the pinnacle of his corporation (though it is for the pure pleasure of it, he tells us, not for the money); the basketball recruiter's transcendent belief in his mission wins out in the end over the persuasive devices and extreme measures of his rivals, where Frank's unswerving belief in the value of a strong general education proves a weak contender. The goal of efficiency and growth is not for a little backwater restaurant like Chez Louisianne. It is an idea ill-suited to the soil—the tradition and location—of this restaurant's business life.

Having briefly summarized the narrative and ideological formulas for many if not all of the episodes of *Frank's Place*, we are in a position to examine the ways in which cinematic codes of representation construct the world and world-view of the series. We will discuss the general cinematic lexicon of the series and then specific ways narrative, ideology, and representation intersect.

## THE CINEMATIC LEXICON OF *FRANK'S PLACE*

The first episode, "Frank's Return," like the others we will examine, uses shooting and editing strategies uniquely tailored to the narrative/ideological conflicts of the show. But "Frank's Return" also establishes a characteristic shooting style, editing pace, and mise-en-scène—a cinematic lexicon, if you will—characteristic of the series as a whole. For example, the series utilizes soft, post-flash color highlighted by a row of sharply defined but softly rimmed lights along the back of the restaurant bar. This glowing soft-color ambience was established in the pilot by the same director of cinematography who lit *Rosemary's Baby* and *Close Encounters of the Third Kind* (William Fraker). It suggests that when we are in the restaurant we are in a special place, a place of warmth, humanity, and quirkiness where wonderful, strange things may happen (for example, the "voodoo" involving the cat Hank Aaron in the first episode). The behind-the-bar lights serve as a back frame to the story-within-a-story narrative structure. The story from the outside world that enters the restaurant enters a stage of sorts. Accordingly, the lights that surround the characters are in this sense stagelights as well as bar lights.

Camera blocking and horizontal field of view, and what we might refer to as "camera choreography," favor an interchange of carefully lit and framed medium shots, two-shots, and close-ups (extreme close-ups are rare) with tracking shots of characters going back and forth from restaurant to kitchen. The tracking shots, which often travel the length of the bar, serve as transitions, entries, exits, or as dramatic relief from stationary scenes of confrontation and contests of verbal repartée. Some episodes rely heavily on these moving shots to move the plot along. Others, the "Businessman" episode for instance, dispense with them as the drama intensifies and the regular series' characters become stationary witnesses to the struggle of ideas and values before them.

Still tableaux are another important feature of the cinematic lexicon of *Frank's Place*. Frank's reactions are at times sustained almost as long as freeze frames. When everyone in the restaurant comes out to see Hank Aaron the cat, they all stand at attention, as if frozen in time. At the end of the show there is always a moment of stillness, heightened at times by an actual freeze frame or a dissolve from color to the sepia-tone black and white that opens the show.

These features of the cinematography of *Frank's Place* are complemented by a lively musical score, musical transitions, and musical "comments" of native New Orleans folk traditions and jazz that underscore movements, turns, and developments in the narrative. Together, cinematography and score establish the tone and feel of *Frank's Place*. They place it, particularly at the beginning and end of the show, in a sort of mythical time and space—a mythical New Orleans.

## "FRANK'S RETURN": CINEMATIC CODES AND POINT OF VIEW

"Frank's Return," the second half hour of the series pilot, pivots on a small tour de force of cinematography. That moment comes at the twist, the precise point where the escalation of Frank's "dream" (his personal goal of making it as a successful restaurant entrepreneur) and the facts of his social reality intersect: he has inherited a small, casual backwater restaurant which will probably never have more than a limited clientele. As viewers, we are encouraged to share

Frank's dream through a skillful wedding of Frank's point of view to both the point of view of the camera (alternately objective and subjective, but always in one way or another seeing things as Frank sees them) and our point of view as viewers. Viewer willingness to enter into the dream occurs step-by-step, reaching a point where, at the precise moment the bubble bursts and the dream shatters, a strong desire to share in Frank's wish fulfillment has developed. In cinematic terms, how was viewer complicity in this fantasy engineered?

As Frank enters the restaurant from his office on what is presumably his triumphant opening night, the characteristic interior soft-color glow of *Frank's Place* is heightened. The color is even more post-flashed, rendering the colors softer so that the characters and decor of the restaurant bar merge and blend in the lights. The lights themselves are refracted by star filters, a Hollywood effect that seems to suggest the way Frank feels at that moment.

Frank sees Anna enter the restaurant. An MTV-like rapture fantasy of the mythic gaze-across-the-room is heightened by slow-motion cinematography, a blazing red neon sign behind Frank's head, and the slow parting of the crowd between them as each moves to reach his/her mind's eye lover. By the time the overblown acting and musical score reach a crescendo—in the "miracle" Frank performs for Anna's mother—it has become clear that the show's increasing cinematic excess has been a ruse. At what point have the intensified effects of this scene twisted the parameters of the series' cinematic lexicon beyond the realm of credibility? By the time Frank's eyes rise out of their sockets and the music has acquired a religious transcendence that is at distinct odds with the conventions of a television comedy of manners (no matter how quirky), it seems unlikely that most viewers are not on to the fact that something is wrong. The cinematographic bubble bursts: Frank awakens with a start to real time, real sweat, real anxiety, and a distinctly low key and unglamorous first night in the restaurant. It is evident, however, that the build, the puncturing twist, and the return to reality are in large part accomplished through skillful manipulation of cinematic codes.

This is a rather flagrant example of how the filmmakers' control of the show's imagery works to accomplish its narrative purposes. But there are numerous more subtle ways camera, editing, and sound articulate the show's values, themes, and narrative point of view. We will take just one element of visual coding—camera angle—and show how it works to shape and reflect one of the show's central themes.

*Frank's Place* characteristically explores, through engaging stories and individual personalities, various forms of social power: the power of ownership (one of the major themes of the first episode); the power of tradition and family ties and the power of hierarchical control of business or corporate interests (the "Businessman" episode); the power of marketable skill (the "Basketball Recruiter" episode); and the power of persuasion (the successful "pitch" in the "Basketball Recruiter," and the businessman's blunt but effective carrot-and-stick persuasion over the phone). Clearly, script and performance explore these themes, but we argue that the camera does as well.

The first view we have of Frank's Place in "Frank's Return," after the opening montage and story of Frank's disasters in Boston, is shot from an uncharacteristically low angle. We are looking up with the camera from the floor of the bar area in the restaurant as it is being mopped. The head waitress towers over the restaurant help mopping the floor. "Look at that," she says. "Get that up. Folks are supposed to eat off this floor. You think the Marines is tough; I'll show you tough." As she speaks, the head waitress' power is underscored by the angle of the camera. Frank enters the door and a shot/reverse-shot sequence begins. The camera angles, now eye-level, are equalized. "Hi," Frank says. "Hi," says the head waitress, warily. "How's it going?" he asks. "I don't know," says the waitress, eyeing the new owner. The mop-wielding employee has stopped his work to listen. "Mop!" she orders, turning on him, and he hastily goes back to work.

As the new owner is introduced to the rest of the staff he appears in the upper right corner of the screen at some distance across the room. Miss Marie emerges on crutches and Frank walks over to her. As Miss Marie gives orders to the others she becomes the central force on the screen. She is treated in close-up, given central graphic weight—she literally "centers" the shots—and begins to interrogate Frank. Frank is placed higher than Miss Marie in the upper right of the screen during this dialogue (Miss Marie is lower screen left). Yet despite his relative position in screen space, Frank is always *smaller* (in medium shots). Thus, for the second time in this brief introductory scene in the restaurant, a power relationship is encapsulated in camera angle and distance. Frank is higher within the screen space (after all, he does own the place) but, in terms of graphic mass within the frame, Miss Marie looms larger (Frank may own the place, but the power of family and tradition runs it), clearly dominating the shot/reverse-shot sequence. In the background, standing in a row, the employees—the chorus—line up to witness the confrontation between these two forms of power.

The introduction of the cat named Hank Aaron manipulates the high-power/low-power equation once more. In confusion and with some surprise, Frank runs downstairs after the others, expecting to encounter yet another form of social power: the celebrity, in this case the star ballplayer Hank Aaron. When he arrives he gazes up to see—a cat.

Frank is at first out of focus and in the background as part of the chorus. Miss Marie again becomes the dominant presence, the interpreter of the scene before them. "This is a good sign, Frank," she says, as the camera dollies in dramatically from a medium shot to a tight close-up. This is the first such camera move in the show and is accompanied on the sound track by a harmonica chord. "The day your Daddy died, Hank took off. Today you come back, he comes back." The cat deliberately leaves his perch on the top of the crates piled high in the alley (a clear pedestal of emblematic power), hops down to Frank's feet, looks up at him (we see the cat from an angle straight between Frank's legs), and meows quietly. The camera cuts to Frank looking down at the cat, then to a close-up as he grins sheepishly, looking around at no one in particular. "Voodoo," he says, and looks down again at the cat. The harmonica cat theme wails its final notes and the scene ends.

The camera again poses and plays upon the question, who has the power? The new owner, in his carefully tailored suit, or the cat, a mysterious harbinger of father and family tradition, the unseen weight of a social and psychological inheritance that accompanies at every step Frank's physical inheritance of the restaurant?

High/low camera choreography also plays a part in Frank's encounter with a member of the kitchen help who at first doesn't know who he is, in his (real life) encounter with Anna, and in the scene between Tiger and Frank as Tiger gets ready to go home at the end of the day, leaving Frank alone in the stifling heat of his room, catching what breeze he can from a small fan.

In this final scene we look in from outside the window after Tiger leaves. As the camera pulls back from the window in a long elegiac move to the other side of the street, we hear gospel music in the distance. The camera comes to rest on a view of Frank through ornate wrought-iron railings. The cat moves into frame, silhouetted on the top of the railing. He hops down and goes through the window onto Frank's lap. Frank, in the still distant shot, smiles and leans over to pet the cat. The scene freezes, but at exactly what point is unclear since everything is so still at this moment, and the color dissolves into the rich sepia tones that saturate the opening stills. The credits roll over the sepia stillness of the scene, frozen in time.

Though not a word is said, much is transpiring in the 45 seconds of this final shot. As viewers, we have already seen a number of instances of Frank's confusion and fear in the wake of his new restaurant inheritance and we perhaps sense the full weight of the nonverbal statement of this scene. It comes to us through picture and sound, through the echoing sound perspective of the gospel music, through camera angle, camera distance, composition and framing, through the rhythm of the camera's intimate revelation as we see Frank in his first moments of silence alone at the end of the day. As the camera pulls back and comes to rest, Frank the character dissolves into the pattern and texture of New Orleans the city, its history and its personality.

We could belabor the symbolism here (the baroque curved railings of the New Orleans balcony in the final shot balance a cross that appears at the top of the window, centered and prominent, above Frank's head). But symbolism is meant to be sensed, not endured; it is polysemic, not unitary. Here in this scene an aura of mystery is felt to attach to the things Frank does not know and understand and we too—disembodied viewers, rationalist echoes of what may or may not be going on in Frank's mind—can neither fathom nor guess the full impact of the moment. One thing is clear, however: Since not a word has been spoken, the mystery that pervades the scene comes to us nonverbally, through the codes of film.

It is not necessary to go into as much detail in describing how picture and sound work in other episodes of *Frank's Place*. Each uses a different cinematic strategy to accomplish its particular narrative purpose and ideological project. The "Businessman," for instance, centers our attention on the powerful CEO of a major corporation through a series of carefully developed two-shots and close-ups, which become more intense as his monologue reaches its apogee. Trucking shots and transitional humor are suspended as we enter the world of the businessman's mind, playing out a dialectic of internal self-conflict. The twist, the sudden rollback of the principle that has captivated his audience at the Chez—that rewards should be equitable and tied to the social value of work (in its own way a quite astonishing idea to hear on American network television, the capitalist medium par excellence)—is activated by a one-minute sequence of quiet musical chords: subtle, ominous, powerful, a musical correlative to the light bulb that starts to glow in the businessman's mind as he begins to see how he can defeat the plot that has been constructed against him. The sequence begins with the words, "That's a mistake, there's always a mistake," and ends with his announcement to his fascinated auditors that the first vulnerable link in the chain of power, fear, and greed encircling him is the affair he suspects one of his former partners is having with a secretary. "The secretary is the key," he says, and his analysis for the open-mouthed audience in the Chez—the comparatively powerless little people who live and work quietly for paychecks and look at the world of high finance and takeovers with varying degrees of skepticism and awe—culminates in a virtual tour de force of writing, acting, and blocking. But the effect of the twist when it occurs would be impossible without that quite spine-tingling set of musical chords, so subtly worked into the background of the scene that many viewers might not be aware of them, and would bring them to consciousness only on a second or third viewing.

Subtle or overt, played out in a detailed sequence like the dream sequence or the final scene of "Frank's Return," or woven integrally into the fabric of the show like camera angle or musical score, the filmic codes of *Frank's Place* sew together the pieces of its dramatic fabric. They create its world and instantiate its worldview. It is by now an unfortunate truism that informed viewings and critiques of television texts too often neglect the role played by the codes of their visual structure. In light of the seeming monotony of much of television's visual landscape, it is particularly important that the remarkable cinematic coding of *Frank's Place*, a coding that plays so integral a role in the intersection of narrative, ideology, and aesthetic, not be likewise neglected.

# 3

## The Sense of Place in *Frank's Place*

*Horace M. Newcomb*

*FADE IN* . . . words that appear on the left margin, one inch from the top of every screenplay. And because they appear on every screenplay they are common and commonplace, overlooked, ignored. In the *production economy* of the film and television industries they signify merely, *start here*.

This, of course, is the technical meaning of the term. Even when filmic representations do not begin with fades the reader is to understand that it is the rising light of exposed film, a technical process, a direction to the camera that is mentioned. To the production staff and crew, even to the actors, even to writers, both the technique and the technical reference to "Begin Here" are important.

But in the *narrative economy* of film and television, in the structure of meanings we critics refer to as *texts*, the words are far more powerful. They foretell. Translated, they could whisper, *Once upon a time*, or even *In the beginning*. They offer a tale, a story. Most likely it is a story told before, and we read/view from this point only to see how the tale is told this time, to see what new discoveries can still be made within this familiar pattern. From such a perspective, then, Fade in is a powerful signifier. More than an invitation, it is both promise and lure. Still, in this economy of pleasure and significance, of emotion and suspense, of carefully selected and limited exposures to a represented human experience, we tend to overlook the fact that we fade *from* somewhere *to* somewhere.

Where are we when we are called upon to Fade in? And to where do we fade? How are we to understand a term of such evocative elegance? Surely our concern is with more than the top left corner of the first page of the screenplay, with more than technique, with more, even, than the first day of principal photography when that first page may be left behind in the production manager's office in favor of the first page actually to be shot. For us, Fade in is entry not to physical space, but to a *sense of place*.

It draws, seduces us into a world like ours but different from it. To judge the world we enter too strictly by the one we leave is to risk grave error—to miss the point of it all. This sense of gentle, gradual, fragile, almost blurred entry suggests a bridge to a world only partially familiar, a world in which to see without being seen, to "listen in," to move about as freely as the camera will allow. We are, as has often been noticed, voyeurs. But we are also visitors, for our entry has been requested, by commercial interests and by creators, artists who without us would wither. We are tourists, for we witness behaviors common to us only in the necessary particulars, comparing the way these "strangers" do "different" things with "our" behaviors, values, practices, and meanings.

The somnolent tone of the words—Fade in—suggests, too, that we are dreamers. We dream in at least two senses of the word. We enter a state in which we explore our own experiences, remade, displaced, altered by what lies (and by the lies) beneath them consciously or unconsciously. And we enter the state of our desires, dreaming of better, ideal worlds.

The kinds of places referred to above—worlds, states—and the activities that are suggested to take place within them—viewing, listening, visiting, touring, even dreaming—demand guides and guidelines, demand maps. In this sense, then, after the initial invitation of Fade in, the screenplay can be seen to serve as such a map. In the production economy of film and television the producer, director, crew, and actors are moved about, guided as it were, by this set of written instructions. This is particularly the case because the "text" is never produced as it is on the page, in a carefully constructed set of causal relationships, movements, and purposeful alterations of time and event. It is created, most often, in the manner cheapest, in every sense of the word, with schedules of actors, crew, and physical environment carefully determined beforehand.

It is therefore essential for the producer or production manager to be able to *extract* the physical environment easily, economically, from the total script. So just as every screenplay instructs all participants to Fade in, every scene has its *slugline*. The slugline denotes interior or exterior, denotes a specific location, and denotes day or night. (Beginning screenwriters, in my experience, are taken with the notion of filming dusk or dawn. Such instructions cause much amusement for experienced production managers and directors aware of the difficulty of filming "golden time," defined as much by physical difficulty, that is, cost, as by aesthetic appreciation.) The sluglines thus become the detailed map of the fictional world we enter. The screenplay, dismantled by the production manager and rearranged into a shooting schedule, is remade into a map of the budget required to create that world. This is to say the sluglines can be read in two ways, as guides to the production economy *and* to the narrative economy of the work. The distinction I wish to make here is one between *location*, essential to production, and *place*, essential to narrative.

Every television series is constructed around a set of locations, some recurring, some altering. In comedy, most locations recur, and the production economy is based in this limited reproduction of, most often, interiors. The narrative economy is grounded in the constant exploration of character as defined, revealed, and altered by events that *can occur within* this restricted physical environment.

All locations have some basic meaning, of course, but that meaning most often results from simple associations established in the worlds of our own experience or, just as often, in our experiences in reading, in viewing films, or other television. That is, we distinguish among the "meanings" of the physical worlds of *Dallas* and *Dynasty*, a distinction based on an assumed knowledge of differences between Texas-rich and other kinds of rich. Or we may distinguish among the worlds of *Dynasty*, *The Cosby Show*, and *Hill Street Blues*, distinctions loosely associated with ideas about class and workplace. Or we may distinguish among *Hill Street Blues, Simon and Simon*, and *Miami Vice*, basing our sense of different place meanings on knowledge of genre.

In some cases, however, location is transcended. It becomes place, or is invested with a sense of place. The distinction, in my view, rests on the fact that place (as opposed to location) is itself imbued with meaning. Thus, characters can be defined, revealed, and altered merely by coming into contact with place. Events, even those we have seen before, are made special because they occur "here."

Given this generalized sense of place meanings, it is clearly in the interest of (the desire and aim of) every television writer and producer to create a location that can, in time, take on far more specific meanings of its own, that is, to transform location into place. This happened with the Bunkers' living room, with the Hill Street squad room, to some extent with the streets of Miami, and powerfully with the Women's bathroom in *Cagney and Lacey*.

When the creators of television shows choose as their locations places that *already* bear significant cultural meaning, then tailor them to have specific meanings capable of adding or establishing significance regardless of character or event, they have contributed mightily to the narrative economy of the series. They have made it possible for writers to construct specific stories based simply on the entry of "strangers," or on the encounter of regular characters with the rules of place, or on the alteration of those rules, the development of those characters or events that are associated specifically with the place. They have thus modified in advance the production economy of the series, not only by working with sets of culturally derived formulas for dramatic action, but also by making it possible for actors, set designers, line producers, camera operators, directors, and production managers to apply those cultural rule systems in their own work. Relatively few television series have managed to begin with this already established sense of place. *Frank's Place* is one of them.

Many of the chapters prepared for this book touch on some of these ideas, on the specific rules and meanings of places available in this series. My purpose here is to outline a set of relationships among them, relationships that enable us to understand *Frank's Place* as a set of cultural meanings constructed by the intersection between existing codes of place and the individualized characters who inhabit those places.

## REGION AS PLACE

The South is place, charged with meaning. It is a matrix of contradiction, a pattern of paradox. The region has its own shaded markers, its internal distinctions. Highland and lowland, tidewater and coastal plain, hill country and delta, swamp and piney woods, are inflected in terms of accent and dress, architecture and crop, hunter and hunted, and, most significantly, class and race.

Even in the wash of mass mediation that has rolled over nations like floodwater since the turn of the century, this region has maintained a sense of place. I will even argue that the influence of mass mediation, while surely altering that sense, has secured it. The region has seen itself represented or forgotten and has chosen to recreate itself in the artifice of craft fairs, local pageants, architectural revivals and renovations. It has established its journals (*Southern Living* and a host of smaller imitators) and its public image, the New Industrial-Information Society South, exemplified in Atlanta.

In the latest version of its populist impulse the South attempts to spread its broad, open, good-face-smile across the chin of the nation. But the corners of that grin remain and bear repetition—class and race. So with gentility and genuine hospitality, with relaxed elegance and good food, with a new, energetic public spirit, come the echoes of violence and demagoguery, oppression, and anger.

In all these patterns it is *memory* that drives the impulse of Southern meaning, memory that regulates the selection and application of image and event. Memory underlies the self-consciously constructed but useful fictions. Still, unwilling and unable to escape the accumulated weight of its own past, its own realization of those fictions, a real history, the education of memory, operates to regulate social interaction.

It is possible that with the decline of the western and the related decline of the meaning of the West, only the South maintains such a distinct sense of region as place. As a result, television shows set there gain in a ready-made set of meanings, but run the risk that those meanings are not as widely shared as they once were. To the degree that the codes of "southernness" must be *explained* they are a liability in the world of television. *Frank's Place*, by activating the codes of race in its most basic premise, recalls much of the sense of southernness, and in exploring those codes explicates them, in the particular version of the show's creators, for the mass audience. The show therefore reestablishes, with a new inflection, the regional meanings in which it is embedded.

None of this is meant to suggest that the show would not be as distinctive if set in another region. It would. But that difference would have to be established for all but a few viewers. A mass audience brings to the show its own varied, but alert senses of the South. To the degree that those senses are played upon, modified, confirmed, or subverted, the narrative economy of the show is enriched.

## CITY AS PLACE

The names of cities clarify this process and add to the riches of place. What would it have meant to have located *Frank's Place* in Ottumwa, Sacramento, East Lansing, or Scranton, in Portland, Fargo, or Brunswick? It surely would have meant something. But again, the burden of definition would have rested on the expository skills of the show's creators.

I have clearly loaded the dice with these examples. Chicago (in a waning Sandburgian sense), Los Angeles, New York, Washington, D.C., we might argue, offer their own compacted meaning structures. But I take it as significant that the strongest set of metropolitan meanings in recent television history has come from *Hill Street Blues*, which simply activated the anonymous code of "urbanness." *Miami Vice* runs a close second, and since Miami eludes southernness this show serves as an excellent example of the way in which meaning can be *constructed* rather than appropriated.

New Orleans offers, by contrast, a thick, dense web of meanings. Many of these have been consciously engaged by the makers of the show. The photographs and sound track of the title sequence present us with one set of meanings. Various plots have instructed us to the existence of others. The show draws stamina from its brew of music, religion, cuisine, custom, and mythology. It can call upon shared, and doubtless stereotypical, notions of voodoo or cooking contests. But it can also modify those notions with special, individualized responses to them and with camera work and sound that break our complacent expectations for the appearance of these types and icons in television comedy.

Moreover, the particular power of meanings specific to New Orleans is directly related to that city's specific inflections on regional meanings mentioned above, most immediately to New Orleanian versions of race and class. The self-conscious history of the city is rooted in the fine distinctions that often appear in the show, distinctions regarding not only black and white, but creole and cajun, white and black creole, and so on. That these "namings" also apply to foods is hardly coincidental in New Orleans or in the show, which makes the choice of the restaurant as setting all the more important. Where else better to explore the gumbos and étouffés, the roux and sauces of racial and social significance?

## COMMUNITY AS PLACE

"Working people don't go out in the middle of the week and white people don't come down here at night."

Tiger's explanation to Frank about why there's no real "night business" at the Chez is an equally clear definition of the community in which the restaurant is located. In one sentence New Orleans has been defined away from its travel brochure romanticism toward a neighborhood specificity, its charm transformed into significant sociology. At this level a mass audience does *not* share a set of specific meanings. What it shares, to some degree, is the sense that a very special set of codes does apply, but that it will have to learn these codes as the show develops.

Some of this is accomplished rather quickly with the establishment of character. We learn easily that Reverend Deal is a type, and what his role in the community is. We learn that there are specific power relationships within the community, that Mrs. Lamour wields a matriarchal authority of more than trifling import. This sense of neighborhood specificity is one of the intriguing attractions that tugs us into the show's continuing narrative. We want (or should want) to see more and learn more about these people, their place, their meanings.

## SET AS PLACE

Thus the circle contracts toward the most specific, and most unique, aspect of place in the series, the physical locus of the actual television narrative. It is far more precise, more material than the other, conceptual aspects of place touched on above. And for these very reasons it is more ambiguous. We will have to come to know it for its meanings to contribute precisely to our full awareness of this fictional world. But because it is a restaurant, certain shared conceptions and meanings surround and inhabit it.

*Frank's Place* could have been a pool hall. It could have been a grocery store or a record store, a barber shop or a book nook. It could even have been another sort of eating establishment, a diner or a hot-dog stand. In any of these cases certain meanings of place would have been associated.

It probably could not have been public premises of a professional nature, a courtroom, say, or a doctor's office. *Place* is too casual a title for such spaces— and too personal. We can't really imagine *Hill Street Blues* as "Frank's (Furillo's) Place." The very application of the name suggests a shift in the meaning of that show, suggests a *mis*nomer. Nor can we think of *Gunsmoke* as "Matt's Place." We probably can't even think of the WJM newsroom as "Mary's Place." Those spaces are defined by their function, generic and occupational. Who would trust a doctor whose shingle read "Marcus's Place"? But a restaurant is given over to meaningful moments. Its menu, its form of service, its staff, its clientele are all forms of expression.

The Chez exceeds even this kind of meaning, though it takes a bit of series development for us to understand these special complexities. It is really five spaces, again calling attention to the production economy of the show, reminding us that this is filmed, TV, on-the-set comedy. Any move off this set, outside the Chez, to the housing projects, for example, or to the boxing arena or Bubba's family dining room for Passover, calls attention to the importance of the Chez as meaningful construct. And within the narrative economy of the series, each of the five interiors bears its own significance. The bar, the dining room, and the kitchen, Frank's office and his apartment each offer the chance for different forms of enactment. Especially important is the fact that Frank inhabits the locus of his labor.

## STRANGER AS GUIDE

Whatever we learn about these rooms, this special community, whatever we learn about the detailed rather than the general version of New Orleans, whatever we learn about new moments of old Southern patterns, we learn with Frank. His sensibility and point of view are ours. When he encounters an instructor—Tiger, or Miss Marie—we, too, are tutored.

The Chez is *Frank's* place because he inherited it. But not one of these rooms will be Frank's *place* until he learns its meanings. Much of the delight many of us have taken in the series comes from the same sense of "being instructed," of learning what it means to be "here." The paradoxical sense of comfort in being guided, as it were, by a stranger in a strange land is fundamental to the structure of television narrative. The close of every episode promises that there is more to come, more to this world than we yet know. In a very real sense the power of television narrative rests in its *untold* stories, in anticipation, in what lies over the hill—or in Frank's case, in what lies in the next room or who comes through the door.

In short, the real sense of place, the sense that makes the show work in its best moments, is our shared sense of learning the rules, the meanings, of the very specifically circled, layered, and overlapped physical and geographical locations I have briefly described. Frank knows southernness, knows New Orleans, the neighborhood, the Chez as generally as we do. True, he has special connections through family, through being black. But he has redefined even these things or is cut off from aspects of them that are crucial to being himself in this new place. Incident after incident could be cited to support this view of the show, but two, from the "Return to New Orleans" episode, stand out for me.

The first is the Boston sequence, when the curse actually "works." Whatever pulls Frank toward New Orleans has destroyed the system of rules and meanings that govern Boston. The laws of nature, the rules of gender, the patterns of civil society have all been broken. Frank leaves, then, a man without meanings. When he walks through the door of the Chez he's the pure initiate. When Tiger asks him "Where you at?" Frank misses any sense of dialect or slang meaning and answers, with his best fraternity pledge's smile, "I'm right here." One can almost hear the "actives" chuckling, "We've got a live one now." It's going to be fun—comedy—to educate this guy.

A second example of the significance of place can be seen in the contrast between Frank's dream of his new life and the reality of "night business at the Chez." The "place" Frank dreams of is easily understandable (at least by every professional academic who has ever dreamed of opening a restaurant). Frank is in control. Athletic and political celebrities wait for his words. Romance is easy, and thorough. Contrary to his recent experiences in Boston, he is now even able to alter nature. Healing Bertha Lamour with a prophet's insistence and a (parodic) shaman's eye, he makes his presence into a rapturous religious moment. Then he wakes to the reality of a few surly drinkers, a sour cook who turns into Sambo to impress his new boss, and an empty set of tables.

What clearer indicator of *misreading* do we need? Instead of being the center, the definer of meaning, Frank discovers he must relearn everything. He does not know where he is, which brings us to the most powerful sense of place in the show.

## SELF AND STATUS AS PLACE

At the deepest level—the level that adds drama to this comedy—Frank does not know *who* he is. Certainly, he does not know it in this new place where all his previous status and authority are undercut by the new rules. The real emotional hook of the series title, then, is that Frank does not "know his place." Frank's dream is of social elevation. It's recognition he's after, and affirmation. Property, prestige, presence in a community rich in friendship as well as money; these are the things he imagines as his deserved "state." The reality of his situation is that being a professor of Italian Renaissance history cuts no ice at the Chez, in his neighborhood, in New Orleans. And for a black man who has given up the sense of status he gained by being successful in Boston, who has given up his place there, his accomplishments mean little in the face of one old Southern reality.

"White people don't come down here at night." How little it takes to remind us that we have far to go.

But in the face of this reality *Frank's Place* reminds us constantly of another, of the richness of place and place meanings. In doing so it reminds us of how far we have come. It suggests that we can get even farther if we acknowledge the texture of this world. We can learn the meanings of place and community found in the numerous touches that run throughout the series: Bubba's pained journey into the projects; the trickster Deal's lovely self-awareness; a Brooklyn-born basketball coach in Mississippi; jazz and African popular music; a black Tulane quarterback-surgeon; a homeless brother who refuses to leave the alley he makes his own; Mrs. Lamour's ruthlessly precise deployment of her power; the subtle and pernicious racism within the black community. All these things could have occurred anywhere but they are made more important by occurring here. Place is the ground on which these meanings are figured.

In the opening episodes, Frank still has these things to learn, and we have to learn at his pace. It is significant, then, that another undercurrent runs beneath all these notions of place and person—the always present sense of Frank's father, the true instigator and premise of this series. For me, the most highly charged moment in Frank's return to New Orleans is the look on his face when he enters the apartment above the Chez. He sees his father's *place* and doubtless contrasts it with his own. In choosing to return he chooses to accept this world.

The spare furnishings, the window over the alley, the chair before the window, the prominently featured bed, all speak of a reality far different from Frank's dream sequence. When he goes back to this apartment after his first, disappointing, real taste of "night business at the Chez" he sits in that sad chair and waits for the cat to come, waiting and puzzling over his place, knowing as we all do that his place waits a few steps away. He must sleep in the dead father's bed.

Because this is a television series, *we* wait to see how he will do it, wait to see how he will come to live here, learn the rules, live the new life. His mistakes will be the most prominent feature of this process, for this is comedy, and misread rules stand as the foundation of most of our jokes.

If we are saddened by the small-minded material decision that has closed off our interest in this world, we can at least hope someone has put a "spin" on the network executives who abbreviated our pleasure—and "we" know what that "means," because we've been "there."

# 4

# Black Music and Television: A Critical Look at *Frank's Place*

*Joe Moorehouse*

## OH, BABY HOW LONG?: A SHORT CONVERSATIONAL HISTORY OF BLACK MUSIC ON TELEVISION

The history of black music on American prime-time television is largely a history of silence. While white pop music has flourished on TV—feeding and being fed by it—blues, rhythm and blues (R&B), and jazz have been virtually nonexistent.

In the late 1950s, a typical episode of *Ozzie and Harriet* might include, after the resolution of the week's plot, Ozzie saying "And now here's my son Ricky to play and sing a song for you," followed by a cut to Ricky on a limbo set with his guitar. Granted, the song he'd play might be "I'm Walkin' " or some other bit of New Orleans R&B, but it sounded distinctly white filtered through Ricky's adolescent pipes.

His success touched off a string of imitators among other young sitcom stars. *The Donna Reed Show* even spawned *two* such crooners—Shelley Fabares ("Johnny Angel") and Paul Petersen ("My Dad")—both of whom contributed embarrassingly sentimental, distinctly white ballads to the pop charts.

It makes sense that in the late 1950s and early 1960s no black music was featured on TV since at that time no black people were featured on TV. The surprise is that, as blacks became more commonplace on the small screen and eventually became lead characters, black music still was only rarely incorporated into the soundtracks. On shows like *Ironside, Mod Squad,* and *Room 222*—shows that featured blacks in important roles—the music remained white and nondescript. Occasionally, when a scene was shot in a poor (read: black) neighborhood, the soundtrack would include a few notes of solo acoustic bass—a nod to black culture via ersatz blues. Young, hip black characters were more likely to frequent rock and roll clubs and listen to rock and roll stations than to champion soul, blues, or jazz. To Hollywood, there was only one music scene for the young, and its 1960s archetype was the Beatles, not Otis Redding. Black music was present only to the extent that it influenced much of the popular white rock and roll; that rock and roll was then (clumsily) mimicked for prime-time drama.

In terms of pop music, the early 1970s were a mirror of the early 1960s. Adolescent crooners were the rage again, but this time most had begun their singing careers offscreen, then starred in their own sitcoms. Bobby Sherman (his nonsinging role on *Here Come the Brides* notwithstanding) was one of these. David Cassidy was another. In 1972, Cassidy's vehicle, *The Partridge Family*, included an episode in which the family/singing group organized and played at a charity block party in a poor, black neighborhood. The black locals on the show were all big fans of the Partridges, of course. With an attempt at soulful panache, Cassidy sang "Oh No, Not My Baby," the old Goffin-King song that Maxine Brown had turned into a hit years earlier. Some solace could be taken from the fact that the show's producers at least incorporated an R&B song into this unlikely scenario, rather than using one of Cassidy's pallid bubble-gum ditties. On the other hand, the end result wasn't much different than Rick Nelson covering a Fats Domino song—except that, on *The Partridge Family*, black characters had to cheer the imitation R&B as though it were the real thing.

Under normal circumstances, there would be nothing particularly wrong with this scenario. Certainly, it's all right—even desirable—for white people to cover songs originally performed by blacks, and vice versa. And in this case, the song was even written by whites. It's equally desirable and realistic to show blacks enjoying music made by whites. The element that rendered this scenario offensive was the history—or better, nonhistory—of black music on television. Given the already offensive context that denied the existence of important black music, it was doubly offensive to show whites aping soul moves and voice mannerisms, because it implied that those mannerisms were the invention of whites.

Interestingly, Cassidy and Sherman were only two-thirds of a teen idol triumvirate in the early 1970s. Their fame among preadolescent girls was shared by a young black singer: Michael Jackson. In retrospect, it's easy to tell that Jackson's talent dwarfed that of the others. At the time, though, all three were considered ephemeral products, more hype than talent. Cassidy and Sherman were granted prime-time sitcoms. Jackson was featured (with his family) only in a Saturday morning cartoon.

The subsequent flourishing of black sitcoms—*Good Times*, *The Jeffersons*, and *Sanford and Son*—did little to bring black music to television. The only music in each was the theme song. *Good Times* and *The Jeffersons* had themes with a strong gospel sound, distinctly black and convincingly written and performed. If in the body of the shows there was no black music and no evidence that the characters had much acquaintance with black music, at least the theme songs were a start.

After the demise of those shows, however, little was done with black music on prime-time television. For all its innovations, the "urban" music on *Hill Street Blues* was often a pale, listless imitation of jazz and R&B. Few other shows of the era included any important black characters at all.

With the arrival of *The Cosby Show*, however, black music established a foothold, tenuous though it was, in prime-time television. On the show, Cliff's father is a jazz musician. He has talked about jazz and played it on screen. Occasionally one of the characters on the show will play a record, usually a mellow, modern soul ballad. Music isn't ubiquitous on the show, as is black visual art, but its presence is felt sporadically which is a big step forward.

There are a few other shows—especially the slick, urban cop dramas—that have occasionally used black music. *Miami Vice* and its clones, as well as *Tour of Duty*, have used R&B, albeit only that R&B that did as well on the pop charts as it did on the black charts. Their use of pop music almost always coincides with a visual style akin to MTV videos. While that may be seen as a small victory, on the whole black music has remained oddly divorced from television's consensus narratives; the message is that black music and, by extension, black culture are not consistent with the culture and values promoted on television.

Oddly, for all the networks' avoidance of black music, advertisers have embraced it, however slowly. In 1967, LeRoi Jones wrote that

TV backgrounds . . . have recently got the rhythm and blues tint via Rock'n'Roll or "Pop," i.e., the soft white "cool" forms, versions, of Gospel-derived rhythm and blues music. . . . The cool was a whitened degenerative form of bebop. And when mainline America was vaguely hipped, the TV people . . . began to use it to make people buy cigarettes and deodorants.[1]

By 1987, the "tint" that Jones referred to had assumed the value of true color. Percy Sledge songs were used in auto commercials; Marvin Gaye songs were in raisin commercials; Aretha Franklin did Chevy spots.

Into this atmosphere came *Frank's Place*, a show that used black music in such inventive, compelling ways that it nearly made up for 35 years of jazz/R&B silence on prime-time television.

## DO YOU KNOW WHAT IT MEANS?: MUSIC AND MEANING IN *FRANK'S PLACE*

The relationship between the narrative text of *Frank's Place* and the music of *Frank's Place* is extraordinarily complex. Perhaps the strangest thing about it is its reciprocity. On most shows, the music enhances the mood, comments on the action, provides transitions, and so on. In short, the music is at the service of the story. All of this is also true of the music on *Frank's Place*. But on this show, the story also comments on the music—and that, in a television narrative that ostensibly has nothing to do with music, is very unusual.

On *Frank's Place* music is a motif, a subtext, even a character. Its relationship to the characters, situations, and settings of the show is intrinsic, not extrinsic. Its role is both traditional and revolutionary.

The next section of this chapter will deal with the way in which music comments on action in *Frank's Place*. Following that will be a discussion of the way in which action comments on music and, so, creates some of the central meaning of the show vis-à-vis culture.

### Music Comments on *Frank's Place*

There has never been, and never will be a juke-box quite like the one at the Chez. It houses a stunning collection of classic jazz, blues, and R&B 45s. Louis Jordan, Tommy Tucker, Slip Harpo, Count Basie, Booker T. and the M.G.'s, Lightnin' Hopkins, and many other legends are represented. The newest songs we've heard from the box are Lee Dorsey's "Ya Ya" (at the opening of the basketball episode) and Booker T.'s "Green Onions" (as Frank and Hannah exit the bar in the Haystackers episode); both are from 1962.

The decision on the part of the producers to use black music almost entirely from the mid-century is an interesting one. It eliminates most of the folk blues of the 1920s, establishing the more urban sound of combos and bands. Given the New Orleans locale, this makes sense. The dearth of recent black music, however, is more telling. On one hand, it creates a kind of nostalgic atmosphere, one in keeping with the style, ambience, and values of the bar. Old people and things are revered. New things are not. Miss Marie, for instance, is held in high regard because of her age. Frank, the show's resident intellectual, was a professor of Italian Renaissance history. And in at least two episodes, modern art is condemned. In "The King of Wall Street," Mitch complains that a decorator has covered his office walls with art he doesn't like. In the Haystackers episode, Frank says to Tiger, "New is not necessarily bad." Tiger replies, "That's where you're wrong. You go to any art museum. . . . " On *Frank's Place*, new *is* necessarily bad, and that includes new music.

Perhaps more important, though, is that using the music of the 1940s and 1950s restricts it to pre-Motown R&B. Mid-1960s Motown is probably the best known, most distinctive black music ever made. It was hugely successful among both the black and white communities and is instantly recognizable to anyone who has listened to pop radio in the last 25 years. That it should be so excluded from a show that uses black music as a near-constant motif cannot be an accidental omission—it is, instead, the point.

The "Motown sound," complete with sweet voices, beautifully crafted pop songs, and strong bass lines, was as much the offspring of white rock and roll as it was of R&B. It was, in many ways, the perfect marriage of white and black popular styles. As Nelson George has said, "Motown in Detroit was black owned [and] totally committed to reaching white audiences. . . . The label seemed hell-bent on injecting itself into the mainstream."[2]

The records on the jukebox at the Chez are less the product of miscegenation than are the hits of Motown. With only a few exceptions, most were popular in the black community but virtually unknown to whites. They are songs whose roots clearly are in gospel and straight blues, not rock and roll or the old Hit Parade. Above all, they are songs written by blacks, sung by blacks, and recorded for black audiences.

The second reason why there hasn't been and won't be a jukebox like the one at the Chez is that it functions as an observer and commentator. Mark Meyerson, one of the show's music directors, has said that his mission was to think of the jukebox not as a machine, but as a character.[3] It's like a wise old man who consoles, supports, mocks, passes judgment, and otherwise comments on the inhabitants of the bar and their actions.

In the Haystackers episode, for instance, the jukebox twice comments as women come to the takeout window and discover that their husbands are sitting at the bar. As the first woman begins to beat her husband, Lionel, with her purse, the jukebox gives him some advice via Louis Jordan's "Caledonia." Jordan sings, "Son, keep away from that woman. . . . " The lyrics not only speak to the situation, but they also provide viewers with a filter through which to view the action; they set up Lionel as the protagonist, his wife as the antagonist. Were the jukebox not commenting on this scene, we would be more ambivalent about the reaction of the woman who, though overzealous in her anger, does seem to have a point—Lionel told her that he was working.

Another Louis Jordan song is playing when essentially the same scene repeats itself. This time, the jukebox simply observes and comments, but doesn't take sides. The lyric goes "Beans and Cornbread had a fight. . . . " This song plays on as the action continues. It acts not only to reinforce the action, but also to foreshadow Frank's confrontation with the music promoter. Beyond this, it is also a counterpoint to the Haystackers' "Pick a Bale of Cotton," using similar rural imagery in the service of a more meaningful story.

Nowhere is the jukebox more actively engaged in commentary than in an episode featuring a New York businessman. As he enters the Chez, Bobby Bland is singing "Stormy Monday," a straightforward foreshadowing of the bad times to come for Mitch Torrence. Of more interest, however, is the jukebox's reaction to the news that Mitch and his cronies (apparently) have been squeezed out of the corporation. An arrogant, racist white yuppie takes a call at the pay phone right next to the jukebox. As he receives the bad news in one ear, Huey "Piano" Smith laughs in his other one. The song is "Don't You Just Know It," but the important refrain is "Ah Ha! Ha! Ha!" Its tone is clearly mocking, a sort of editorial about the businessmen that everyone in the bar might agree with, but not have the opportunity to voice. This is accentuated when, the businessman having (rudely) asked Tiger to turn down the volume, Tiger accidentally turns it up, nearly drowning out the phone conversation with the song's mocking laughter. The volume doesn't decrease until the businessman is back at his table.

As he is about to give the bad news to his cronies, Tiger unplugs the jukebox. The sudden winding down of the sound is a metaphor for the sudden collapse of Mitch's fortunes.

This entire scene is one in which the jukebox is clearly functioning as a character. It's observing the scene, passing a moral judgment on the guests and giving its point of view to the other characters. In suggesting that the businessmen's misfortune is to be celebrated, the box clearly indicts not only these particular characters, but large corporations in general. The political message is that the interests of big business are at odds with the interests of the kind of people at the Chez.

The scored music in this episode helps to reinforce essentially the same theme. At the center of the show is Mitch's diatribe against big business. While he delivers it, there is no music playing, either on the jukebox or on the soundtrack. He is allowed to explain his position with no imposed editorial shading, because his position is the same as the show's—it's to be taken at face value. After Frank asks if the takeover is a fait accompli, however, both Mitch and the soundtrack go through changes. As Mitch says (almost to himself), "Pending details. That's always a mistake," somber, almost eerie strings are brought in. This unsettling music continues as Mitch, thinking out loud, comes to the realization that he can blackmail one of his partners.

The same music is used when Mitch is in the act of carrying out his plan over the phone. It returns as he speaks the line, "I'm gonna squash you like a bug." It stays in as he implies that he has "pictures, tapes, the works" with which to prove the other's adultery, and continues as he says "I didn't come up from the street. I came up from the gutter."

Apart from the largely inscrutable reactions of the other characters to Mitch's plan and subsequent carrying out thereof, the music provides the viewer with the only filter through which to read this scene. Given that, by the beginning of Mitch's resurrection, we've come to like him, it would be easy to read his actions as positive—they lead to a victory for a "good" character. The music, however, suggests that his reentry into the world of power business is, more than just regrettable, actually tinged with evil. The soundtrack makes a moral judgment—just as the jukebox did earlier—and finds Mitch wanting.

Although it's not the most prevalent music on the soundtrack, traditional scoring does play a role on other episodes as well. The opening of the Haystackers show includes "Do You Know What It Means to Miss New Orleans?" played sadly on a single violin. Treating the theme song—the one piece that viewers automatically associate with the Chez—as a lament immediately establishes the idea that the bar is in trouble. It's a more precise, more evocative, and more instructive choice than would be one of the wealth of "money's tight" R&B or blues songs.

Traditional scoring is used to good effect in other episodes as well. "Frank Returns" (the show's second episode) opens with voice-over narration by Frank, explaining the disasters that befell him in Boston as a result of the "spin" that was put on him. Pleasant, slightly sad orchestration accompanies scenes of his toilet spouting like a geyser, his girlfriend leaving him for a woman, and so on. The music is ironic, suggesting that (1) all of these disasters are funny, and (2) they are funny in a low-key way, not as slapstick.

The same episode also features several other scored pieces: There's a harmonica leitmotif for Hank Aaron, the cat, which establishes his character; a gospel choir singing as Hank Aaron jumps through the window to comfort Frank at the end of the show (suggesting, among other things, that the cat is in some way divine); a rather mundane string and oboe piece as Hannah tells Frank that she's engaged; and a brilliant and very complex series of pieces that accompany Frank's daydream of success.

At the opening of Frank's daydream, he's dressed in a tuxedo. Classical music plays on the soundtrack. Given the abundance of twentieth-century black music on the show, it seems surprising—and a bit reactionary—that classical music would be used to evoke elegance. The justification is that this is *Frank's* dream and he is a classicist. As Frank leaves his room and goes to the bar, where Hannah is waiting for him, we hear "Ain't No Mountain High Enough"— the only Motown song ever used on the show—to set the intensely romantic mood. As Frank and Hannah move to the dining room, the music shifts to cool jazz, then to church organ and bells as he miraculously persuades Bertha to eschew her wheelchair and stand. Throughout this sequence, the music does the bulk of the emotional work. It sets the tone, changes the tone, and pulls us slowly along as Frank's dream becomes more and more absurd. The musical choices are just overstated enough to add humor without overshadowing the action. It's a perfect complement.

The episode featuring Adele, the African musician, is the most dense and eclectic musically. Included are rhythm and blues ("High Heeled Sneakers" is on the jukebox as the show opens), American jazz (Dizzy Gillespie performs), African music (an African band performs a song called "Akiwowo"), and traditional dramatic scoring (a poignant string passage is used several times, and a few notes of "The Way You Look Tonight" are heard on brass). There are also several examples of musical punctuation on rhythm instruments. When Dizzy Gillespie is mentioned, there is a brief drum tattoo. When Miss Marie is confused with Anna May, we hear a few notes on upright bass. Remarkably, the variety of musical genres and devices don't get in one another's way. The music is always at the service of the story. But then, in this episode (and occasionally in others) the music *is* the story.

### *Frank's Place* Comments on Music

Rich as is the relationship of music to action on *Frank's Place*, the relationship of *Frank's Place* to music—and, by extension, the larger culture—is even more telling. The show's themes and its attitude toward race, class, and culture are all, to some extent, embedded in its treatment of music.

Music is the most prominent symbol of culture on the show; at times, it is accorded almost mythic power. Music can either bring cultures together or drive a wedge between them; it can break down barriers or erect them.

Popular black music, predictably, is a positive force in *Frank's Place*. The use of juke box songs as commentaries has already been dealt with. The implication is that black lore and wisdom are maintained and disseminated, at least in part, by black music; it has the power to instruct and advise. Music is also seen as celebratory. When Miss Marie discovers that Frank has come to take possession of the bar, she says, "Shorty, put a quarter in that box." She doesn't suggest that he play a specific, overtly festive song—it's *music* as a whole, not *songs* that are valued.

Musicians are held in high esteem. When Cool Charles is talking about celebrities dining at the Chez, he mentions Cab Calloway as his example. When Frank wants to increase his night business, it's not a big screen TV, or drink specials, or a wet T-shirt contest that he offers, but a live band. And the artist that he first hopes to get is guitar legend Bo Diddley. Interestingly, viewers are expected to know who Bo Diddley is. There is no explanation proffered for the ignorant. Knowledge of musical giants, no matter what genre they've worked in, is taken for granted.

This same assumed knowledge is exploited by Frank's promoter when he brings up the wittily named Guitar "Fat" Brown. "The problem with Guitar 'Fat,' " he tells Frank, "is that very, very square white people have never heard of him." Frank is intimidated into pretending that he is familiar with Brown. The implication here is that black music and musicians are necessarily "hip," while white music and musicians are not.

This is made more explicit later in the same episode, when the Haystackers appear. As the Haystackers enter the kitchen in their matching red-checked outfits, an instrumental blues boogie is playing on the juke box, further juxtaposing the folk singers with their environment. Judging from their looks and repertoire, it is unlikely that the Haystackers have heard of Bo Diddley, much less the mythical Guitar "Fat" Brown. Their total insensitivity to black music and black people is made apparent when they perform an old slave song as though it were a culturally meaningless hootenanny tune. Were the Haystackers to sing the titular "Oh, baby how long?" signature line, they would rob it of its slave spiritual echoes ("How long, oh Lord, till freedom?").[4] These are, indeed, "very, very square white people," but their ignorance is not harmless, it is culturally damaging.

The largely black audience reacts to the Haystackers by glaring, or sitting dumbfounded. They don't move at all, as a few of the white people do. Their utter stillness conveys their rejection of the music, a rejection that the music well deserves. It contrasts with scenes from the African musician episode, in which listeners—both those at the African musician's practice and those at the Gillespie concert—move in time to the music. Their love of and feeling for the music is shown in reaction shots in which they bob their heads, tap their toes, and smile. Movement indicates pleasure.

If the Haystackers debacle indicates that white Americans don't understand black music, then another, more subtle moment suggests that black Americans want no part of white music. Bob Coleman, the State Department representative who is chaperoning Adele and his companions tells Frank that "Adele is a national treasure in his country. If he were to stay here it would be like Elvis Presley defecting to the Russians. Now you know the good old boys back home wouldn't go for that." What Coleman doesn't say, but implies, is that black people wouldn't much care—it's white rednecks who are interested in Elvis Presley. There is no mention here, however, that black indifference to white music is culturally damaging. The chasm between the cultures is simply pointed out, not analyzed.

There is clearly, however, a close relationship between black African culture and black American culture. The Americans love the African's song; Adele loves Dizzy Gillespie. In fact, jazz seems nearly magical for Adele. The line most central to his story is, "Your father's record collection is *truly amazing*, Frank. I am *not* going home." That such a momentous decision should be triggered by something as simple as a couple hundred jazz albums speaks to the power of music and to the affinity that black musicians feel for black music of any culture.

The mad leader of Adele's country prohibits jazz on the grounds that it is "ethnically polluting." *Frank's Place* argues that cultural commerce between African and American blacks is desirable; the two groups find a common language in music, and come to understand one another better.

The show also argues that no such bond operates between black Americans and white Americans. Even though they speak the same language, there is no cultural communication between the two groups and, perhaps, no hope for it. The white restaurant consultant advises that Frank raise the price on the juke box from twenty-five to fifty cents—thus, whites not only keep their distance from black culture, they also try to distance *blacks* from black culture.

After enduring a generation of television that tried to pretend black music didn't exist, it shouldn't come as a surprise that *Frank's Place* treats jazz and R&B as prized things, private to their own race.

## NOTES

1. LeRoi Jones, *Black Music* (New York: William Morrow and Co., 1970) p. 204.

2. Nelson George, *The Death of Rhythm and Blues* (New York: Pantheon, 1988) p. 86.

3. Mark Meyerson, interview with author, October 19, 1988.

4. In the same interview as listed above, Mark Meyerson said that the signature was from a 1920s song entitled "How Long Blues." Steve Tyrell, the other music director, sang and recorded it for use at the end of the show.

# Part II

International Authorship Studies

# 5

# Television Authorship in France: *Le Réalisateur*

## *Susan Boyd-Bowman*

> We have a fault in our television, a fault that INA has not avoided and
> which relates to French sociology. We are authors. We are always trying
> for the masterpiece, and we forget the program.
>
> Jacques Pomonti, INA's president, 1984

This chapter discusses authorship in French television, where creativity is deemed
to lodge with the director. My argument is that French broadcasting inherited
from film culture a form of the *politique des auteurs* which means that the
director of a program is perceived as the originator. In British television, by
contrast, the institutional power has resided with the producer and creativity with
the writer, as opposed to the director. Thus the name attached to a British program
in the case of TV fiction is generally the screenwriter's, and in documentary
features it is the series editor's or individual producer's. In France, the person
who *realizes* the program and *proposes* it to the viewing public, is the director,
whose authorship is enshrined in the 1985 Copyright Law (alongside the screenwriter's and composer's) and in the covenant of the TV directors' syndicate. I
will return to this contrast at the end of the chapter, after an extended consideration of the bastion of the director-as-author in French television: INA.

## INA IN FRENCH TELEVISION

French broadcasting legislation in 1975 broke up the old ORTF (*Office de
Radiodiffusion-Télévision Française*) and incidentally created the Institut National de la Communication Audiovisuelle (INA) with a specific mandate to

experiment in TV output. This provided the infrastructure of a cadre of freelance *réalisateurs* who would carry over a tradition of innovation from the cinema into broadcast TV.

Among state-funded broadcasting organizations, INA has been in the unusual situation of having both responsibility for the national audiovisual archives, and a specific brief to produce creative and experimental productions for the national networks. The conception it adopted is one of "memory as a source of creativity," with the audiovisual, like other works of art, being a firm part of the national heritage. This patrimony was put at the disposal of a host of filmmakers recruited from the cinematic (and later video) avant-gardes, whose work was influenced by the structuralist intellectual climate.[1] There was a period of highly innovative production before cataclysms took place in the political economy of French television, culminating in the recent expansion and deregulation of television channels, which has seriously jeopardized INA's production budget. The programs it makes have been transmitted on a quota basis on the first three French networks; its impetus is now likely to be taken over by the forthcoming "cultural" channel, La Sept, in European coproductions with comparable channels such as Four in the United Kingdom.

Fredric Jameson[2] describes the energetic texts of late capitalism as embodying advanced communications technology to mesmerize the audience with sheer technique of representation itself: a rocketing into "postmodern hyperspace." Some of the later work done by INA can be considered as "energetic" in this way. Its project was the attempt to disrupt the discourses of French public service broadcasting and to problematize its concepts of popular memory, cultural heritage, and narrative, in the same way that such texts, according to Jameson's thesis, challenge official culture by veering toward the attenuation of dominant ideology. The collages transmitted under the series titles *Rue des Archives* and *Juste une Image* contested the literary values and signifying practices which predominated elsewhere on television. They broke down the demarcation between high art and popular culture, for example. But they also represented a technicist fetishization of the *Image*, a postmodernist play that is less interested in what its original materials may once have meant, or signify to viewers today, than in the radical polysemy of the text. In the period I am describing, the mid-1970s to the early 1980s, French culture witnessed a waning of a modernist belief in problematized historicity and communication and a turn to ironic parody. As I will argue, the two anchors in this drift have been the abiding auteurism of French television—the retention of faith in the subjectivity of the author and the viewer—and a cultural nationalism.

When INA's president, Jacques Pomonti, made the remark which prefaces this chapter, its future policy was posed as a choice between originality, which ran the risk of an elitist address, and a mass appeal which meant homogenization with the rest of television; a choice between creativity and industrial production. "Our role," he said, "is invention and research. We aren't going to amuse ourselves in retailing production like a factory."[3] Here as elsewhere in French discourse on television the subtext is the specter of American imperialism, crystallized at the time around the impact of *Dallas* on national culture.

INA's documentaries based on archival sources negotiate a contradiction between production as a form of communication, with its implied mimetic qualities—the transparency of the national storehouse of the audiovisual, and its salability as part of TV's parasitism on its own past—and on the other hand as a form of expression, with its insistence on textual production.

## EXPERIMENTATION IN THE AUDIOVISUAL

My thesis is that in the three audiovisual magazine series produced by Thierry Garrel and Louisette Neil (both of whom have since moved to La Sept) between 1975 and 1984, there was a shift from a modernist approach to the archaeology of the image, with its concern with history, style, and didacticism, to a "hypermodern" reification of the image, in which history and logocentrism are suppressed in favor of an attempt at "inner speech," a play of verbal images addressing a collective unconscious. Stephen Heath has observed that "independent, avant-garde, and political filmmakers have turned to inner speech and its verbal images to produce alternative institutions, different 'viewings', new hearings."[4] Across these three series, Garrel, Neil, and their collaborators have tried to reconcile the individualized languages of authorship with the collective dreamwork of film and television. As Willemen defines inner speech in relation to psychoanalysis: "The traces of inner speech in the visual, in the figuration of a narrative or a tableau, take the form of, precisely, *loci communi* of the socially and linguistically commonplace. This would be one more argument why 'images' should be considered products of secondary elaboration, that is, displaced enunciations invested by/with unconscious discursive processes."[5] The problem to which I will return is the cognitive dimension of these enunciations. "We were the very first to 'decipher' the image," coproducer Louisette Neil commented in 1984. *Hiéroglyphes*, made on film in 1975/76 demonstrates the main principles of the audiovisual magazine which would be carried over to the later video series *Rue des Archives* and *Juste une Image*:

1. a celebration of authorship; each item will be "signed" by the *réalisateur* who made it

2. the etiolation of the presenter, and eventually of a commentary voice to situate the items in relation to each other

3. an eclecticism in use of material (spanning the entire history of film and television, the popular and the avant-garde, the foreign and the domestic, etc.) enabled by the liberalism of the archive policy

4. the emphasis on radicalism in form: an aversion to anything which fits within the norms of television

John Ellis points out that the magazine format of items running ten to twelve minutes in a program of one hour, has now become habitual on French television (it is used on Antenne–2's *Cinéma, Cinémas* which began in 1981), and remarks that the "advantage of the formula is its consistent possibilities for surprise, both in the nature of the material that can be shown, and in the possibilities for startling juxtapositions."[6] The dethronement of verbal language in favor of the pleasures of the image has only rarely been experienced on British television: video art showcases like *After Image* and *Ghosts in the Machine* on Channel Four have been much debated in terms of media representations of the visual arts.[7]

## RUE DES ARCHIVES

*Rue des Archives* was a series of individually authored archive compilations which ran for four series of six editions each from 1978 to 1981. Before *Rue*, archive compilations had been primarily illustrative, often with a new commentary provided. As Theirry Garrel explained:

We decided not to treat the Archive as a kind of meccano collection from which one assembled a film to illustrate a historical thesis or whatever. What we did was to go to a certain number of directors and ask them to say something with the Archive, without reducing it to a simple collection of stock shots, just putting together so many minutes of television.[8]

The new series was made on video, and unlike *Hiéroglyphes* before it or *Juste une Image* after, it relied entirely on archive material, rather than mixing found with commissioned work. The result was a highly impressionistic series of montages. To quote from INA's press release for the first series in 1976:

Named after the Paris street housing the National Archives. This series is exclusively composed of extracts from the archives of French television and provides the audience with an opportunity of strolling around that vast collective memory.
   Departing from the conventional classifications according to genres, specific themes, historical periods, it gives these documents a different dimension and a new resonance.
   The first six programmes of the *Rue des Archives* series are original essays in which the authors/filmmakers confront—according to their personal vision—striking and singular moments from television's past. While the emotion of the rediscovered images is preserved, reflection is also [aroused] on the reality of television yesterday and today [INA's translation].

We can note that the objective of the series is the attempt to yoke the affective and the cognitive dimensions of the audiovisual. The metaphor of the promenade is conveyed in the series titles, which show a silhouetted figure walking up a cobbled street, the rue des Archives. The words are represented as the classic blue Parisian street sign; each episode (transmitted on Sunday evenings at 20:30 [8:30PM]) is cued by "today: . . . [title]" and of course the name of the author.
   The most critically celebrated *Rue* essay of 1979 was the two-part "Petit

Manuel d'Histoire de France,'' directed by the exiled Chilean filmmaker Raul Ruiz, who brought to this commission some of the stylistic fabulism for which he was becoming known in avant-garde cinema. (He would later get commissions from INA for feature films, most notably *Trois Couronnes pour le Matelot*.)

Ruiz gave an account of the project to *Cahiers* in 1981:

INA was interested in developing relations between the cinema and television, and so tried to bring to television some *auteurs*, people who had a distinctive approach. . . . At the time they wanted to call on foreign *auteurs* (there were Terayama, Angelopolous, etc.). I realized that they considered us as authors, as a little apart from the others.[9]

Garrel was producing *Rue des Archives* at the time, and proposed the subject of French history to Ruiz: "It was a matter of editing together clips from serials and historical dramas, putting them in chronological order, and showing the history of France as television saw it."[10]

Ruiz chose to span the time from the Gauls to the invention of the cinema, often intercutting between several versions of the same event, as in the sequence about Jeanne d'Arc, in which five different actresses interpret the character. Whereas other *Rue* directors used montage in discrete sequences, Ruiz attempted to juxtapose images within the frame:

I wanted to take into account the multiplicity of interpretations of history and I had the idea of making a film with two bands of images in parallel. I showed two (and sometimes three) films at a time, which I could mix at the last minute on video by a simple wipe passing between one and another, in such a manner that you could feel that while you were watching one event there were others happening. Not just different versions of the same events, but events in parallel.[11]

Ruiz began by viewing programs and studying history textbooks, and located very strong stereotypes. Fredric Jameson has commented on "la mode retro": "it seems as if we are condemned to seek the historical past through our own pop images and stereotypes about the past, which remains forever out of reach."[12] Ruiz, too, made a postmodern diagnosis:

I saw that these stereotypes were used by directors of the Right as well as the Left. An historian friend helped me to understand that these stereotypes had their origin in the nineteenth century. . . . All of French history was that of the formation of the State and all moral discussion in these films bore on that theme. Most of the films I saw—what we call "the Buttes-Chaumont school"—were in effect bits of the same discourse. Everything that works for the centralized state, no matter what the means employed, is good, and everything against it is bad. . . . For that reason, I chose to work with the actual school-texts [four manuals running from the end of the nineteenth century to 1968] and to have them read by children of from eight to sixteen years old, girls. I adopted the idea of having them read these texts for the first time. . . . Then I played with these three elements: the double image, the maladroit readings of the schoolbooks, and the very stereotypical mise-en-scène of the history of the formation of the State.[13]

Another element of parody in "Petit Manuel," which consists entirely of these quotations from television plays and reenactments of French history, is the digital date of the given event which appears in the upper-right corner of the frame. (As usual in *Rue*, almost each extract is provided with a provenance in screen writing). The proliferation of stereotypical representations reaches a subversive pitch when Ruiz gets to Napoleon, and follows a clip from Gance's *Napoléon* with his own frenetic montage of shots from the preceding parts of the program, what Jonathan Rosenbaum describes as "a helter-skelter heap of near-subliminal flashes, one shot per era, which effectively reduces all French history to a hysterical flood of incoherent clichés."[14] (Those who followed the 1988 presidential election campaign may have seen Mitterand's use of the same technique in his political ad, which featured 800 images in 90 seconds.)

Is this parody of French history an act of subversion or does it exemplify the postmodern tendency to undermine the very possibility of authority and origin? Does Ruiz's parody of this official grand narrative imply that there can never be one? In his comments to *Cahiers* it seems he did have a view of history heavily colored by his Latin American origins. But the problem with his INA programs is that the spectators cannot orient themselves within the text. Ruiz's thesis about the formation of the state implies a logic to the radical heterogeneity of clips which I suspect is not evident even to a French viewer, and the sole basis for our perspective of this depthless, kaleidoscopic spin through history is simple irony.

## DOCUMENTARY FEATURES

Another Latin American director working in Paris, also associated with the cinematic equivalent of the "magic realism" movement in literature, was Edgardo Cozarinsky, who was commissioned by INA to make a one time only documentary based on archival material. It would get wide distribution outside France, increasing the prestige of the organization and the stable of film directors it patronized. *La Guerre D'Un Seul Homme* would also inaugurate another strand in the Garrel-Neil output: film documentaries which juxtaposed public images (newsreels or fiction cinema) and written texts (by the famous and the obscure) to demythologize French history.

Edgardo Cozarinsky, an Argentinian filmmaker living in Parisian exile, had produced four shorts for INA from archive footage, in the form of "cartes postales." "In all four of them fictional texts (messages written on postcards) explode the raw document and make it yield to something else." Cozarinsky describes the technique as "putting into conversation the strands of lies that are the substance of History."[15] These "stolen" postcards were the prototype of what has become a dominant form at INA, breaking that convention of the documentary that insists that sound and image tracks move in parallel.

*La Guerre D'Un Seul Homme* (INA, 1981) had its origin back in 1978, when Cozarinsky flicked through the INA catalog of Actualités Françaises, an independent newsreel company operating between 1939 and 1969, when its archives were bought by ORTF. In addition to noticing that some items were "faked," he was surprised by the amount of content on daily life. He also knew the wartime diaries of Ernst Junger, the military commandant of Paris from 1940–44, an aesthete and intellectual who observed the Occupation of the city with detachment. (Junger is still alive, and his writings are well-known in France.) Cozarinsky became interested in "cantilevering" the newsreel images and the writings of the German officer. The principle of his feature-length film would be a dialogue between the trivialities of the propaganda newsreels and the subtle self-deceptions of a *littérateur*.

At the time, INA had withdrawn from international coproductions on experimental films, and so Cozarinsky was obliged to make a 55-minute video for television transmission. It took him a further two years to put together the ideal that emerged as the 109-minute film financed by INA, ZDF, and Marion Films. It was edited over twelve weeks in May 1981, dubbed with the voice of actor Niels Arestrup, and the music of four German composers (the "Aryans" Strauss and Pfitzers, and the "Degenerates" Schoenberg and Schreher). It was shown in eight film festivals, won a lot of prestige for INA, and launched (or revived) a subgenre of the compilation film, in which the found footage is manipulated in a fictional way.

In an interview for *Cahiers* in 1982, Cozarinsky said he never felt he was making a documentary. It is impossible to capture truth with a document, because truth is in fiction. *Golddiggers of 1933*, for example, tells us more about the New Deal than any documentary. Or as he put it in a later interview with Thomas Elsaesser for *Framework*:

As far as documentary is concerned, I always feel that fiction films are the best documentaries of any period, for they allow the imaginary to speak, which in the bad sense of documentary is forbidden. . . . The stock footage of any period is meant to be a recording of reality but it is completely open to the imagination. For me there is a kind of displacement of roles, the fiction film becomes a document and the would-be document opens itself to the imaginary.[16]

As we have seen, this inversion of the fictional and the documentary was typical of INA's attitude to moving images. The highly coded quality of the Actualites newsreels meant that they had to be forced to reveal what they suppressed. Like Marcel Ophuls's *Le Chagrin et la Pitié*, *La Guerre* returns to what Cozarinsky calls "the neuralgic point of the national conscience," but he isn't interested in statistics about collaboration with the Nazis, and the film doesn't pretend to tell the truth about this period. It breaks with almost every convention of the compilation genre. If Bazin disparaged archival montages as lies about history, Barthes was writing thirty years later of history itself as the Big Lie. As Cozarinsky recalls it:

I wanted to study the play of lies . . . and reproduce on a small scale the contradiction and blind spots of an epoch without ever assuming the voice of history, but rather, to recreate the difficulty of seeing clearly in which people live in any period. From that point of view, it was the strongly encoded aspect of the news films that interested me: precisely through the censorship, they betrayed all that was repressed. At the same time, when you construct a small-scale model with forty years' hindsight, you know the historical outcome of the situations you are examining. Hence the sense you get of making a film about the present, by rediscovering the lines of force, finding behind the image that remains of that period, the problems and anxieties of the present.[17]

Cozarinsky told Pascal Bonitzer he was trying to capture some of the post-Cambodian shock and disillusionment with Left ideology which he felt was absent from mainstream cinema. But most of the film critics missed any polemical intent, ascribing *La Guerre* to what is usually called a montage film, while reflecting on the fictionalization of the documentary form entailed by Cozarinsky's method of juxtaposition—for example, his editing by association on a symphonic musical structure, rather than by chronology, subject matter, or other expositional device. The *Positif* critic argued that the links between thought and image were so oblique (as in Junger's dream illustrated by a tornado) as to be Borgesian (a literary comparison often made, due to Cozarinsky's nationality). The film, he argues, does not produce a reality effect, but a truth effect.[18]

British critic Thomas Elsaesser also had reservations about the implications of the method. He published an interview with the filmmaker in *Framework* in the summer of 1983, which while on the one hand inviting Cozarinsky to expand on his critique of the intellectual frivolity of Parisian life (fashion, he believes, was and is the model for French culture), nevertheless expresses disquiet with the film's ambiguities:

The malaise the film provokes stems from the sense that, as a spectator, we cannot orient ourselves. We are not given an opposition, we cannot work on simply irony, as the basis for our perspective. . . . The malaise is nonetheless never released, the irony never leaves the audience in a position of knowledge.[19]

Cozarinsky replies that while he hopes that certain "rhymes" will become apparent on repeated viewings, and that reiterating some shots with different editing and soundtrack will show them to be constructed, nevertheless his prime objective was to disrupt the process of reading the film:

What I was most afraid of, on aesthetic grounds, was that the film would be systematic in the wrong sense, in that it would become obvious to the viewer from the start how it worked, the rest following on the same principle. I was very much afraid that the film would have a method which people could pinpont.[20]

It could be argued, given the polyphonic quality of the text and the lack of any clear perspective, that the viewer is left identifying with the voice of Junger, the visitor from another planet. Cozarinsky denies that Junger's voice is the overarching discourse:

The voices I would have liked to listen to are not those of such "stars," however engrossing their account, but those of the nameless "extras"—I have frozen the image on their faces (literally, the faces in the crowd) to let us fantasize what roles they would have played, what their "one-man's-war" may have been like.[21]

The "voice" chosen by Cozarinsky is that of a compromised cosmopolitan intellectual; the images seized from the flow are valued for their qualities as images. Elsaesser picks up a contradiction which runs throughout INA's experimental work (though he is speaking here of *La Guerre* only):

We have, in our fascination with the image, no responsibility to what the image "in reality" might have signified. We appropriate the image in a way that perhaps writing does not allow itself to be appropriated, for when language is used in such an appropriable way we call it bad writing, propaganda.[22]

Cozarinsky concurs, admitting that he wanted to preserve the faces of people in order to possess them himself: "I allowed myself to engage in some kind of necrophilia by making them the object of my desire." Wartime images are particularly fascinating because they are so violent. Cinema has a vampiric relation to life: "When I want to allow people to really see the face of the prisoner about to die, my film feeds on his victimization." He goes on to echo a view widespread at INA: lamenting the contemporary saturation with images because of television. Images have lost the aura they had when people had to go to the cinema (as to church) to see them, and when they had a greater capacity to impress people's imagination. This experience is lost from watching films on television, and there is a strong but implicit argument that *La Guerre* (and later films in this series), though made for television, ought to be seen on the large screen.

## CHANGING DISCOURSES

In France, the television documentary does not hold the same prestige as it does in the UK. The artistic impulse is almost always to deconstruct it. Like many of the auteurs who came to INA for funds, Cozarinsky had a low opinion of the capacity of television to handle grand themes. At Jacques Derrida's 1979 philosophy colloquium, Régis Debray chaired a workshop on teaching and the media, which concluded that television, by its ephemerality, lack of reciprocity, and appeal to the affective rather than the cognitive, could not be used for doing philosophy.

The mass media are not neutral forms susceptible of carrying no matter what cultural material. They entail necessarily a regression of discursive forms, a decomposition of analytical procedures inherent in critical thought, the progressive abandonment of a certain number of constraints proper to the philosophical effort such as demonstration, definition, or interpretation.[23]

A series of similar objections to the medium are made in the 1981 TV supplement of *Cahiers*; here is critic Sylvie Blum:

Speed [of images] makes intelligibility disappear, or rather makes it difficult to find meaning, except to show that meaning is an addition, appliquéd on color put into a coloring book. The essence of television is speed, a flow which denies the possibility of going back. . . . You can't talk of truth if you can't talk of meaning.[24]

Thus far the critique is a traditional literary one, but Blum goes on to anticipate what will soon become postmodernist orthodoxy:

At the moment I'm watching, I renounce the real so that television offers me another world seen by another in my place. Which is why television is never in truth, but always in fiction. Because this other reality is not a copy of the first, but functions as a model of it. Television does not return us to a preconstituted reality. It manufactures a language of images which has its rules, its rhythms, its own time. . . . We could say that the new space is perhaps that of dream or poetic space. And flux, liberty or poetry. Analogic associations, syntactical disorder, indeterminacy of meaning. Television discourse is contrary to any classic propaganda.[25]

If television is to be rescued from this homogenization toward the simulacrum, she says, it will be by the eruption of the Unknown, almost unimaginable in the present institutional context—one must leave to the *réalisateurs* the task of playing with time, with form, and with fiction. "The principle of reform will be to allow the unexpected to be produced and transmitted—things which (outside of all utility) make television lie, break all the rules, escape the flux and the oblivion where one amuses oneself."[26]

By 1986, however, INA was obliged to retrench and consider carrying the Unexpected into the marketplace. In a speech to the CNCA (Conseil National de la Communication Audiovisuelle) Blum said that INA's *réalisateurs* must, in the future, "reintegrate formal research into its proper place and perhaps into works which retackle the real, the text, and stories." Survival for INA would henceforth depend on involvement in international coproductions and its ability to cope with the constraints which inevitably follow from an attempt to address a multinational audience.

## LES RÉALISATEURS

Who are these television directors? Entry into the profession is strictly regulated; there are 940 TV directors, and within their ranks there is a hierarchy of genres, means, and access to airtime. Many won entry through the film school, others won "homologation" through having directed a certain quota of material. Garrel's introduction to the dossier *Profession: Réalisateur* (1986) lists the many skills a director (always spoken of in the masculine) must possess. His conclusion gives a good idea of the professional ethos at INA:

The director is an intellectual. He is, in the communications world, a mediator of ideas, of facts, of people and values. Invested with social responsibility, he is neither a teacher, a policeman, judge, journalist, priest, doctor of souls, even if all these dimensions pertain—for better or worse—to the manner in which he practises. The director is also a creator. Endowed with a particular sensibility, he imprints images, by means of an invisible alchemy, with something of his own personality. Which is why he insisted on the status of "image writer" and could win, in addition to his function as craftsman, his position as author, confirmed by the Lang law in 1985. But is it really an Art, like music or painting, or art in the sense in which cuisine is, in which case direction is limited to a savoir-faire accompanied by more or less good taste? If the baker makes bread and the painter his canvas, the Director makes—often simultaneously—a work, a film, a broadcast, a message, a product, a program. So he can scarcely pretend to the "artistic liberty which has no other limits to its expression than the exploration of what he wants to say" [my translation].[27]

The contradiction between artisanal and industrial modes is an issue that preoccupied Manette Bertin, INA's head of production, in an interview with Thierry Garrel for the same 1986 dossier on directors.[28] She bemoans the fact that INA has seemed unable to reconcile the exigencies of industry and the "subtlety necessary to any cultural enterprise," which results in the lumping together of disparate workers: beginners, technicians, real authors, specialists in video, etc. In order to renew the moribund creative function of INA, she recommends a politique of prototypes, modelled on the industrial sector, which would be well financed enough to attract the best professionals ("to them should go the honor of trying out things which allow you to establish new genres and to invent formulas which good artisans can then develop into series; up to now they have preferred to devote themselves—despite their militancy in favor of the public service—to their personal work"). *La Propagande: L'Image et son Pouvoir*, a coproduction for French, Swiss, Belgian, and Canadian TV, was the last INA series in the prototype inaugurated by Garrel and his *réalisateurs* ten years before. TF1, now privatized, did not take up its option to transmit the series; there was to be no vindication of INA's policy of audiovisual memory as a source of creativity.

## AUTHORSHIP IN BRITISH TELEVISION

If in French television, the phrase "propose par . . . " or "réalisé par . . . " [director's name] appears in the opening titles, in British broadcasting it is the producer's name which holds pride of place as the last name of the end credits. In a debate on the role of the director held a couple of years ago at the Edinburgh

Television Festival, the complaint was made that "over the years, the director has lost his importance in television. Today, the director comes third or fourth after the editor, the producer, the series producer and even the scriptwriter."[29] Changes in the politics of British broadcasting have meant a further diminution in the status of the director. On the one hand there is a pendulum swing away from observational documentary—those ciné-verité studies of institutions which have dominated documentary output for over a decade, making the reputations of a number of British equivalents of Frederick Wiseman—toward the authored, composed documentary, with the writer's byline and face on the screen. In fiction, there has been a backlash among television critics to what is perceived as the self-indulgence of directors who are attempting to bring to the small screen the aesthetics (and *longueurs*) of feature film production. The contradiction is that many of these larger budget series and serials, particularly those transmitted on the publishing-only Channel Four, are the result of European coproduction, where the ideology of "art" cinema and "art" television favors the director-as-author, the sort of "names," French and foreign—and even embracing American video artists like Robert Wilson—who have been fostered by INA.[30]

Translation of film authorship into television has led to a precarious balance between eclecticism, didacticism, and postmodern manipulation of the audio-visual heritage. France's emphasis on the quality of the individual auteur's creativity is to be contrasted with Britain's lingering commitment to the spoken word, the acting performance, and the public service profile.

## NOTES

I would like to thank David Russell for his comments on the drafts of this paper.

1. Among the filmmakers commissioned by INA were Rivette, Godard, Marker, Duras, Syberberg, Angelopolous, Varda, and Akerman.

2. Fredric Jameson, "Postmodernism & Consumer Society," in Hal Foster, ed., *Postmodern Culture* (Pluto, 1985).

3. Jacques Pomonti, quoted in Jill Forbes, ed., *I.N.A.: French for Innovation* (BFI Dossier 22), 1984.

4. Stephen Heath, quoted in Gregory Ulmer, *Applied Grammatology* (Johns Hopkins, 1985), p. 298.

5. Paul Willemen, "Cinematic Discourses—The Problem of Inner Speech," *Screen*, vol. 22 (1981).

6. Ellis, quoted in Forbes, *I.N.A.*, p. 33.

7. See Philip Hayward, ed., *Picture This: Media Representations of Visual Arts & Artists* (John Libbey, 1988).

8. Garrel, quoted in Forbes, *I.N.A.*, p. 20.

9. "Entretien avec Raul Ruiz," *Cahiers du Cinéma*, Television Supplement, 1981.

10. Ibid., p. 41.

11. Ibid.

12. Fredric Jameson, "Postmodernism, or the Cultural Logic of Late Capitalism," *New Left Review*, no. 146.

13. Ruiz, *Cahiers*, p. 42.

14. Jonathan Rosenbaum, "Beating the Labyrinth," *Monthly Film Bulletin*, vol. 52, no. 612 (January 1985).

15. Pascal Bonitzer, "Entretien avec Cozarinsky," *Cahiers du Cinéma*, March 1982, p. 12.

16. Thomas Elsaesser, "Discourse and History: *One Man's War*: An Interview with Edgardo Cozarinsky," *Framework*, no. 21 (Summer 1983).

17. Cozarinsky, in Bonitzer, p. 12.

18. Emmanuel Carrere, "La Guerre D'Un Seul Homme," *Positif*, no. 264.

19. Thomas Elsaesser, "Discourse and History," p. 21.

20. Ibid., p. 21.

21. Ibid., p. 22.

22. Ibid., p. 21.

23. Régis Debray, quoted in Ulmer, *Applied Grammatology*, p. 302.

24. Sylvie Blum, "Y a-t-il quelqu'un qui regarde?" *Cahiers du Cinéma*, TV Supplement, 1981, p. 89.

25. Ibid., p. 90.

26. Ibid., p. 91.

27. Thierry Garrel, ed., *Profession: Réalisateur* (INA Dossier de l'Audiovisuel) no. 7, 1986, p. 15.

28. Manette Bertin, "Le point de vue d'une productrice," in Garrel (ed.), p. 42.

29. David Cunliffe, Head of Drama, Yorkshire Television, at the Edinburgh Television Festival, 1985.

30. In December 1988 the Media 92 program of the EEC set up the European Script Fund to finance preproduction of projects from writer-directors which would be of interest to at least two member states.

# 6

## Authorship Conflict in *The Prisoner*

*Tony Williams*

Originally screened on British television, *The Prisoner* concluded its brief 17-episode run amidst great controversy. Although it began in a spy series format, the course of the formula transcended the original structure subverting not only agreed concepts of what a television series should be but also accepted definitions (pre-1968) of viewer identification with narrative and hero.

*The Prisoner*'s importance extends far beyond the original viewing experience. It breaks down the rigid television barriers between subject and object as the final segment, "Fall Out," reveals. Thus the temptation arises to ascribe the splits and tensions within the series to a battle between two "authors": script-editor George Markstein, who initiated the idea, and star, Patrick McGoohan, who later gained full control. In popular criticism the series' vitality became the latter's property. Did he not embody the most comprehensive figure of the auteur? McGoohan was not only the star but also directed, produced, wrote certain scripts, edited others, supervised the re-shooting of "unsatisfactory" scenes and even attempted composing the theme music.[1] So, in terms of a loose use of auteurism, it appears "natural" to credit McGoohan as the individual author of the series.

However, this not only neglects *The Prisoner*'s production history but also certain significant insights of post-structuralist theory which question any individual author's role. Controlling personalities are less important than the dynamic complexities of meaning inherent within the textual process. *The Prisoner*'s significance in terms of television studies may be more appropriately investigated by referring to contemporary works on textuality.[2] These investigations emphasize the demotion of the creative individual in favor of understanding more crucial issues of subject identity, both of director and audience.[3] In examining

*The Prisoner* we shall see that its value lies less in assigning its status to any particular individual source but more in terms of its questioning accepted ideas of a television series and individual creativity.

A comparison with the average television series is useful here. No matter what the intentions are, any series is a product of capitalist conspicuous consumption designed to be devoured in one evening and forgotten the next.[4] Any series has an ephemeral value unless the components take on a nostalgic or "popular memory"[5] force that results in its reappearance at a later date. The usual series format is a random number of episodes which may or may not continue over several seasons depending on the ratings system. Usually, the stars appear in several episodes with no connecting link between them. Each week we view the adventures of Maverick, Cheyenne, Crockett and Tubbs, the Enterprise crew in segments which have no connection with either past or future episodes. The Lorimar soap operas *appear* to be exceptions in their continuing sequences. But low ratings may bring cancellation even when several enigmas remain to be solved as in the case of the concluding episode of *Flamingo Road*. One appropriate model is *The Fugitive*'s conclusion in which Richard Kimball finds his one-armed man and is declared innocent. Other examples are *Route 66*, which had a perfunctory winding coda to the series, and *The Survivors*, which attempted *The Fugitive*'s comprehensive conclusion formula but at the cost of making incoherent previous narrative segments.[6] In both cases the attempt is made to round everything up, like the Aristotelian well-made play where nothing remains for audience consideration after the climax.

*The Prisoner* attempted the second formula but violated the definitive conclusion concept making assimilation into television narrative canons impossible. If the climax appeared to engender confusion no less so is the question of any definitive authorship inscription. Indeed, both text and "author(s)" form a complementary matrix.

Patrick McGoohan's resignation from the mid-1960s popular British spy series, *Danger Man* (in the U.S., *Secret Agent*) formed the initial act in the drama. Created by Ralph Smart, *Danger Man* began as a half-hour episodic series featuring the weekly adventures of special agent John Drake. McGoohan abruptly departed just as the series extended into an hour long format. At the time *Danger Man* had eclipsed another Lew Grade I.T.C. series, *The Saint* (featuring Roger Moore), in popularity. The I.T.C. company was desperate to find a new vehicle for McGoohan.

*Danger Man*'s story editor, George Markstein, provided the answer. Exploiting the real-life situation of McGoohan's resignation, he envisaged the idea of a secret agent retiring at the height of his career. From his past experience as a British intelligence officer Markstein knew of institutions that contained ex-spies who could never be allowed freedom. The inmates often suffered highly sophisticated brainwashing techniques. In his sixty-page treatment Markstein conceived the idea of a former agent's abduction to a strange Kafkaesque environment which had vague parallels to his previous society. While his captors wish to know the reason for his resignation the Prisoner attempts to learn the identity of a mysterious unseen Number One who controls the place. All his fellow prisoners are either ex-agents or pawns of the administration. Each episode involved a battle of wills between the Prisoner, wishing to retain his individuality, and the wardens, who attempt to break him. The proposed series would be a natural sequel to *Danger Man*. However, since "John Drake" was still Ralph Smart's copyrighted property, McGoohan's persona became "Number Six."

As Chris Rodley describes it, "*The Prisoner* was conceived as a spy thriller consciously constructed around more 'profound' notions of the individual versus the system, personal freedom and personal prisons."[7] This double edge set it apart from its nearest relatives such as *The Saint*, *The Avengers*, *The Baron*, and *Man in a Suitcase*.[8] With its commercial perspectives of overseas sales (especially American), *The Prisoner* would belong in the context of those non-serious espionage formats such as *The Man from U.N.C.L.E* and *I Spy*[9] but colored by an uneasy amalgamation with the British realist tradition and Orwellian satire.[10] Markstein added other elements to his concept creating the ideas of the prison as a village (modelled on the lines of the Butlins holiday camps),[11] a twenty-four hours surveillance system, the prisoners' identity by numbers, a currency credit card system known as "units," hallucinatory drugs used in sophisticated brainwashing, a new Number Two every week, and his silent butler appearing in each episode.

McGoohan took the proposal to Grade who immediately accepted it. The star's addition involved selecting Portmeirion in North Wales as the village location, refusal of 1960s' action spy thriller formats such as fast guns and cars, no Ian Fleming-influenced female sexual partners, and specific visual designs such as the penny farthing bike and piped blazers. Art director Jack Shampan included the mini-moke taxis and cordless telephones.

George Markstein first heard about his project's acceptance when he read the evening paper on the railway journey from Shepperton to Waterloo.[12] It was advertised as Patrick McGoohan's idea!

Location filming began at Portmeirion in September 1966. But although the series arose from a combination of Markstein and McGoohan's ideas there were other salient factors at work.

The production company was Everyman Films. Named significantly after the medieval allegory of a man who must confront his own death, the company comprised two directors—Patrick McGoohan and television director David Tomblin. Both men had worked together on a Portmeirion *Danger Man* episode.[13] A wider circle of people became active in the conception. George Markstein became script-editor and collaborated on the opening episode, "Arrival," with Tomblin. Jack Shampan had also enjoyed a long association with *Danger Man*. He had also worked on Ealing Comedies, well-known for their gentle satire of English characters and institutions, as well as Hammer productions such as *Circus of Horrors* (1960) and Joseph Losey's spy send-up *Modesty Blaise* (1964). Shampan designed Number Two's inner sanctum and the village control room in a group decision process.[14] Director of photography Brendan J. Stafford had worked on all the *Danger Man* shows, feature film productions, television series designed for an international (that is, mainly American) audience, and documentaries.[15] Film and television director Don Chaffey directed the first four episodes with the exception of "Free for All," an allegorical treatment of Parliamentary democracy scripted and directed by McGoohan.

Chris Rodley describes *The Prisoner* as being "a prime example, although by no means exclusively so, of a constant cross feeding of talent between television and feature film production which thrived in the 1960s."[16] We must remember that this was a period of liberal radicalism within television drama experimentation which often questioned the status quo. The contemporary benevolent regime of BBC Director-General Hugh Carleton-Greene provided a fertile environment. Thus *The Prisoner* found a favorable climate to emerge at that particular time in which it could engage in a subversive attack upon authoritarian institutions, especially the British establishment.

This is most evident in the casting. From the time of the second episode, "The Chimes of Big Ben,"[17] it became clear that Number Six's own side wanted to break him. European Nadia Gray arrives in the village which is run by Leo McKern's Number Two (this is well before his *Rumpole of the Bailey* days). The vague geographical location (contradicted in following episodes) appears to be somewhere in Eastern Europe. However, the main figures in the episode are actors familiar for their portrayal of establishment types in contemporary British film and television—Richard Wattis and Kevin Stoney.[18] Number Six finds that the village has recreated his superior's London office. In "Arrival," Guy Doleman played Number Two. Doleman was Michael Caine's spy boss in the 1965 *The Ipcress File*. He repeated the role in *Funeral in Berlin* (1966) and *Billion Dollar Brain* (1967). George Baker's second Number Two contained echoes of that actor's 1950s contender status for establishment "stiff upper lip" hero roles usually associated with Jack Hawkins and Anthony Steele. By design or unconscious accident Patrick Cargill[19] appeared as a British secret service executive in "Many Happy Returns" and later as Number Two in "Hammer into Anvil." In "Free for All" Eric Portman was the Number Two who engaged Number Six in a "democratic" election for his job. Portman could play both sturdy establishment types as in *The Colditz Story* (1954) as well as sinister, sometimes foreign roles.[20] In the same episode, character actor George Benson appears as the civil servant, Number Fifty-Eight, grilling Number Six. There is some visual ambiguity in that scene since it is the latter's shadow which appears behind the former. It tentatively hints at the projection of an unconscious fantasy even in the earlier, more "realistic" episodes.

The initial idea was to shoot thirteen episodes with a production break, then return to complete a probable season of another thirteen. What actually happened was contrary to everyone's expectations.

The first location episodes were "Arrival," "Free for All," "Dance of the Dead," and "Checkmate." Then followed "The Chimes of Big Ben," "The

Schizoid Man," "The General," and "Hammer into Anvil." The last episode shot was "Once Upon A Time" on a black set involving an Oedipal duel between Number Two and Number Six. This unconsciously paralleled a struggle between Markstein and McGoohan for control of the series. For Markstein the writing was on the wall. He left after this episode which was acted, written, and directed by McGoohan.

An eight-month production gap followed. McGoohan went to America to film *Ice Station Zebra* leaving Tomblin to set up the last four episodes for an early termination of the series. According to a strict application of the auteur theory, McGoohan should be the acknowledged victor in terms of the conflict with Markstein. But this argument is problematic in terms of the circumstances surrounding the final episodes.

It was actually Tomblin who set up "Do Not Forsake Me O My Darling," an episode designed to compensate for McGoohan's physical absence from the set. Tomblin and scriptwriter Vincent Tilsey solved the dilemma by having another actor, Nigel Stock, play a Number Six deprived of his body by mind transference. Number Six thus has to return to the world he has left. Like the other episode, "Many Happy Returns," it was designed to suggest that the forces controlling the British establishment and the village were identical.[21]

Two other "padding" episodes were conceived by Tomblin. They were pastiches modelled respectively on the popular 1960s television genres of the western and spy thriller. Although designed as "light relief" these episodes had significant threads relevant to the whole series. Both take Number Six out of the village only to return him there. In "Living in Harmony," Number Six discovers that the western town is only a set, a fiction designed to entrap him in an imaginary world. He also finds that the actors in the western drama (gunfighter Alexis Kanner and saloon girl Valerie French) become so entrapped in their roles that they cannot discern fiction from reality. This anticipates "Fall Out's" premise. "The Girl Who Was Death" makes explicit both Number Six's misogyny as well as the village's sexist structure which rarely has a female Number Two. At the climax we discover that the narrative is in reality a bedtime story which Number Six tells to the village children. Number Two (Kenneth Griffith) and his female accomplice (Justine Lord, Number Six's fictional adversary) have hoped that the "bedtime story" would result in an unconscious slip of the tongue revealing the reason for his resignation. However, by this time, the resignation has attained the status of Hitchcock's "MacGuffin." It is insignificant in comparison to the play of forces involved in the signifying process of Number Six's identity.

In "Fall Out," written and directed by McGoohan, the series concludes with a postmodernist discourse on the processes of subject construction and viewer identity. The viewer wishes to know Number One's identity in the manner of a normal spy series. Instead, the spectator is prompted to reread and reevaluate everything that has preceded this episode "in the light of a barrage of comparatively indigestible material."[22] We move away from the manifest level of the text toward a latent discernment of the figural constituents inherent in every episode that both transcend and explode any ascription of individual authorship.

A brief examination of these figural elements reveals the dominance of circular imagery—the penny farthing, the Rover balloon, the light over Number Six's head which often hypnotizes him with some brainwashing process, a television monitor's eye, hidden cameras in his room and the rest of the village, the circular arena inside Number Two's dome as well as those two cameras beneath monitoring the movements of the village moving round in a circular direction. With its sense of observation and entrapment the circle forms a powerful structuring element around which the text of the whole series gravitates. The final episode involves an eye watching in Number One's rocket.

Number Six is under constant observation in his circular home. Each episode ends with his face zooming toward the screen before prison bars abruptly close on it. The village is in the background. A direct look at the camera breaks the diagetic code of realist representation. Only the clanging of the prison bars prevents his gaze invading the viewer's. The final credits construct a penny farthing bicycle wheel before Rover emerges from the depths into complete circular construction. The circle is usually understood as the symbol of roundness, coherence, and implying wholeness and identity. But it is this imaginary ego that the series seeks to destroy. No answer is given to the hermeneutic code of the validity of Number Six's epistemological quest and the preservation of individuality. Under the series's textual construction this is an impossibility.

Each episode begins with a recapitulation of Number Six's incarceration until the final one breaks the imprisoning structure. The format of the previous sixteen episodes has a dominant repetition-compulsion sequence with overtones of Freud's "fort-da" game involving the viewer in a frustration of the Prisoner's request for release.

This quest involves a revelation and vindication of individuality. However, "Fall Out" suggests that the search for a Cartesian ego free from social and unconscious constraints is a myth. The climactic image is the opening scene of the first (and subsequent opening scenes of the initial sixteen) episodes. It asserts that the quest for individuality is little more than a neurotic repetition compulsion as is the quest for original authorship.

"Fall Out's" format involves not only the viewer's active interpretation of events but also a reinterpretation of previous episodes. This is especially so with the reintroduction of previous characters in new (Alexis Kanner, Kenneth Griffith) and familiar (Leo McKern) roles.

"Once Upon A Time" concluded with Number Two's (McKern) death after his unsuccessful attempt to reconstruct Number Six's social identity.[23] "Fall Out" commenced with the supervisor (Peter Swanwick) leading Number Six away to finally meet Number One. They enter a tunnel ending up in a changing room. Inside we not only see Number Six's original suit but *moving* coat hangers. This alerts us to the fact that the series concerns everyone not just one individual. Others have obviously preceded (and will follow) Number Six in his battle against the social construction of individuality. The audience naturally expects Number Six to emerge as the eventual victor, an expectation that the climax will deny. Throughout the series the village attempts to change not only Number Six's mind[24] but also his body.[25] A tailor's dummy in the changing room resembles Number Six with his original pre-village clothes. The supervisor's ironic words—"We thought you'd be happy as yourself"—precedes a juke box recording of the Beatles' "All You Need is Love." At the time this was the anthem of the hippy nonconformist revolt against establishment values, a revolt which was to collapse into futility after "innoculation" by bourgeois ideology.[26] The role of Alexis Kanner's Number Forty-Eight illustrates this, his number being an inverse of "Nineteen Eighty-Four" as well as representing one of the peak years of the British baby-boom era whose representatives would be the beneficiaries of 1960s youth culture.

Number Six emerges into a chamber occupied by a president (Kenneth Griffith) who significantly wears the ceremonial robes of the speaker of the House of Commons. Also within are other establishment figures: the military, surgeons, and a jury composed of white-hooded figures all representing various movements that capitalist society has safely categorized and rendered ineffective. They are identified by labels such as "Welfare," "Activists," "Pacifists," "Identification" (among whom the supervisor sits), "Defectors," "Therapy," "Reactionists," and "Anarchists."

The president then begins a discursive address which represents authority's final attempt to overpower Number Six by co-opting him into the status quo. "This session is called in a matter of democratic crisis. And we are gathered together to resolve the question of revolt."

He turns in a *circular direction* in his podium to the jury's applause. Quieting his audience he speaks of the threat to the community, speaking constantly in the plural. "We desire that proceedings be conducted in a civilized manner. . . . The community is at stake and we have the means to protect it." Although he applauds Number Six's survival the mise-en-scène reveals the still existing threat to Number Six. He is dwarfed by a high-angle shot with surgeons (perhaps from "The Schizoid Man," "Dance of the Dead," and "A Change of Mind") standing prominently behind him. The following reverse low-angle shot of the president stresses institutional dominance. "Indeed, he must no longer be referred to as Number Six or any number of any kind [shot changes to mid-shot]. He has gloriously vindicated the right of the individual to be individual [jury figures prominently behind]. And this assembly rises to you sir." At this point the jury immediately stands in applause.

The president then speaks of a "tedious ceremony" involving the "time of ultimate power": inviting Number Six to "observe the preliminaries from the chair of honor." Number Six then seats himself to the musical strains of the British establishment ruling-class anthem, "For he's a jolly good fellow."

Unease appears on his face. He observes the cage where his psychological battle with Number Two occurred and a rocket marked "Number One." The observers on two cameras from Number Two's surveillance chamber are also present.

A parallel exists between Number Six's enthronement in the chair as *passive* observer and the average television viewer. The latter believes in an artificial screen separating him/herself from the dominant ideology contained in the media apparatus. Is not the television screen seemingly under control? Is it not "just entertainment" which the viewer could switch off? The question is far more complicated. Both Number Six and the viewer are presumably individuals in full control of their destiny. But Number Six's enthronement in the viewer's chair presumes a royal control that is illusory. As we shall learn, Number Six is not a coherent individual but a divided self. The same is no less true of the average viewer.

In an afterword to the work of H. L. Dreyfuss and Paul Rabinow,[27] Michel Foucault speaks about the second phase of his explorations involving discursive practices in relation to individual subjectivity. "I have studied the objectivizing of the subject in what I shall call 'dividing practices'. The subject is either divided inside himself or divided from others. This practice objectivizes him."

In its entirety *The Prisoner* text is an important example of this argument. Its premises extend far beyond any level of individual authorship attribution since the entire work opposes the facile nature of any form of subjectivity that is supposedly either coherent or free from social dominance.

Foucault's work about the devices that dominate the subject within all phases of human society forms a crucial background toward understanding the series. It relates to certain aspects of postmodernist thought involving the death of individuality and the role of power-knowledge structures in everyday life. The village is a microcosm of society, particularly in the devices it uses to attack Number Six's mind and body. It is more than accidental that the underground chamber has more than a passing resemblance to Bentham's Panopticon described in *Discipline and Punish*. The television apparatus has now taken the place of the original structure. For Foucault, the Panopticon is "a generalizable model of functioning; a way of defining power relations in terms of the everyday life of men. . . . It is in fact a figure of political technology that may and must be detached from any specific use. It is polyvalent in its applications."[28]

In Number Two's version of the Panopticon we see a parallel to Bentham's original surveillance cells. However, there are now television screens both below and above Number Two's chamber. Foucault's description reveals the power of this observation apparatus not only on the observed but the observers. All the Number Twos in the series are constantly under observation. In this mechanism that "automatizes and disindividualizes power,"[29] making the rituals of a sovereign's power useless, a central tower (Number Two's dome headquarters?) is a "privileged place for experiments on men, and for analyzing with complete certainty the transformations that may be obtained from them."[30] Number Two's chamber is certainly the observation area for Number Six's mental and physical ordeals. Foucault also points out, "The Panopticon may even provide an apparatus for supervising its own employees.''[31] This parallels Number One's observation rocket and his own interior chamber. The Panopticon functions as a "laboratory of power" that can be integrated into any function by being closely linked with it, making "power relations function in a function, and of making a function function through these relations."[32] Foucault's description of the Panopticon's operation closely resembles that of the village.

Hence the major effect of the Panopticon: to induce in the inmate a state of conscious and permanent visibility that assures the automatic functioning of power. So to arrange things that the surveillance is permanent in its effects, even if it is discontinuous in its action; that the perfection of power should tend to render its actual exercise unnecessary; that this architectural apparatus should be a machine for creating and sustaining a power relation independent of the person who exercises it; in short, that *the inmates should be caught up in a power situation of which they are themselves the bearers*. To achieve this, it is at once too much and too little, for what matters is that he knows himself to be observed; too much, because he has no need in fact of being so. In view of this, Bentham laid down the principle that power should be visible and unverifiable. Visible: the inmate will constantly have before his eyes the tall outline of the central tower from which he is spied upon. Unverifiable: the inmate must never know whether he is being looked at at any moment; but he must be sure that he may always be so (emphasis added).[33]

Certainly, this describes the whole village situation: from its occupants who are either prisoners or warders, to a Number Two constantly observing and under observation, to a Number Six who discovers that he is his own jailor. Number Six thus has to learn that he is the bearer of the look, a look returned by him and returned by his alter-ego in the unmasking sequence.

In the meantime he observes the adjudication of two forms of revolt—Number Forty-Eight and Number Two. Alexis Kanner's Number Forty-Eight represents the 1960s hippy revolt of disruption. He initially upsets the assembly by rushing through its confines singing "Dem Bones." However, both his hippy language and song are taken up by the judge and assembly temporarily under Number One's direction. Subjected to Barthes's "innoculation" process, Number Forty-Eight's revolt fails and he is led away.

The next revolutionary is Leo McKern's Number Two. Resurrected from the dead he was obviously once an important establishment figure. His speech explains his use-value and village incorporation.

It has been my lot in the past to wield a not inconsiderable power. Nay, I had the ear of statesmen, kings and princes of many lands . . . sweeping policies defined and revolutions nipped in the bud at a word from me in the right place and at the propitious time.

Not surprising, therefore, that this community should find a place for me, not altogether by accident that one day I should be abducted and wake up here amongst you.

What is despicable is that I resisted for so short a time, a fit tribute to your methods (applause follows).

It is obvious that Number Two is an older version of Number Six. He antic- ipates his successor's later activity in staring at Number One before being led away, arms in a crucified position similar to those of Number Six before the office doors in the pre-credits sequence. The only revolutionary left now is Number Six. He receives an invitation to join the establishment. Rejecting this, Number Six is asked to make a farewell address. "Remember us, don't forget us. Keep us in mind. Sir, we are all yours."

This invitation is significant. It is a last attempt to incorporate Number Six, particularly in its use of the plural and the communal inducement, "we are all yours." However, Number Six still attempts to assert his individuality. Each time he begins his address with "I" the jury interrupts, echoing it back to him three times. Obviously, had he said "we" he would have been a lost cause. The number "three" has, also, significant associations. It not only is half his village number but anticipates the three part repetition of each episode's con- cluding pre-credits segment when he unmasks Number One.

Number Six makes his way to Number One's chamber. On the way he passes Number Forty-Eight and Number Two imprisoned inside glass chambers. He passes an empty one, obviously his destination if he fails in his mission. He then ascends the stairs to a control room containing globes and television mon- itors. A hooded figure sits in front of the screens. The chair turns round remi- niscent of the motion of Mrs. Bates's chair in *Psycho* before the final revelation which also mocks the viewer's epistemological quest.[34]

Number One watches a television screen showing what would be a subjective point-of-view shot from his perspective of Number Six's entry. The lines of Number Six's refusal speech begin. "I will not be filed, indexed, numbered, stamped, briefed, debriefed," etc. It speeds up reiterating the "I" similar to Hitchcock's celebrated stream-of-consciousness effect in *Blackmail*.[35]

Number One hands Number Six a crystal globe. The circle corresponds with the observation tower globes as well as those other figural motifs within the series. A close-up of the crystal globe follows "I" repeated mockingly speeded- up on the soundtrack as Number Six takes it. Then Number One stretches out his arms satirizing Number Six's defiant gesture as he opened the office doors prior to his resignation and challenging any claims to freedom and individuality.

Number Six drops the globe. As it smashes on the floor there follows a succession of three shots of each episode's concluding coda. This repeated sequence denies the supposed freedom that Number Six hopes to gain. It also denies any realistic epistemological narrative resolution that the viewer would expect from the concluding episode of a television series. Both aurally and visually the sequence anticipates the following schizophrenia of Number One's unmasking.

Number Six tears off the mask finding a monkey visage beneath. This stresses the primeval level of human consciousness. But this is not all. Removing this he then confronts his own face jeering at him and repeating his cherished symbol of individuality, "I." The unmasking is shot in reverse shot alternating close-ups of each character. Number Six repeats Number One's facial grimace before chasing him around his observation chamber and locking him inside the rocket.

The final village scenes show the three "revolutionaries" escaping to the ironic theme of "All You Need is Love" as they shoot their way out. Assisted by the butler, they flee in the cage that had witnessed the Oedipal duel between Number Six and Number Two. This setting already hints at a return to square one despite the anarchic behavior of all three inside. Number Forty-Eight's theme "Dem Bones" returns temporarily, diverting the attention of an establishment figure driver before he once more gains control of his car and drives away. "Dem Bones," with its motif of the interconnectedness of all elements within society (in that each unit needs the other and cannot exist independently), has somber undertones in view of what will follow.

Number Forty-Eight leaves to thumb a ride on the highway. Number Two departs near the Houses of Parliament, the area from which he was presumably originally kidnapped. The butler enters Number Six's London house. However, the door ominously opens like his village domicile and has the number "1." As Number Six gets into his Lotus automobile, the undertaker's car of each pre-credit opening sequence passes him.

The preceding revolt is already undercut. Number Forty-Eight hitchhikes on the highway in an opposite direction from where he started. It is obvious that the aimless direction of his revolt will continue. Number Two is last seen with his establishment attire of striped trousers, dark jacket, bowler hat, and briefcase before he enters the House of Lords. Thunder once more occurs on the sound-track, the same thunder that heralded each episode. The Lotus races down the runway. A close-up of Number Six which opened every episode is the final image. The wheel has turned full circle and is about to resume again.

*The Prisoner* thus concludes in denying the Cartesian concept of the ego, its ideological crux of freedom and individuality, and the television series' role in providing a coherent, epistemological resolution for the viewer. It is irrelevant as to who is the original author. We are all the "authors" trapped in the ideological matrix of individuality. The whole text of the series is structured on the denial of subjectivity, hence its unpopularity as a mainstream television series on both sides of the Atlantic and its relegation to "cult" status. In many ways its trajectory has much in common with Lacan's definition of the subject. According to Lacan, the imaginary, the symbolic, and the real constitute subjectivity.[36] In the "mirror phase" a young child's identity bases itself upon a narcissistic sense of unity with its mirror image. This image becomes projected on the surrounding world. However, this unity must be broken up by the world of difference before the child can take its place in culture as a sexed object.

In "Once Upon A Time" Number Two reverses Number Six to the pre-Oedipal stage to discover the secret of his resignation. "The Father" fails due to his opponent tenaciously clinging to his imaginary identity. It is significant that Number Six never has any sexual relationship throughout the series or any long-standing female companion. Unless they are victims or "castrating mother" types ("Free for All," "Dance of the Dead") women are inevitably betrayers of male freedom as in the opening episode "Arrival," "The Chimes of Big Ben," and "The Schizoid Man." Although McGoohan stipulated Number Six's "loner" status as part of the deal for making the series, Number Six's sexual isolation is a barrier in his development. He will remain entrapped in his own paranoic fantasies much of which have to do with narcissistic individuality and his refusal to recognize himself as a "split subject."

For Lacan, it is necessary for the child to move from the imaginary to the symbolic in order to learn difference. In the "splitting" process it has to become a language-using subject in order to make demands. Instead, Number Six narcissistically guards his individuality in an almost psychotic fashion.[37] But the series questions whether his perception is true in a world in which isolation is impossible. The village is his own psychotic fantasy of the outside world. One of the remarkable features of the "Fall Out" episode is Number Six's Yugoslav maid (Rachel Herbert) who speaks an incomprehensible language in an episode stressing misinterpretation of individuality and language by the media. "Arrival" features a Chinese girl who also speaks French and a grocer who communicates initially in nonsense language.

The series premise is thus pessimistic. Number Six questions a society that has not only incarcerated but produced him as a subject from which he vainly attempts to resign. He finds his individuality is useless in a quest for freedom and knowledge. The key to the solution, the identity of Number One really does not exist. Number One merely gibbers back at Number Six. His "I" is a mirror image stressing that his imaginary sense of unity does not exist.

Lacan's analytic solution is to attempt to orientate the subject in language to ensure full access to the symbolic and desire. But if the child is not produced as a differentiating and differentiated subject finding its place in culture, illness results. If the imaginary ego idea remains, " 'I' am not a number. 'I' am a free man," the movement toward the symbolic would only be the endless narcissistic identification of the mirror image. In "A, B and C," Number Six sees his own face in a mirror anticipating the climactic moment in "Fall Out." He is aware of the constant view of the camera and reacts accordingly. But as a Cartesian subject thinking himself aloof from the society that produced him, and which he reproduces in his fantasy, he does not exist. It takes "Fall Out" to learn this. Hence the return to the opening image at the finale hints at another circular descent into madness.

*The Prisoner*'s textual process is a complex one. It cannot merely be reduced to a sketch of conflict between two "authors." Conflict resides within the text as well as the producing subjects. It involves the complex system of power relations and is a warning rather than an answer to the question of struggling against state power. Critical of individual hero and entertainment apparatus that lulls the consumer into easy acceptance of fictionalized narrative resolution, it implicitly argues for a new type of subjectivity in which the old individuality becomes redundant.

"The conclusion would be that the political, ethical, social, philosophical problem of our days is not to try to liberate the individual from the state, and from the state's institutions, but to liberate us both from the state and from the type of individualization which is linked to the state. We have to promote a new kind of subjectivity through the refusal of this kind of individuality which has been imposed on us for centuries."[38]

## NOTES

1. See Chris Rodley, "Degree Absolute," *Primetime* 1,3 (March-May 1982): 16; "Inside Out," *Time Out*, no. 622 (July 23–29 1982): 11.

2. For a survey of relevant approaches see Dudley Andrew, *Concepts in Film Theory* (New York: Oxford University Press, 1984), pp. 123–24; and "Papers from the *Enclitic* International Conference on the Textual Analysis of Film, May 15–17 1981," *Enclitic* 6,1 (1982).

3. Ascription to any one individual director is now recognized as problematic in film as well as television studies. This is particularly so in the light of the various intersecting forces involved in *The Prisoner*. For an overview of various authorship theories in relation to film see John Caughie, ed., *Theories of Authorship* (London: Routledge and Kegan Paul, 1981).

4. Such is the case when guest Hollywood directors control individual episodes such as Samuel Fuller did in *The Virginian*'s "It Tolls for Thee." How many viewers would have read Fuller's intention to reversing the formula to make Lee Marvin's outlaw the hero and Lee J. Cobb and James Drury as "villains" in that one single intercession? No matter how destabilizing the director may have intended the intervention it is usually re-incorporated back into the text. The same is true of the Godardian conclusion to the Christmas 1986 *Moonlighting* episode which revealed studio crew and audience to the viewers at the climax.

5. On the problematic nature of "popular memory" see the Cahiers du Cinema interview with Michel Foucault in "Film and Popular Memory: Cahiers du Cinema/ Extracts," *Edinburgh 77 Magazine*, Edinburgh Film Festival (1977): 18–36.

6. Rodley recognizes this in "Degree Absolute," p. 17.

7. Rodley, p. 15.

8. Rodley, "Inside Out," p. 11.

9. Mike Gold in "The Prisoner," *Fantastic Films* 8 (July 1980): 66, notes the peculiarity of *The Prisoner*'s scheduling by the CBS network as a summer replacement series in 1968 since the spy boom was wearing off. Possibly memories of *Secret Agent*'s successful runs on both sides of the Atlantic may have been the reason.

10. British cinema (and, to some extent, television) has always existed between the twin poles of sober realism and visual excess, the latter most notably represented by Powell and Pressburger, Ken Russell, Nicolas Roeg, and Derek Jarman. The Monty Python comedic technique has also a respected ancestry.

11. This institution appears as a textual reference in Claude Whatham's *That'll Be The Day* (1974) and Russell's *Tommy* (1975). Developed by Billy Butlin in a British

climate of post-World War II austerity it was noted for its regimentation of holiday makers into various daily activities under the supervision of male and female "redcoats" who wore piped blazers.

12. Rodley, "Inside Out," p. 11. This was also confirmed in a private conversation with Markstein at the London Institute of Contemporary Arts in April 1982.

13. Rodley, "Degree Absolute," p. 15.

14. Ibid.

15. Ibid., pp. 15–16.

16. Ibid., p. 16.

17. Naturally, the shooting sequence differs from the scheduled showings. Rodley gives the following order: "Arrival", "Free for All", "Dance of the Dead", "Checkmate", "The Chimes of Big Ben", "The Schizoid Man", "The General", "A, B and C", "Many Happy Returns", "It's Your Funeral", "A Change of Mind", "Hammer into Anvil", and "Once Upon A Time", the last episode filmed before the production break. An index of screened episodes appears in Gary Gerani and Paul H. Schulman, *Fantastic Television* (New York: Harmony Books, 1977), p. 125. These list the order for the American market. Most sources display confusion about the actual number of episodes envisaged and the departure of key personnel. Mike Gold ("The Prisoner," p. 70) reports that McGoohan originally wanted to do a seven-part serial but Lew Grade wanted twenty-six shows so that he could sell them on a package deal to CBS on a first season basis. They compromised on seventeen episodes, McGoohan adding the additional ten plots over one weekend. However, Gold's information appears dependent upon later myths about the series built up by McGoohan in his presentations before North American college students. Rodley's sources of information appear more accurate (confirmed also by George Markstein in conversation). An initial season of thirteen episodes was planned with a probable second season of another thirteen after a production break. This was the standard format at the time (Rodley, "Degree Absolute," p. 15). "Many Happy Returns" was designed as the model for the second series with the Prisoner out in the world and discovering that the village is in fact everywhere. A contradiction exists in Rodley ("Inside Out," p. 11) where in contrast to stating that Markstein left after the originally envisaged concluding episode of the first season, "Once Upon A Time," he states on the preceding page that "Markstein parted from the series after six episodes following McGoohan's virtual complete appropriation of every creative avenue"! In view of the complexity of the series one should expect some degree of contradiction about what *did* actually happen.

18. Richard Wattis was a character actor who specialized in playing comic roles usually epitomizing the pomposity of British middle-class snobbery. His role as the vain neighbor in the fondly remembered 1960s television series, *Sykes*, starring Eric Sykes and Hattie Jacques, was one key example. Toward the latter end of his television career Kevin Stoney also gravitated toward establishment roles. His casting as traitor Mavic Chen in the twelve-part Dr. Who episode screened before *The Prisoner* in 1965 would form the basis for his role as one of Number Six's London supervisors.

19. Although later known for his comedy role in the British TV series, *Father Dear Father*, Cargill's range as an actor in the early 1960s was much more extensive. Although he appeared in Chaplin's *A Countess from Hong Kong* (1962) he could also play roles such as William Franklyn's spy boss in the short-lived British television ITV series *Top Secret* (1960).

20. His casting as the Nazi officer in *The 49th Parallel* (1942) and the "glue man"

in *A Canterbury Tale* (1944) show that Powell and Pressburger recognized a sinister side to this actor as well as a heroic one in *One of Our Aircraft is Missing* (1943).

21. From my memory of this episode's initial screening in 1967, it opened in contrast to the others with the English spy bureaucracy, represented by Donald Sinden, Patrick Cargill, and Richard Caldicot, discussing a situation necessitating Number Six's reappearance. The conjunction of this sequence to the opening credits was an explicit signifier of the village's relationship to the status quo. This sequence has never been screened since.

22. Rodley, "Degree Absolute," p. 17.

23. This episode was a play on Shakespeare's *The Seven Ages of Man* but with the emphasis on Number Six's social construction as an individual from childhood to adulthood involving the ideological state apparatus instruments of school, work, and law. For the role of this concept see Louis Althusser, *Lenin and Philosophy*, trans. Ben Brewster (New York/London: Monthly Review Press, 1971), pp. 145–82.

24. "The Schizoid Man," "A, B and C" are salient examples as well as "Once Upon A Time."

25. The division between the two is not always clear-cut. Since Number Six is physically imprisoned we may also include the above episodes along with "Do Not Forsake Me O My Darling," "A Change of Mind," "Living in Harmony" as well as "Fall Out."

26. For this concept see Roland Barthes, *Mythologies*, trans. Annette Lavers (London: Jonathan Cape, 1975).

27. H. L. Dreyfuss and P. Rabinow, *Michel Foucault: Beyond Structuralism and Hermeneutics* (Chicago: University of Chicago Press, 1982), p. 208.

28. Michel Foucault, *Discipline and Punish*, trans. Alan Sheridan (New York: Pantheon Books, 1977), p. 205.

29. Ibid., p. 202.

30. Ibid., p. 204.

31. Ibid.

32. Ibid., pp. 206–7.

33. Ibid., p. 201.

34. See here William Rothman, *Hitchcock: The Murderous Gaze* (Cambridge: Harvard University Press, 1982), pp. 340–41.

35. On the significance of this experiment see Rothman, *Hitchcock*, pp. 58–59; Elizabeth Weis, *The Silent Scream: Hitchcock's Soundtrack* (London and Toronto: Associated University Presses, 1982), pp. 44–49.

36. See Jacques Lacan, *The Language of the Self*, trans. Anthony Wilden (Baltimore: Johns Hopkins Press, 1968); *The Four Fundamental Concepts of Psychoanalysis*, ed. Jacques Alain Miller, trans. Alan Sheridan (London: The Hogarth Press, 1977); and *Ecrits: A Selection*, Trans. Alan Sheridan (New York: Norton, 1982).

37. At several points his behavior almost verges on the insane. See particularly "Hammer into Anvil" where his successful breakdown on Number Two reveals elements of savage psychosis.

38. Dreyfuss and Rabinow, *Michel Foucault*, p. 208.

# 7

# Program Production for Export and the Domestic Market: Authorship in *The Avengers*

## *Jonathan David Tankel*

Any discussion of television authorship focuses quite naturally on those individuals responsible for the creation (origination and production) of the particular television program. While this examination of authorship in the 1960s British television series *The Avengers* will describe the contributions of various creators in some detail, it is important to recognize that implicit in this perspective is a recognition of the role played in the process of creating television programs by the historical circumstances of production (historical and industrial). For example, marketing decisions made by the executives of a television production company can be viewed as part of the collective authorship of the television program. Marketing decisions reflect a sense of the implied audience, and when the implied audience for the program includes those located in other countries, then questions about authorship collide with questions about authenticity and cultural autonomy. This study of authorship in the production (and distribution) of *The Avengers* assesses what the domestic audience may gain or lose from the domestic production of television programs for export.

This view of authorship also permits a larger theoretical interrogation. The interaction of domestic audiences and the local production of entertainment programs for export has often been relegated to a minor role in the larger theoretical construct described as *media imperialism*. Both dominance (international or transnational imposition of alien values on native culture) and development (the national or dominant class goal of cultural unity) have been explored extensively, yet little attention has been paid to the dynamics of specific international program trade transactions. By determining the motivation of program *sellers* and *buyers*, it becomes possible to reconstruct the layers of "cultural compromise"—the intrusion of cultural values into commercial transactions and the influence of commercial realities on cultural decisions—that comprise international program trade (see Schlesinger, 1986, for an overview of British trade in television programs).

*The Avengers* is an appropriate object of study because it was popular with regional and national audiences in Great Britain and with national audiences in the United States.[1] The series was produced in three successive phases identified by the implied audience, beginning with early videotape production without full British commercial television "network" support (1961).[2] The second phase involved national transmission of videotape episodes and the origins of the *Avengers* cult following (1962–64). Finally, the program shifted to film production in anticipation of sale to an American commercial television network that altered the overall circumstances of production (1965–69). The changes in the industrial context of the production of *The Avengers* provide an appropriate opportunity to consider the British strategy of production for export and the problems it creates in defining what constitutes domestic television production in the context of media imperialism.

## MEDIA IMPERIALISM AND PROGRAM TRADE

The sale of television programs is, among other things, an act of trade. Value is exchanged between partners willingly because both parties perceive an advantage; the economic principle of comparative advantage dictates that both parties to an international transaction can derive benefits regardless of the economic size of participants. In order to explain the consequences of program trade, the researcher needs to find the value attendant to each party. In the literature of international program flow (Schiller, 1969, 1976; Nordenstreng and Varis, 1974; Tunstall, 1977; Nordenstreng and Schiller, 1979, among others), the effect of export sales on domestic commercial television production is a secondary issue—the focus is on the sale of British and American programming to third party nations (Salinas and Padden, in Nordenstreng and Schiller, 1979, are notable exceptions). Program trade between the United States and the United Kingdom flows only from Hollywood to London. The impact of American programming on British audiences and the homogenizing effect of American media economic power are still important considerations, yet the more mundane motivations of seller and buyer need also be considered. The motivation for trade exchange should be first identified. Schiller (1969) and others who contributed to the development of the media imperialism paradigm (Green, 1972; Read, 1976; Wells, 1972) focused on the U.S. seller's motivation for program trade. In using an economic model to describe program flow, television programming was divided into two categories: foreign and domestic. These theorists assumed the primacy of a domestic production that presumably represented native culture. The two categories of television programming were presented as polar opposites, with little attention paid to the range of utilities the program might offer to both trading partners. Using this perspective, the entertainment function was seen as reinforcing the process of exploitation; no intrinsic value was perceived in the process of producing domestic programs similar to those which are imported.

Production designed to Hollywood specification was more than a tangential concern to Tunstall (1977). He ultimately blurred the distinction between American and British production by referring to both as "Anglo-American." The research does not, however, generally recognize the possibility of competition for the Americans. This chapter views the British as competitors to American producers—competitors in the British domestic market and in the American network market—in order to identify factors other than domination in the trade process.

## ANGLO-AMERICAN PROGRAM TRADE: THE MID-ATLANTIC

Even before the first night of transmission, Independent Television made a commitment to high-quality "networked" television series produced domestically.[3] ITV executives, particularly at Associated TeleVision (ATV), were convinced that the American audience would accept British programs. To that end, producers needed programs that conformed to American network production standards (to attract American television network programmers) and to British regulation (to meet ITA, later IBA, content guidelines). Because of incompatible video transmission line standards, the format for exportable programs had to be film. ATV was the only company to invest heavily in television film production in the 1950s. Some small success was achieved during the western phase of American network television, since British series of the 1950s about outlaws, pirates, and crusaders were similar in a narrative sense to tales of the Old West.[4]

An unusual confluence of forces in the 1960s resulted in the domestic popularity of British television film action series involving espionage and international intrigue. These series produced the greatest volume of sales to the American commercial networks in the history of British television to date (see Rogers, 1988, for an encyclopedic overview of ITV adventure series). The ability of British producers to place programs on the American commercial networks was based on the production of television film series matching the expectations of those American network executives. The ATV series were dubbed "mid-Atlantic" by British television critics, and were viewed as a threat to British cultural autonomy in the realm of television production (for example, Hood, 1983).

The mid-Atlantic television film series was similar to the international theatrical film. The guiding principles included removal of strictly local references and insertion of elements designed to appeal to different markets. Eric Paice (1966), who wrote for a number of British television film series, offered the perfect description of the mid-Atlantic series format.

The formula is well known. It must be on film so that print copies are available. Picture quality and definition must be [good], story structure modified to include the maximum number of action sequences—thus partially surmounting the language barrier. Story content must be reduced to a simple contest between good and bad, instantly recognizable and unequivocal in resolution.

The specific British content of these ITV adventure series was guaranteed by regulation in terms of personal and financial participation (see ITV, 1957). Still, to some, a domestically produced series was seen as no different than a foreign-produced series because domestic production was perceived to adhere to an alien standard.

Disagreement over the value of producing programs conforming to American production standards was constant in British public criticism of British commercial television during the 1960s. The conflicting positions ran along a continuum from the strong negative warnings voiced by Stuart Hood in *The Spectator* and Peter Black in the *Daily Mail* to the support offered by *Television Mail* and *The Economist*.[5] These perspectives represented differing interpretations of the value created by the export transaction. There was rarely a question that these programs might not be British by regulation; the question was whether they were British by inspiration.

ATV interpreted the regulations in a broad manner: service to its public, regional or otherwise, was defined by ATV as providing entertainment programs. Murdoch and Halloran (1979) identified the corporate culture of ATV as "a commitment to mass entertainment as an end in itself . . . and an insistence on the highest standards of technical excellence in every aspect of program making"(p. 278). The cost of technical excellence was high, and ATV engaged in large-scale program production suitable for export as the means to bring this type of programming to its domestic audience. That these programs were created primarily to entertain should not overshadow their value as domestic television production that could compete with the dominant producer, the United States. Political and Economic Planning (Pratten, 1970) and the Prices and Incomes Board (in Smith, 1974) issued reports noting the positive aspects of the ITV thriller. The process of exporting these film series provided valuable marketing and distribution experience to ITV companies. The high-quality production values of British commercial television programs sold overseas is partially a result of the competition with American producers at home and abroad.

ATV's efforts in financing domestic production by export sales included the production of series designed for export, such as *The Saint*, and series that had export potential, such as *Danger Man*. The export of the ABC (later Thames) production of *The Avengers* was not predetermined by corporate trade policy. While ATV and Lew Grade invested heavily in film series with the hope of export sales, ABC was primarily concerned with providing entertaining programs for its regions and the network. In following this policy, ABC (the smallest of the original ITV companies) developed the most popular British film action series exported in the 1960s from an original, regionally produced drama. *The Avengers* became an international success by combining the essential formal elements of the "mid-Atlantic" film style with a quintessential British sensibility.

## AUTHORSHIP AND *THE AVENGERS*

The origins of *The Avengers* can be traced to two men: Howard Thomas and Sydney Newman, but it is unclear as to the specific participation. While Newman was in charge of dramatic production for ABC, Thomas was the chief executive. Newman would be gone by the end of 1962, while Thomas remained with ABC, and became chairman of Thames Television (ABC's successor). The two different stories have common elements, and it is these common elements that illuminate the complexities of discerning authorship in the television production industry. Howard Thomas's claim to authorship is based on his serving as chief executive officer of the company during the evolution of the series (Thomas, 1977; Tankel, 1984). He suggested to Newman that he develop a different type of drama to balance the generally realistic (read: working-class) single-play dramas that were the company's specialty (see Black, 1967; Hood, 1966, Schulman, 1973, for discussions of the ITV style of drama innovated by ABC's *Armchair Theatre*). The model for this new series, according to Thomas, was the movie series based on Dashiell Hammett's *The Thin Man*. The characters in the new series were to be sophisticated, elegant, and fashionable. Newman responded by suggesting a series that combined two popular television genres—*Police Surgeon*, which went on the air on September 10, 1960.

*Police Surgeon* was not *The Thin Man*. A standard cops-and-robbers show with a medical twist, it was not compelling drama (even by television standards) and it did not meet the expectations of Howard Thomas. The series lasted only twelve episodes, although Ian Hendry, who played Dr. Geoffrey Brent, displayed the talent and rugged good looks that deserved a second chance. When *Police Surgeon* was cancelled, ABC executives decided to pair Hendry with another actor, Patrick MacNee, in a new series called *The Avengers*. According to Thomas, then, *The Avengers* was a direct spin-off from *Police Surgeon* (Thomas, 1977).

Rogers (1983, 1985, 1988) has presented ample evidence that casts doubt on the specifics of Thomas's version of *The Avengers*' origins. Patrick MacNee did not appear in *Police Surgeon*, as Thomas wrote in 1977, so the pairing of MacNee and Hendry could not have been a direct result of the failed medical crime series. MacNee's connection to the series, according to Rogers, was Sydney Newman, who had met MacNee in Canada before Newman was hired by ABC. Newman and Leonard White (who became the producer of the new series) decided to cast MacNee as the mysterious secret agent who aids Dr. David Keel (Hendry's new role) in avenging his fiancee's death, hence the origins of the series' title. But whether or not *The Avengers* was spun off directly, the series was indeed an outgrowth of the Thomas directive that led to the creation of *Police Surgeon*. Also, a number of creative personnel (including White, who had been coproducer of *Police Surgeon*, Don Leavner, who was the director, and a third performer, Ingrid Hafner, who portrayed the doctor's secretary) moved quickly from one series to the other, since there was only one month from the demise of *Police Surgeon* to the arrival of the first *Avengers* series in January 1961. (Ironically, Newman left ABC in late 1962, while Thomas remained to become chairman of Thames Television, ABC's corporate successor.)

One aspect of the *Police Surgeon/Avengers* controversy is agreed: Both series were produced live on videotape, as were all ABC dramas not produced live on the air.[6] Since ABC transmitted only on the weekend, some means of preserving performances for weekday transmission by the other ITV companies was necessary. Thomas recalled that ABC purchased some of the first videotape recorders manufactured by Ampex (Tankel, 1984). In addition, kinescopes were made from the videotapes to demonstrate the program to buyers from television systems not compatible with British line standards. A second point of agreement involves the ITV networking arrangement. Neither series cleared the whole network: *The Avengers* itself was transmitted originally only in the North and the Midlands (ABC's regions) and by some of the smaller regional ITV franchises.

The turning point in the new series came as the result of an Equity strike against the commercial television production companies that ran from January to May 1962, shutting down production. When the series returned to production in May 1962, Hendry left the series and was replaced by Honor Blackman as Mrs. Catherine Gale, a beautiful anthropologist whose skill in martial arts always came in handy. The male-female chemistry of *The Thin Man* was finally achieved. John Steed (MacNee) was now an Edwardian dandy, with double-breasted, three-piece suit, complete with bowler and umbrella. Steed's attire exploited the fashion trend among the teddy boys, a teen subcultural style that was soon to be adapted by Carnaby Street (1964–65). Cathy Gale affected a style that ranged from tailored suits to leather and boots. The plots began to include large doses of parody and humor, as was noted in a comment in *Contrast* (1963):

*The Avengers* is British television's first popular myth. As extravagant as an old Feuillade serial, shameless in its symbols and send-up eroticism, sharply contemporary in its attitudes, it gaily ridicules its own most sacred conventions (p. 82).

The regional popularity of the new film *Avengers* permitted ATV to begin transmitting the program in London by late 1963, thereby achieving full network status.

But all was not well with all the critics. A number felt the program had gone too far, and the parody was becoming the end rather than just the means. Philip Purser (1963) wrote in the *Sunday Telegraph* that "A.B.C. are nurturing what begins to look suspiciously like a cuckoo in the nest," and goes on to decry the need to get bolder each season, this being the third. Ivor Jay (1963) lambasted the program in the *Birmingham Evening Mail* (where ABC and ATV shared the transmission time), concluding that "*The Avengers* is a bore of banal tarradiddles much less amusing than the sort of programme it presumably guys." The "gruff realism" of the regional program had been transformed into a self-conscious spoof in order to broaden its appeal to a national audience.

Honor Blackman left the series at the end of her second year (March 1964) in order to take the part of Pussy Galore in *Goldfinger*, one of the James Bond movies that *The Avengers* was intending to satirize. Ironically, her departure coincided with the decision to produce the series on film. The search for the new female lead became entwined with the conversion to film production. Thomas persuaded Associated British Pathé (ABC's parent company) to invest one million pounds in film production for *The Avengers*. The investment was predicated on the program's export potential, but only at this point, nearly three years after the original series, did export potential become linked to the mechanics of production.

On one hand, Thomas charged Julian Wintle, a theatrical film producer, with the authority to make the series "look right." Technical quality equal, or even superior, to Hollywood became a matter of corporate policy. On the other hand, the new female lead, Diana Rigg, was meeting resistance from American network executives to whom the series was being offered. Thomas went to New York City to lobby for the program as film production began. CBS and NBC rejected the series, probably because they already had their own spy dramas. ABC lacked a strong spy drama at the height of the genre's popularity. Thomas used his acquaintance with Leonard Goldenson, president of ABC (U.S.) to make a deal including Diana Rigg as Mrs. Emma Peel and 26 monochrome episodes—*The Avengers* has the distinction of being the last monochrome program bought by an American network.

In Great Britain, the sale of *The Avengers* to the United States was received with mixed reviews from the British press. Its national success had been because of its Britishness, and the program had served as comparison to ATV series such as *The Baron* and *The Champions*. The switch to film was seen as a ploy to obtain an American sale. British television critics feared the new series could not now be supported without a U.S. sale, and that U.S. network pressure would force the producers to undermine the essential Britishness of the program.

The new film version of *The Avengers* was a ratings success in both the United States and Great Britain. Peter Black (1966) wrote in the *Daily Mail* that the new series "showed what a high-budget film technique can do when it is assisting talent." Diana Rigg became an international star as the enigmatic Mrs. Peel as the plots became even zanier with more international backdrops: the characters maintained the cultural authenticity of the program unlike the ATV characters who affected the mid-Atlantic accent. The program was consistently in the top twenty in the regions where ABC transmitted. In the United States, ABC (U.S.) first used *The Avengers* as CBS and NBC used other British spy dramas—as replacement series. Finally, in 1968 *The Avengers* appeared in the fall network schedule as the first totally British hour-length television film series to do so.

The irony for British critics is that the series did become dependent on American revenue, but with unforeseen consequences. Thames (corporate successor to ABC) would have ceased production in 1968 when Diana Rigg quit before the American fall premiere season; Howard Thomas was tempted to end the series rather than replace Rigg. But financed by the guaranteed network sale, Thomas decided to continue production with a new female lead, the less athletic, but more buxom Tara King (played by Linda Thorson). The foregrounding of Steed as a more protective figure (or better, more paternalistic) changed the male-female chemistry toward a more conventional sex-role stereotype. While *The Avengers* declined in popularity in the United States as it competed in prime time with *Gunsmoke*, the series achieved its highest ratings ever in Great Britain. But American network cancellation in 1969 ended the production of *The Avengers* and what the (Manchester) *Guardian* called "Britain's single television export success story" ended as a result of the fear shared by many observers of ITV—dependence on revenue from the United States—but only after the Americans paid for an additional year of production. In that final year, the program became as diffuse as its audience, while its cultural integrity became affectation. In the final analysis, *The Avengers* became the perfect international television program: in its historic time, it was simultaneously all things to all people and nothing at all.

## PROGRAM PRODUCTION FOR EXPORT AND THE DOMESTIC MARKET

The case study illustrates various dynamics of program trade. The export transaction contains positive and negative aspects for each partner, with the ultimate result being an increased pool of available programming for the domestic audience. Audiences in British regions were able to view domestically produced series equal to the American imports. Foreign programmers compared British programming favorably to American series, leading to greater interest. Series financed by export sales also did not seem to drain funds from domestic production, although a more detailed examination of the relationship of export revenue to domestic production would be an important area for further research.

The most extreme critical perspective on the ITV film series would not consider that production of film action series comparable to a Hollywood style would have any benefit to the British audience. But the entire process of export created marketing expertise and product recognition throughout the world. Negative criticism of ITV film series has to be subsumed under the larger context of the negative criticism of advertiser-supported entertainment media. As the Pilkington Report stated in 1962, those "who criticised the production in this country of mid-Atlantic programmes were, we note, also especially critical of independent television" (H.M.S.O., 1962, p. 67). After all, domestic audiences in countries engaged in international program trade are, by definition, included within the international audience.

Economic motivations interact with sociocultural decisions when television systems import television programming. To produce programming for the export market, creative decisions must be tempered by an awareness of the cultural barriers that must be surmounted. As audiences expand, the more successful programs deal in broad strokes, in order to invite multiple readings (for example, see Liebes and Katz, 1986, for a study of various decodings of *Dallas*). This raises a question about the authentic nature of collaborative television production: do television fiction series offer audiences the capacity to create their own authenticity? *The Avengers* seemed to alter what it offered its primary audience. As a regional drama, it was realistic. At the national level it was presented as a national myth, or at worst, a national joke. As an international hit, it maintained its British audience, while offering foreign audiences visual style and broadly drawn characters.Those who created *The Avengers*, just like those who created *Dallas*, found national myths (or stereotypes) permit the broadest possible international audiences. The case study indicates that the industrial context inherent in commercial television production makes problematic the designation of authorial intent. Furthermore, the production and distribution of television programs for export consists of multiple levels of compromise: economic, technological, and cultural, making authorial control subject to multiple levels of market expectation. A television program can exist successfully in any cultural context that offers that program an environment that permits the making of meaning; the trick is to find the appropriate template for the proper audience, as did the authors of *The Avengers*.

## NOTES

1. The standard unit of measurement for popularity is the nationally supervised ratings undertaken by commercial polling organizations such as Arbitron and Neilsen in the United States and JICTAR in Great Britain. The determination of the popularity in Great Britain of *The Avengers* was made reviewing the regional ratings for the period of transmission and noting how many times the program appeared in the top ten. Popularity in the United States was determined by the continuing renewal of the program by American network executives.

2. Independent Television (ITV) does not provide programming from a central source as do the American commercial networks. The system does provide "networked" programs during prime time, produced by the primary broadcasters. Individual regional broadcasters decide whether to "buy" a network offering. This system becomes problematic when the regional broadcaster is also a competing network program producer.

3. The structure of Independent Television created a de facto network programmed by the first four program companies to begin transmission in the metropolitan centers. London was served by Associated-Rediffusion (weekday) and ATV (weekend), Manchester by ATV (weekday) and ABC (weekend) and Liverpool by Granada (weekday) and ABC (weekend). This arrangement did not change until 1967, when Lord Hill oversaw and arranged the restructuring of ITV markets.

4. ATV was able to sell a number of half-hour monochrome film television series to

the American commercial television networks from 1954 to 1962. Series sold included *The Adventures of Robin Hood*, *The Adventures of Sir Frances Drake*, *Ivanhoe*, and *The Buccaneers*. The lack of a strong demand from the American networks led ATV to pursue another sales strategy—syndication. This practice continued throughout the late 1960s and early 1970s, the period of greatest ITV presence on American network television.

5. The views expressed by Hood and Black later surfaced in their respective books about television (Hood's *On Television*, 1980/1983, and Black's *The Mirror in the Corner*, 1972). Some critics were more sympathetic, such as Milton Schulman, whose *The Least Worst Television in the World* (1973) was one of the few popular defenses of ATV/ITV export production. The views expressed by the industry press were evident in the author's review of newspaper clip files held in the Library of the Independent Broadcasting Authority, which were unpaginated.

6. Rogers states that the original series (1961) was transmitted live by ABC. Thomas's recollections do not preclude Rogers's claim, since Thomas might easily have been referring to the male/female *Avengers* (1962) in response to questions asked twenty years later (see appendix to Tankel, 1984 for a transcript of the Thomas interview).

## REFERENCES

Black, P. (1966, March 23). Untitled column. *Daily Mail*, unpaginated.
———. (1967). Money, rubbish and T.V. hopes. *Encounter*, 29, 3: 196.
———. (1972). *The mirror in the corner*. London: Hutchinson and Co., Ltd.
*Contrast*. (1963). Vol. 3, no. 2 (Caption under picture of Steed and Mrs. Peel), p. 82.
Green, T. (1972). *The universal eye: World television in the seventies*. London: The Bodley Head.
H.M.S.O. (1962). Report of the Committee on Broadcasting. Command paper 1753.
Hood, S. (1966). Export backlash. *The Spectator* 217: 676–77.
Hood, S. (1983). *Stuart Hood on television. 2nd ed. London: Pluto Press Ltd*.
Independent Television Authority. (1958). *ITV 1957*. London: I.T.A.
Jay, I. (1963, December 2). *The Avengers* creaks, contrives and bores. *Birmingham Evening Mail*, unpaginated.
Liebes T., and E. Katz. (1986). Patterns of involvement in television fictions: A comparative analysis. *European Journal of Communication* 1: 151–71.
Murdoch, G., and J. Halloran. (1979). Contests of creativity in television drama: An exploratory study in Britain. In H. Fischer and S. Melnik, (eds.) *Entertainment: A Cross-cultural examination*. New York: Hastings House.
Nordenstreng, K., and H. Schiller. (1979). *National sovereignty and international communication*. Norwood, NJ: Ablex Publishing Corporation.
Nordenstreng, K., and T. Varis. (1974). *Television traffic—A one way street?* Paris: UNESCO.
Paice, E. (1966). TV's export drive—What it means to the writer. *Screenwriter*: Spring (unpaginated).
Pratten, C. F. (1970). *The economics of television*. London: Political and Economic Planning.
Purser, P. (1963, November 10). Television: Vengeance is whose? *Sunday Telegraph*, unpaginated.
Reid, W. (1976). *America's mass media merchants*. Baltimore: The Johns Hopkins Press.

Rogers, D. (1983). *The Avengers*. London: Independent Television Books in association with Michael Joseph Ltd.

———. (1985). *The Avengers anew*. London: Michael Joseph Ltd.

———. (1988). *The ITV encyclopedia of adventure*. London: Boxtree Ltd. (TV Times imprint) in association with Independent Television Publications Ltd.

Salinas, R., and L. Paldan. (1979). Culture in the process of dependent development. In K. Nordenstreng and H. Schiller (eds.) *National sovereignty and international communication*. Norwood, NJ: Ablex Publishing Corporation.

Schiller, H. (1969). *Mass communication and American empire*. Boston: Beacon Press.

———. (1976). *Communication and cultural domination*. White Plains, NY: M. E. Sharpe.

Schlesinger, P. (1986). Trading in fictions: What do we know about British television imports and exports. *European Journal of Communication* 1, 3: 263–87.

Schulman, M. (1973). *The least worst television in the world*. London: Barrie and Jenkins.

Smith, A. (1974). *British Broadcasting*. Newton Abbot: David and Charles.

Tankel, J. D. (1984). The ITV thriller: The interaction of Media systems and popular culture. Ph.D. diss., University of Wisconsin-Madison.

Thomas, Howard. (1977). *With an Independent Air*. London: Weidenfeld and Nicolson.

Tunstall, J. (1977). *The media are American: Anglo-American media in the world*. New York: Columbia University Press.

Wells, A. (1972). *Picture-tube imperialism?: The impact of U.S. television on Latin America*. Maryknoll, NY: Orbis Books.

# Part III
## The Studio as Auteur

# 8

# Negotiating the Television Text: The Transformation of *Warner Bros. Presents*

*Christopher Anderson*

During the evening of September 12, 1955, one night before the network premiere of *Warner Bros. Presents*, ABC President Robert Kintner wired a telegram to his new business associate, Warner Bros. President Jack Warner. Kintner was deliberately writing before the debut of the studio's first television production, he explained, because he wished to express his gratitude and confidence during this moment of tranquility before Warners and ABC faced the reaction of the public, the critics, and their peers in the entertainment industry. Whether the program was judged a success or a failure, Kintner assured Warner, ABC planned to order another Warners' series for its schedule next season. Warner thanked Kintner for his kindness and promised that the studio was prepared for the challenge of supplying more TV programming in the future.[1] Judged by this exchange, it might appear that both executives presumed their companies had engineered a mutually beneficial exchange, that ABC was pleased with the series it had purchased, that Warners successfully had navigated the transition to television production by the time its first television series premiered.

*Warner Bros. Presents* was an omnibus program featuring three rotating series based loosely on Warners' films from the 1940s: *King's Row* (1942), *Casablanca* (1943), and *Cheyenne* (1947). Each weekly hour-long installment of *Warner Bros. Presents* offered a complete narrative episode from one of these series and concluded with a twelve-minute segment titled "Behind the Cameras at Warner Bros." Designed to promote the studio's current theatrical releases, this portion of the broadcast offered television viewers a privileged backstage glimpse of stars like John Wayne, Gary Cooper, and Elizabeth Taylor, or demystified the practical aspects of movie production, such as the problems encountered while shooting *The Searchers* (1956) on location. Host Gig Young introduced the episode, bridged the transitions between the program and commercials, and led the backstage tour of "Behind the Cameras." The series debuted with an episode of *King's Row* in which the protagonist, a young, small-town psychiatrist, dispels the townspeople's suspicion of psychotherapy by curing a woman whose paralysis is the symptom of a childhood trauma. The "Behind the Cameras" segment featured *The McConnell Story*, a film directed by Gordon Douglas and starring Alan Ladd. The episode captured a respectable thirty-four audience share, but it triggered an immediate critical barrage from the press, which felt that the series failed to demonstrate the production values and storytelling skills associated with a major motion picture studio.[2] When the first installments of *Cheyenne* and *Casablanca* sank below fifteen in the ratings, the sponsors—General Electric, Monsanto, and Liggett & Myers Tobacco Company—joined the press in attacking the studio. "Their criticisms are so persistent and so severe," Kintner informed Warner, "as to raise the most serious problems for both Warner Bros. and ABC. *King's Row* and *Cheyenne* are far below the quality of most TV. The series represents a below-standard operation that can only detrimentally affect the advertisers, ABC, and Warner Bros. The series has gotten off to such a bad start that it will take emergency measures to make it a success."[3]

Instead of marking a smooth passage in television production, the premiere of *Warner Bros. Presents* sparked a new, and often acrimonious, round of negotiations between Warners, ABC, and the program's sponsors. Informing Jack Warner that the sponsors had demanded immediate conferences to discuss the fate of *Warner Bros. Presents*, Kintner joked with the studio chief, "This is worse than the picture business, isn't it?"[4] Warner undoubtedly agreed. Since the studio's production agreement with ABC expressly prohibited any sort of interference from the network or the sponsors, Jack Warner had not fully considered the possibility that the conditions of commercial television might compromise his studio's customary autonomy in the conception and execution of its motion pictures. Indeed, Warners had accepted the contract only after network assurance that, contrary to standard industry practice, sponsors would not be allowed to meddle in programming produced by the studio.[5] Only after the program premiered, however, did Warner executives realize just how substantially the studio's traditional production practices would be altered by the intricate set of relations that bound together the studio, the network, and the sponsors.

*Warner Bros. Presents* wouldn't be simply a Warners product, but the product of this new economic affiliation and of the stakes and expectations that each participant carried into the relationship. As the studio, network, and sponsors struggled to define *Warner Bros. Presents* in accordance with their own economic goals and conceptions of television entertainment, the ongoing negotiations made the series a virtual text, one in a perpetual state of contestation and transformation. What type of text should a major motion picture studio such as Warners produce for television? How would this text resemble or differ from the feature films that the studio produced for theatrical exhibition? How would a studio-produced narrative series serve the commercial goals of network television? In a sense,

*Warner Bros. Presents*, which one Warners executive described as an "experiment," served as a laboratory for testing answers to these questions.[6] The negotiations that swirled around its production provide a unique opportunity to examine the film and television industries' discourse about television textuality during the transitional period in which major motion picture studios entered television production and the industries attempted to establish the dominant forms of prime-time television programming.

During the past decade, a number of scholars have reoriented the issue of television textuality and the production of meaning by shifting attention from the TV industry's activity to that of the television viewer. John Fiske, for instance, reminds us that the TV program and the TV text are not homologous; the program is merely the site of potential meanings that may be activated by a socially situated viewer.

To understand television in this way, we need to see it and its programs as potentials of meaning rather than as commodities. A program is a clearly defined and labeled fragment of television's output. It has clear boundaries, both temporal and formal. . . . Programs are produced, distributed, defined by the industry: texts are the products of their readers. So a program becomes a text at the moment of reading, that is, when its interaction with one of its many audiences activates some of the meanings/pleasures that it is capable of provoking.[7]

Although this chapter focuses primarily on the media industry's production of a single program, or what Stuart Hall describes as the media's "encoding" practices, it doesn't assume that a unified culture industry produces coherent texts able to manipulate passive audiences, nor does it deny the productivity of the viewer's "decoding" practices in the generation and circulation of meaning.[8] Instead, this case study examines how certain historically situated media companies conceived of the TV text, the TV audience, and the relationship between economic and textual practices during a period in which the dominant practices of network television were being contested by networks, advertisers, producers, government regulatory agencies, and viewers. As each of the major participants attempted to translate its ideas about TV into specific encoding practices, the conflicting industrial strategies contradicted the image of a cohesive, rationalized "television industry." Similarly, the conflicting discourses that run through *Warner Bros. Presents* belie the traditional image of the closed text, in which a determinate set of signifying practices, the stable and coherent product of a unified culture industry, are able to control a viewer's ability to make meaning or derive pleasure from a TV program. Indeed, *Warner Bros. Presents* exemplifies the instability of media texts *and* media industries.

Due to its history in motion pictures, Warners was least concerned with the practices of commercial television as it attempted to create its first TV program. Warners had two primary goals in producing the series. First, the studio wanted to diversify its production operations with a dependable revenue source that

would counterbalance the mounting expense and uncertain fortunes of a production schedule now dominated by blockbuster features like *Moby Dick* (1956)
and *Giant* (1956). Second, after successfully plugging recent Warners features
on *The Ed Sullivan Show*, studio executives saw *Warner Bros. Presents* as a
free-flowing promotional pipeline wedged deeply into the American home. As
Jack Warner explained in September 1955, the studio's primary rationale for
engaging in television production "was chiefly and only to secure advertisements
through television."[9] Warners certainly wouldn't get rich on the series itself.
The production agreement with ABC required the studio to produce 39 original
episodes, with 13 repeats during the summer. In return, ABC paid $65,000 per
original episode and $32,000 per repeat, for a total of $3 million. To place this
figure in perspective, $3 million might have provided the budget for two of the
studio's moderately priced feature films, but in this case it was used to produce
programming equivalent in length to 19½ feature films. In other words, the
budget for *Warner Bros. Presents* was equivalent to a feature-film budget of
only $150,000.[10] In 1955, even the most disreputable Poverty Row potboilers
cost more.

Due to the financial restrictions inherent in television series production, the
studio conceived of the individual episodic series as undistinguished B-grade
productions. Strict standardization of the product and the production process
took precedence over the goal of differentiating the individual series from others
on TV. Warners hoped to produce the least expensive program possible, regardless of its merits, conceiving of it solely as a framework from which to
suspend the studio's promotional messages. This relatively restricted vision of
television's potential usefulness framed the studio's practices during this first
season of production. Stringent economic regulation shaped the studio's development of *Warner Bros. Presents* because studio executives thought that the
program would be differentiated from other TV programs not by the narrative
series, but by the allure of motion-picture stars in "Behind the Cameras." In
fact, ABC marketed "Behind the Cameras" as the program's "high point,"
"the most glamorous and looked-forward-to feature of the program."[11] Due to
its past experience and its economic interests, Warners conceived of the program
as a bounded formal unit, unrelated to other TV programs or to the sponsors'
commercials. Consequently, the studio was concerned with the questions most
relevant to the production process. Within the financial and temporal constraints
of network television, how should a studio produce an episodic series based on
a general narrative model?

ABC and the sponsors demonstrated a more complex conception of TV textuality because of their familiarity with broadcast industry practices. ABC's
approach to the TV text was more audience-oriented, defining the text in relation
to the network's conception of TV audiences and their practices. How should
the TV text's mode of address relate to its mode of reception—the domestic
conditions of television viewing? The network felt both that the family, gathered
around the living room TV set, was the subject of address for the TV broadcast

and that the home viewer was an inherently distracted viewer whose attention had to be focused actively on the TV screen.[12] While ABC clearly granted the studio its promotional ambitions, the third-place network intended to attract these home viewers by broadcasting the first filmed television series with production values and narrative strategies matching those of major studio feature films. With all filmed TV series produced on a shoestring budget, ABC hoped that Warners would distinguish its product from existing television fare by delivering to the video screen the Hollywood cinema's commitment to spectacle. ABC touted the series in its publicity by claiming: "In coming to the home screen for the first time, Warner Bros. will throw all its resources behind *Warner Bros. Presents* to give the TV production all the craftmanship and quality that has been the hallmark of Warner Bros. motion pictures."[13] ABC also assumed that the studio's skill in producing such Hollywood genres as the melodrama (*King's Row*), the romantic adventure (*Casablanca*), and the western (*Cheyenne*) would give the network an edge by providing an alternative to CBS's and NBC's dominance in such traditional broadcast genres as situation comedy, variety shows, and live drama. In its quest for a competitive audience share, ABC conceived of *Warner Bros. Presents* as a type of fishing expedition, with each individual series a lure designed to attract a vaguely defined demographic segment of the audience: *King's Row*—adult women; *Casablanca*—young men and women; *Cheyenne*—men and children. In the event that any of these series failed in the ratings, the production agreement stipulated that ABC and Warners would replace the program with one from a different genre. In the days before demographic ratings, this experimental strategy represented ABC's first unsystematic efforts to locate and appeal to segments of the mass audience, rather than to the audience as an undifferentiated mass.[14]

While the studio conceived of *Warner Bros. Presents* as a discrete product, the network and sponsors also recognized that the series as a text should be conceptualized in terms of its intertextual relations with other discourses of commercial television. They were concerned about the program's fragmentation, the immediate juxtaposition of the episodic narrative and Warners' self-promotion with discourses such as commercials and network promotions. How, they asked, could the textual strategies employed in *Warner Bros. Presents* best ensure viewers' attention during the abrupt shifts from one discourse to another? Similarly, ABC was concerned with the program's position as a unit in the larger textual organization of network schedules. How would the series "fit" with other programs in ABC's schedule and with competing programs on other networks? These concerns demonstrate ABC's interest in promoting two of commercial television's most significant textual characteristics: segmentation and flow. Raymond Williams first suggested that, in spite of the fact that TV listings imply that programs are separate from one another, the television experience actually is not one of single, discrete programs interrupted by commercials and other intrusive discourses. Rather, commercial television consists of a planned, continuous sequence of often unrelated images and sounds which Williams refers to as "flow." John Ellis subsequently noted that television's flow consists of a series of discrete segments that lack internal closure and a causal connection with contiguous segments. From the network's perspective, flow developed as a programming strategy designed to hold the attention of distracted viewers by minimizing the shocks and providing a sense of continuity during abrupt shifts among these arbitrarily connected segments.[15]

The Warners program played a prominent role in ABC's strategy for managing the flow of its prime-time schedule. The network intended to counter-program against the other networks by scheduling a highly differentiated, hour-long program—a "keystone" program—in the 7:30 PM time slot each evening, and then to build the evening's programming on the foundation provided by that initial program.[16] NBC and CBS scheduled relatively uncompetitive programs before 8:00 PM. NBC, for instance, split the 7:30–8:00 time slot with a fifteen-minute newscast and the Dinah Shore variety show, while CBS aired a game show, *Name That Tune*. ABC hoped to capitalize on the time slot's minimal competition in order to capture viewers early and hold them throughout the evening. The strategy had given ABC its first hit with *Disneyland* on Wednesday nights in 1954, and now the network hoped to repeat its success with Warners on Tuesday. Because of the large percentage of children viewing television at 7:30, however, Warners also would have to repeat Disney's success with the younger age groups if it hoped to garner competitive ratings and to set the stage for the remainder of ABC's Tuesday night schedule.[17]

Although the sponsors were not concerned with the scheduling of *Warner Bros. Presents*, they wanted the Warners series to provide a suitable "environment" for their advertisements. They resented the fact that their sponsorship provided Warners with a forum for free publicity, but they had agreed to the deal once ABC had satisfied their doubts by promising a miracle in which Warners would use its meager budget to produce something greater than mere telefilms.[18] By completely denying the economic base of film production, the network's sales pitch to advertisers promised: "The production values Warner Bros. will put into each of these new 'pictures-for-television' will exceed many times their selling price."[19] Expecting the same stars and production values as those of the studio's theatrical features, a seemingly acceptable trade-off for the free publicity of "Behind the Cameras," the sponsors agreed to tolerate Warners' self-promotion as long as the program delivered the highest possible ratings—at least equal to *Disneyland*'s thirty-nine rating during the previous season.

Following meetings with the sponsors during the program's first weeks, Kintner sent a pessimistic telegram to Warner that turned up the heat in the laboratory of *Warner Bros. Presents*. The episodes came under attack for their impoverished sets and generic costumes, their amateurish acting and cliched writing, their styleless direction and confused editing. The sponsors complained most vociferously about the "overcommercialization" of the program, represented primarily by host Gig Young's incessant plugs for studio features. The sponsors felt that, like Walt Disney in his series, Young should manage the textual flow more gracefully, weaving the diverse discourses of narrative, commercials, and studio promotion into a seamless unity. Instead, Young's brusque narration contained constant references to the "Behind the Cameras" segment that concluded the program. Because the studio lacked an understanding of flow, the program's segmentation seemed too obvious, its organization too arbitrary; viewers tuned out during the broadcast. The sponsors' solution to this "overcommercialization" was to decrease the emphasis on "Behind the Cameras," a reaction they justified citing the decline in ratings that occurred during the last quarter of the program.[20]

The critics and sponsors weren't alone in grumbling about *Warner Bros. Presents*. Even studio personnel recognized that it was less distinguished than other low-budget filmed TV series. Hectic production schedules caused by an August Screen Actors Guild strike, the demands of television's weekly broadcast schedule, and the difficulty of organizing the new television production unit left little time for perfection, or sometimes even for simple craftmanship. *Cheyenne* made an inauspicious debut when writer Maurice Geraghty asked to have his name removed from the premiere script, which he felt had been ruined during the episode's production and postproduction.[21] The pace at Warners was so frantic that *Casablanca* director John Peyser didn't view the final cut of his episodes until they aired over his home television set. Like the sponsors, Peyser complained that Gig Young's insistent studio promotion created the impression that "Behind the Cameras" was the real subject of each episode, and that *Casablanca*'s narrative was little more than an unfortunate intrusion. He was even more startled to witness the results of the obvious rushed and haphazard process of postproduction. Glaring errors, the product of carelessness, appeared obvious. Black leader used during editing was left in the final cut; as a result, the image intermittently disappeared, replaced by a black screen. In other instances, dialogue and action begun in one shot were repeated in the succeeding shot as the editor cut to a reverse angle, yet picked up the character's movement or speech at a point prior to the moment when the cut occurred.[22] Since professional editors working for a major studio generally wouldn't make such evident mistakes, these problems indicate the studio's initial difficulty in adapting to the pace of TV production.

Throughout the opening weeks of the TV season, ABC and the sponsors applied relentless pressure to Warners, reminding the studio that less expensive new series like *Gunsmoke* were drawing much higher ratings. Representatives of Monsanto actually flew to Los Angeles for a three-hour meeting with Jack Warner and the studio's television production supervisor, William Orr. Since Monsanto never before had advertised on television and had been drawn to this sponsorship deal by the tradition of motion picture production associated with Warners, it became the most demanding sponsor because it expected the studio to make good on all of ABC's vague marketing promises. Surprised that Warners had not delivered the promised production values or stars, Monsanto requested that the studio give the show a "shot in the arm" by adding major stars on a one-shot or recurring basis, thereby enabling the network to publicize the series more heavily. "In my opinion," Warner told Kintner, "[the sponsors] expect too much. They left me feeling that they would be pleased only if we could get John Wayne to play the part of 'Cheyenne' and comparable stars for *Casablanca* and *King's Row*.'' Warner countered ABC's exaggerated assurances by explaining to Monsanto's representatives the economic realities of the entertainment business. ''I told them that if we could secure the Wayne type of star we would be happy to,'' he said, ''but for the money they are paying us it would be just impossible. . . . These people are getting a good bargain for the $65,000 they are paying us.''[23]

As early as mid-October distress signals echoed through the soundstages of Warners and in the hallways at ABC. ''We are in a most serious crisis,'' Kintner told Warner, ''and by 'we' I mean both ABC and Warner Bros., because neither of us can afford to fail in TV.''[24] On the West Coast, Jack Warner, Bill Orr, and the four *Warner Bros. Presents* producers huddled with ABC's vice-president in charge of West Coast programming, Robert Lewine, and the network's Warners liaison, J. English Smith, to concoct a plan for salvaging the program. The participants reached two conclusions. First, Warners had to make a greater effort to unify the four different discourses contained within the program's general structure. The host's direct-address segments, the episodic narrative, the commercials, and the studio promotions should be restructured so that transitions among them seemed less arbitrary. If the differences among these discourses were less apparent, *Warner Bros. Presents* would have a better chance at holding viewer attention throughout the hour. Second, the studio had to clarify the narrative strategies of each individual series, both to generate more compelling stories from the series formula and to hold the attention of audience members by increasing their investment in the episodic narrative.[25]

At this point, Warners adopted a number of textual practices that had been established in broadcast radio. The studio began by introducing a dramatic ''vignette'' to lead off the program, a ''teaser'' that offered an enigmatic trace of the impending narrative to provoke the viewer's desire to experience the entire program. Orr described the structure and function of the vignette to his producers: ''This is to be a visual device narrated by Gig Young consisting of exciting film, perhaps one or two shots, placing a slab of drama before the audience to tell them what our show is about. It should be brief, exciting, and dramatic.'' The vignette should not be merely an excerpt from the episode, he argued, but should be conceived at the time of scripting as a structured prologue to the narrative's first act. ''The action in the vignette,'' he added, ''can take place some time prior to the story's actual opening, from seconds to hours, days, or months, as long as it predicts the story to be told in the main drama and is itself dramatic action.''[26] The adoption of a narrative vignette to focus the attention of distracted television viewers at the beginning of the broadcast represented the studio's first concerted effort to devise a mode of address that responded to the conditions of television viewing, rather than to those of the cinema.

Though forced upon the studio by the sponsors and the network, the initiation of the vignette marked another important stage in the development of series television at Warner Bros. For the first time, the program's primary emphasis shifted, however slightly, from studio promotion to the narrative episode that filled the bulk of the broadcast. Whereas the viewer initially had been faced with a seemingly arbitrary spectacle of narrative and advertising, this structural feature was meant to direct a viewer's attention to the primacy of the narrative. By planting this enigmatic sequence prior to any other discourse in the program and by giving it authority through the host's narration, the studio hoped that the narrative would become the program's organizing frame, that the text's flow would be orchestrated by the narrative. Desire for narrative closure would hold the viewer's attention for the length of the program, regardless of transitions among the program's discourses.[27] By subtly shifting emphasis away from self-promotion, therefore, Warners hoped not only to appease the sponsors, but to serve its promotional goals more effectively by ensuring that viewers still would be watching when "Behind the Cameras" aired.

Along with the effort to integrate the program's various discourses by encouraging investment in the narrative, the studio made other significant changes. Most of them were borrowed from radio and were designed to support the text's flow by providing less abrupt transitions between the narrative and the commercials. It was agreed that Gig Young would appear more frequently and would begin "to project more warmth and sincerity" in his role as mediator between narrative and advertising discourses. His introductory comments would be directed more toward the narrative episode and his segues returning from commercials would be used to reiterate the plot—another change designed to organize the program's discourse for the distracted television viewer. The studio and network agreed also on a standard format for transitions into commercials and back to the narrative. The musical score would punctuate the scene, bringing it to a definite conclusion, before a gentle fade to black and a fade-up would lead into the commercial—thereby providing a "graceful and unhurried presentation" of the commercial. ABC negotiated another change designed to encourage viewer interest throughout the hour. Instead of being divided into three segments, the narrative would now consist of four segments. With this alteration the network could schedule three commercial breaks during the program's first half-hour, when competition on the other networks wasn't as strong and more viewers tended to be watching. This structural change also ensured that the third segment would not end until at least thirty-nine minutes into the program—well beyond the 8:00 PM starting time of NBC's and CBS's more competitive programs. In other words, the network hoped that the narrative's second-act complications would be compelling enough to carry viewers beyond the point where they might switch to the other networks. ABC's liaison with Warners, J. English Smith, hoped that these changes, taken as a whole, would "provide a more smoothly integrated presentation which will result in a better pace, greater sustained viewer interest, and a reduced possibility of tune-out during the last fifteen minutes of the program."[28]

While ABC and Warners restructured the program's format, they also examined each of the individual series, since all three had come under attack. *Casablanca* was criticized for its routine plots, its superficial, undifferentiated characters, and its slow pace. As partial remedy, Warners picked up the pace by chopping over three minutes from the second episode. Of course, this last-minute editing further offended the sponsors because the lost time had to be recovered by padding "Behind the Cameras."[29] The network felt that *King's Row* should branch out from its central character, a psychiatrist, and generate future narratives by focusing on other characters in the community. "I suggest this possibility," Kintner remarked, "because there has been so much question about whether the stories directly tied to the young psychiatrist can have an interest for the entire family, including children." Jack Warner responded, "We do not and never did intend to make *King's Row* a series on psychiatry. It is and will be more of an anthology . . . with stories of different residents of the city."[30]

The negotiations over *King's Row* explicitly introduced the question of the intended audience for *Warner Bros. Presents* and suggested to studio executives that ABC had conflicting impulses about how to use the studio most effectively. ABC had signed the production agreement with Warners in part because of the studio's reputation for sophisticated genre films. The network had selected *Casablanca* and *King's Row*, a romance and a melodrama, because of their appeal to a mature audience. Later, the network had marketed the program to sponsors by emphasizing that the studio's legacy of high-quality production would provide a sophisticated environment for their advertisements. At the same time, however, ABC primarily wanted to build a unified schedule that would attract steady, routinized viewership. Instead of developing a few random hits scattered throughout the schedule, the network intended to structure its schedule around nightly blocks of programming anchored by the lead-off "keystone" programs.[31]

Studio personnel argued that the network had unfairly exploited Warners in order to achieve conflicting goals: On the one hand, ABC wanted to market a "mature" program in order to entice new advertisers to television; on the other hand, the network wanted to carry out its comprehensive programming strategies by placing the series in a potentially unfavorable time slot. Warners attributed the program's low ratings not to its questionable quality, but to what the studio perceived as ABC's misguided scheduling practices. From the studio's perspective, the audience for *Warner Bros. Presents* existed, but not in the particular exhibition venue that ABC had forced upon it. This argument began to arise after a late-September article in *Variety* claimed that the program had faced a difficult journey from the outset because dramatic programs had never been successful before 9:00 PM.[32] Story editor Richard Diggs began a running debate with ABC's Robert Lewine about whether *Warner Bros. Presents* would find an audience in the early time slot. Through contacts at the Young & Rubicam advertising agency, Diggs had learned that the TV industry considered the 7:30 PM TV audience to be immutably top-heavy with children, and that television industry wisdom stated that no program could achieve impressive ratings during this period without appealing primarily to children. He complained to Lewine, "I feel that in our time slot we are in very much the same position the Theater Guild would be in if Barnum and Bailey asked it to play *Death of a Salesman* in the center ring of the circus. I question if the finest script in the world would have much of a reception in this situation."[33] As Warners' personnel saw it, ABC gambled in the face of clear precedent by forcing *Warner Bros. Presents* into the 7:30 time slot when a later slot "would have almost automatically guaranteed a higher rating."[34]

After listening to his advisors, Jack Warner confronted Robert Kintner with these criticisms of network programming policy and chastized ABC for its contradictory attitude toward *Warner Bros. Presents*. Warner asked Kintner to explain why the network expected narratives that attracted mature viewers, while broadcasting the program at a time when high ratings were possible only if the program appealed to children. In his response, Kintner never mentioned the general network strategy that justified the decision to situate *Warner Bros. Presents* at 7:30, but he advised Warner that the time slot from 7:30–8:00 PM represented the greatest potential in television because it had not yet been dominated by the other networks. "Actually, 7:30–8:00 PM has the minimum competition that you can find in television, with only *Name That Tune*, Dinah Shore and John Cameron Swayze against you, and this is the real reason we have done as well as we have," he said. "If you moved to the 8:00–9:00 PM spot, you would be on against Milton Berle, Martha Raye, and Bob Hope, and, I must be candid, but I believe that would really knock your rating down." Because the network simply wouldn't move the program from this time slot, the problem of targeting an audience remained—and Kintner merely rearticulated the contradiction. "I agree with you that there is confusion concerning an 'adult' show vs. a 'children's' show," Kintner admitted. "I think that what we were groping for was an adult show that would hold the attention of children who were older than nine or ten years of age."[35]

*Cheyenne*, in particular, suffered from the tension of trying to create a series that would appeal to both children and adults. When the market for television programming opened in the late 1940s, the producers of B westerns were among the first to fill the new programming needs. By the mid–1950s, low-budget cowboy stars like William (Hopalong Cassidy) Boyd, Roy Rogers, and Gene Autry had resurrected their careers by becoming TV stars. As their older theatrical films began racking up huge profits in the new medium (with only Boyd actually owning the rights to his older films), these aging heroes produced original programming for television. In short measure, new TV western series, such as *The Lone Ranger, The Cisco Kid, Wild Bill Hickock*, and *Rin Tin Tin*, filled the airwaves. As more independent telefilm producers turned to the western genre because of its adaptability to low-budget production, the B western's backlot landscapes, shrieking Indian raids, and stolid lawmen virtually epitomized the worst of television programming to those who disparaged the new medium.[36]

At the same time, however, the motion picture industry was developing a contrasting variation of the western genre, a type that came to be known as the "adult" western. As postwar conditions in the film industry encouraged increased differentiation within the movie industry's traditional genres, Westerns began to employ narrative strategies more commonly associated with modernist fiction or the contemporary American theater, strategies such as formal self-consciousness, a revisionist attitude toward generic conventions, more ambiguous characters and conflicts between these characters, and explicit social and political allegory.[37] The industry began to distinguish westerns such as *The Gunfighter* (1950), *High Noon* (1952), and *Shane* (1953) from grade-B westerns by referring to them as adult westerns. While it is not clear how the term "adult western" originated, the industry quickly cultivated it as a marketing device, and the popular press regularly discussed the defining features of this type of western.[38] Managed to a certain degree by studio publicity, this discourse constructed the adult western as a generic category with appeal to moviegoers who had grown tired of the genre's most common conventions, especially as they were displayed nightly on TV.

Although the point here is not to define the adult western, nor to contrast it with other types of westerns, one might roughly describe the early TV westerns as emphasizing the same qualities that had always characterized B westerns: action and plot take precedence over dialogue and characterization. Characters are seldom elaborated by identifying them with collections of traits, long-term goals, or a past that impinges upon present action. Instead, they exist primarily as plot functions. Represented through stereotypical, easily identifiable traits, their narrative agency provides the most expedient support for the narrative's conflict-to-resolution structure. For this reason, narrative conflicts are generally unambiguous, enacted by clearly distinguishable antagonists—hero versus villain, cowboys versus indians. These intrinsically defining characteristics, however, are no more important than the extrinsic cultural discourse that surrounded and defined the western genre. The active construction of the adult western subgenre is important to recognize because critics often have discussed the adult western as though it were an objective narrative form, a product of inherent generic evolution. Critic J. Fred MacDonald represents this approach when he discusses the rise of adult westerns on TV by remarking that "adult westerns were recognizable immediately by their [TV] sponsors."[39] The point is not that the adult western was an ideal type that sponsors were able to recognize, but that entertainment industry forces actively constructed the concept and category of adult westerns as a mark of product differentiation. Consequently, the category of adult western was not a stable, objectifiable concept, but a construct that became the site of ongoing struggle to define the term, to debate which films should be included and excluded. Since the term came to represent a certain exchange value, the stakes in this debate were high.[40]

Discursive strategies for constructing the adult Western subgenre become apparent in the conflict that surrounded *Cheyenne*. It is no coincidence that the first three TV series that were labeled adult westerns premiered in September

1955—*Cheyenne* and *The Life and Legend of Wyatt Earp* on ABC, *Gunsmoke* on CBS. *Cheyenne* was described in ABC's sales presentation as an "adult western—featuring a mature story." The network invoked this term to identify the series with a type of Hollywood feature film that had been constructed in the first place partially as a means for differentiating feature-film westerns from their TV counterparts. By distinguishing their new westerns from the low-budget telefilm westerns that had been sold primarily in terms of their appeal to children, the networks hoped to attract more prestigious sponsors with the promise of a more desirable audience of consumers. The contradiction for *Cheyenne* was obvious; the series was sold on its promised appeal to an adult market, and yet was designed according to network specifications to draw an audience of children, an audience that would inflate the program's rating even if it didn't supply the type of audience most desirable to the sponsors.

For Warners, the 7:30 PM time slot initially meant that *Cheyenne* should follow the narrative model provided by the existing television westerns. When the first episode featured various conventions of the B western, such as infallible hero Cheyenne Bodie (played by inexperienced actor Norman Walker, rechristened "Clint" by the studio), a comic sidekick, an extended Indian attack, and conflict based on action rather than character psychology, the sponsors were not pleased. According to Kintner, the sponsors repudiated the series because it didn't provide the proper setting for the products advertised in their commercials. Liggett & Myers, which also sponsored the other new adult western, *Gunsmoke*, cried that they had purchased an adult western "along the lines of *Hondo* or *Gunsmoke*," but they had received instead a mere "Cowboys and Indians story." Kintner immediately asked the studio to reformulate the series. Warners agreed without hesitation. "Some Indians may pop up now and then," Jack Warner assured Kintner, "but we are going to adult westerns." Kintner returned to the sponsors with news of the change, and explained how the mistake had occurred. "While *Cheyenne* was attempting to attract an 'all-family audience'," he said, "it will turn to an 'adult western' conception rather than a program that is mostly designed to hold younger people. Perhaps the first *Cheyenne* was an error, but it was a legitimate error whose purpose was to try to hold as many sets at 7:30 as possible."[41]

For Warners, the first adjustment in salvaging *Cheyenne* was to fire producer Harvey Foster and replace him with *King's Row* producer Roy Huggins. At the same time, Warners authorized larger salaries for writers on all three series, and although script payments were still only $2500-$2900 per episode, this enabled the producers to recruit more experienced writers who previously had been too expensive. After Huggins became producer, an effort was made to rid *Cheyenne* of its B-movie conventions and to emphasize adult-western conventions. Cheyenne's humorous sidekick was unceremoniously dropped from the series. Since the revisionist adult westerns had attempted to remove the western from an unspecific, mythic West and place it in a space invested with historical authority, Huggins tried to bring a sense of verisimilitude to the series, going so far as to order a dozen historical reference books, a "minimum reference investment" for the series.[42] He also commissioned scripts with plots motivated by character psychology, not simply by conventional action. The most successful of these was an adaptation of the studio's 1948 film, *Treasure of the Sierra Madre*. Once these changes had been made, Warners tipped off the industry press that *Cheyenne* had been transformed into an adult western, hoping that publicity would help to re-situate the series in the public discourse. *Variety* reviewed the new *Cheyenne* on November 2, just one month after it had called the series "strictly kiddo fare." While the reviewer admitted that the episode "resembled a watered-down *Treasure of the Sierra Madre*," he also applauded the "astonishing" change in the series, calling the episode "the most adult of the 'adult westerns' seen this season on TV."[43]

By mid-November the effort expended to acquire the "adult" label appeared to have been justified. Although still action-oriented, the more reflective *Cheyenne* episodes began to pull higher ratings than competing NBC and CBS programs over the course of the entire hour.[44] In spite of the improvements in *Cheyenne*, however, ABC and the sponsors continued to apply pressure on Warners because the overall rating for *Warner Bros. Presents* remained between fifteen and twenty. Kintner promised that the sponsors would stop complaining when the series regularly reached a rating between twenty-five and thirty.[45] While ratings for *Cheyenne* easily hit the mark, those for *King's Row* and *Casablanca* were seldom much more than half that figure. In order for the entire program to achieve ratings that would satisfy the sponsors, both Kintner and Warners agreed that the weaker series—both of which had been designed to appeal to women—would have to undergo further alterations.

After meeting with sponsors, Kintner complained to William Orr that *King's Row* had become too nostalgic and sweet-tempered, that the series was not "sufficiently lusty to be true to the era or to be attractive to the viewer." Later, he warned Warners that the series "may lack appeal for the male element unless the stories are very lusty and combative." Following the network's suggestions, Warners commissioned scripts that introduced violent conflict and threats of danger into the pastoral melodrama of *King's Row*. Its soothing tales of moral welfare became "lusty and combative" as both studio and network sought "to minimize the serenity and gentleness inherent in the series." In one typical script written under this new policy, an escaped criminal seizes control of the local elementary school and holds the teacher and students captive during a lengthy confrontation with the police. Soon Warners adopted a new policy in acquiring stories for each series. In the words of *King's Row* producer Ellis St. John, the episodes for all three series now had to be "action stories that also appeal to adults."[46] This involved a startling departure from the original conception of *King's Row* and *Casablanca*. Although neither Warners nor the network ever explicitly articulated the new policy, its unspoken goal was to make *King's Row* and *Casablanca* more "masculine," more like *Cheyenne*, by adding action and the element of jeopardy to both series. ABC used the comparative failure of

*King's Row* and *Casablanca* as a rationale for ending its efforts to appeal to female audience segments.

While some of the changes in these series involved mere shifts in tone, the most interesting changes required major transformations in the narrative structure of *King's Row* and *Casablanca*. These changes compelled the network and studio to question the development of narrative strategies for TV series. In general, the structure of *Cheyenne*, on the one hand, and those of *King's Row* and *Casablanca*, on the other, represented two alternative forms of series narrative. *Cheyenne*, with its redeemer figure wandering from community to community through the old West, proved to have an ideal structure for generating series narratives and for appealing to male viewers. In essence, this type of structure gave the series many similarities to the anthology format, in which a series consists of diverse, unrelated narrative episodes. In the case of *Cheyenne*, each episode contained conflicts involving new characters, and these episodes were unified only by the recurring character of the protagonist who functioned as the force of moral order able to resolve any narrative conflict. Each time Cheyenne entered a new community, he either witnessed or provoked a new story in which he would participate to varying degrees. Like many of the telefilm genre series developed at this time, including most westerns and crime series, *Cheyenne* could be described as a disguised anthology series.

*King's Row* and *Casablanca*, on the other hand, took place in the very sort of community through which Cheyenne merely wandered. Centered around a single location, a community with a recurring set of characters, these series generated stories through the ongoing interaction of an established ensemble of characters. Although other characters occasionally entered the community from outside, these external characters were always peripheral to the episodic narrative. Like the conflicts in TV's situation comedy, therefore, those in the prime-time melodramas, *King's Row* and *Casablanca*, generally involved the potential disintegration and ultimate reintegration of the community structure. Warners and ABC began to feel that this community imposed major restrictions on the series. Because of its episodic structure, with a single locale, a limited set of characters, and the need to impose closure at the end of each episode, the series didn't offer the potential for a wide variety of stories. In addition, because conflicts were restricted to a small cast of recurring characters, the series presented few possibilities for violent conflicts or jeopardy. *King's Row* director Paul Stewart had warned the studio about these narrative constraints before the series even went into production. Stewart worried that the studio's contractual commitment to five actors in recurring roles might restrict the narrative possibilities for the series, especially if Warners demanded that all of the actors be used in order to get the most value from them. "I cannot be too emphatic about this," he explained, "since I feel that as we progress with the writers, and we place upon them this restriction of having to create stories only about these individuals, we will have an ingrown quality in our shows."[47] The network and studio might have solved this dilemma if they had been willing to sacrifice episodic closure and transform these melodramas into the serial format of the daytime melodrama. At the time, however, soap operas were a somewhat disreputable form of programming locked in the women's ghetto of daytime TV. In spite of its concern with demographics, ABC seemed convinced that the appeal of soap operas was too limited for prime time and, in the production agreement, expressly prohibited Warners from producing open-ended serials for *Warner Bros. Presents.*[48]

Eager to escape the limitations of the episodic format, ABC repeatedly requested the studio to move beyond the cafe setting of *Casablanca* and the town of *King's Row* in order to stir up more diverse, action-filled stories. *Casablanca* episodes began to change in ways similar to the siege story on *King's Row*. Narratives were structured around murder mysteries and characters in peril; deadlines were added to provide a thrust to the narrative. In an episode entitled "Killer at Large," for instance, an assassin stalks a diplomatic conference taking place in the city and the protagonists discover that the villain has planted a bomb scheduled to detonate at precisely 11:00 PM. Kintner offered the most fascinating strategy for diversifying the episodic narratives when he suggested adapting the screenplays of old Warners features to fit the series. *Cheyenne* had successfully adapted not only *The Treasure of the Sierra Madre*, but also *Rocky Mountain* (1950), *Along the Great Divide* (1951), *The Charge at Feather River* (1953), *Bordertown* (1935), and *To Have and Have Not* (1944). *Cheyenne*'s structure, however, made this sort of adaptation easier, since the lone protagonist either could be inserted into these narratives as an active participant or could be added as an observer. But the structure of *King's Row* and *Casablanca* did not allow such facile narrative transposition. Anxious to guide these series in the direction of *Cheyenne*'s disguised anthology structure, Kintner offered an ingenious solution. "Story lines from previously made Warners pictures might be adapted," he said, "even if a technique like flashbacks were used to get away from the set characters and into a different story setting. . . . "[49] Kintner's suggested use of flashbacks to diverge almost entirely from the established characters would have transformed *King's Row* and *Casablanca* into anthology series in everything but name.

By early December, ABC and Warners considered *King's Row* moribund. To salvage the series and add variety to its episodes, Warners weighed the possibility of shifting *King's Row* away from its established characters and making it a full-fledged anthology of stories situated in and around the town, featuring new characters and unrelated stories each week. From the studio's standpoint this seemed like a shrewd maneuver. According to the industry's agreement with the Screen Writer's Guild, Warners retained all subsequent rights to scripts written for an established episodic series, including serialization, sequel, and merchandising rights, but held only TV film rights to an anthology script. In addition, minimum payments and residuals for an anthology script were $200-$300 higher than those for an episodic series script. Warners thought that it might retain all rights to future scripts and circumvent the extra payments by making *King's*

*Row* an anthology series without officially declaring the change in format. They quickly realized, however, that this strategy would not be accepted by the Guild, because the union agreement clearly defined an episodic series. A setting alone could not serve as the basis for an episodic series. According to the agreement, " 'Episodic series' means a series of films each of which contains a separate complete story with a character or characters common to each of the films." Since episodic series were contractually defined as being organized around recurring characters, and nothing else, Warners feared that if the series changed in midstream from an episodic to an anthology format the Writer's Guild might claim payments for future episodes as anthology scripts, and also might demand retroactive payment for completed episodes, claiming that the series had always been an anthology.[50]

Since Warners was thwarted in its attempt to transform *King's Row* into an anthology series, it is not surprising that in mid-December ABC, Warners, and the sponsors agreed to drop *King's Row* from *Warner Bros. Presents* and gradually phase out *Casablanca*, while replacing them with an anthology series given the blunt title, *Conflict!*. Nor is it surprising that the anthology premiered with an episode based upon the school siege script written but never produced for *King's Row*.[51] In spite of the fact that *Cheyenne* did not appear weekly, and that each of its narrative episodes was buried within Warners' self-promotion, the western series emerged as one of the season's most popular new programs. By mid-February its ratings reached thirty-three. If its individual ratings for the entire season had been calculated separately from those of the other series in *Warner Bros. Presents, Cheyenne* would have finished the season among the twenty top-rated programs.

In spite of *Cheyenne's* ratings success, however, the first year of television production at Warners was one of confusion and uncertainty, a protracted period of unsystematic trial and error. Warners lost nearly $500,000 during its first year of television production because it couldn't produce the program for the price that the network paid. As the industry trade papers noted, this financial setback was compounded by the fact that the studio had completely ignored the established telefilm practice of recovering losses through subsequent sales in syndication. Due to the time alloted to "Behind the Cameras," the episodic narratives contained in *Warner Bros. Presents* had running times of approximately forty minutes. Since this length couldn't fill standard one-hour or half-hour time slots on local stations, the Warners program was unmarketable in syndication. Blinded by its immediate plan to promote feature films on prime-time TV, Warners produced something rare in the telefilm industry—"properties with little or no residual value."[52] Since deficit financing supported by syndication revenue was standard practice in the telefilm industry by 1955, this strategic oversight, more than any other event during the first season, suggests how haphazardly Warners had planned its entrance into the field of television production.

The popularity of *Cheyenne*, a solid hit in a year that saw the emergence of a number of popular westerns like *Gunsmoke* and *The Life and Legend of Wyatt*

*Earp*, demonstrated that the negotiations between Warners, ABC, and the sponsors had at least generated a tentative strategy for producing popular series television. Still, Warners was never satisfied with its unwanted collaborators. Once it became apparent that the studio would suffer financial losses, Jack Warner lost patience with the network and the sponsors. He complained to Robert Kintner that Warners had not received adequate financial compensation for its program and that the series was still handicapped by its time slot. He also requested that ABC simply dismiss the disgruntled sponsors from their contracts and replace them with more congenial companies.[53] While the sponsors, ABC, and Warners never reached agreement about "Behind the Cameras," however, other elements of the negotiations provoked Warners to consider the TV text as something different than the cinema text. Prompted by its partner's knowledge of broadcast practices, the movie studio began to consider such issues as television's modes of reception, the TV text's flow, and the implications of series narrative. ABC and the sponsors convinced Warners to emphasize its episodic narratives as a means for unifying the program's unrelated discourses and sustaining the home viewer's experience of flow. After gradually rejecting the ensemble series, *Casablanca* and *King's Row*, Warners and ABC found that *Cheyenne*'s disguised anthology structure proved to be the most effective conjunction of economic and textual practices. As a narrative function, the lone, wandering, redeemer protagonist enabled Warners to create a disguised anthology series which provided the differentiation of anthology episodes and the standardization of an established character and a narrative formula. Because the series relied on only a single recurring character who moved freely through a backlot western landscape, episodic narratives could be generated easily and produced at a relatively low cost. At the same time, the moral certainty associated with this redeemer hero proved appealing to the male segment of the television audience at a time when westerns were becoming the dominant television genre.

Due entirely to the popularity of *Cheyenne, Warner Bros. Presents* was renewed for a second season. Neither ABC nor Warners, however, suggested scheduling the western series into its own time slot. Instead, it was agreed that the format for *Warner Bros. Presents* would alternate *Cheyenne* and the anthology series *Conflict!* The decision to juxtapose *Cheyenne*, an emerging hit, with the anthology format's unproven potpourri of stories provides a most revealing image of the ambivalent relations between Warners and ABC at the end of this first season. Kintner's rationale for the switch to an anthology format indicates that *Warner Bros. Presents* was still something of an experimental laboratory for both ABC and Warners. "Making these anthology episodes will not only bolster up the series," he explained while cancelling *King's Row* and *Casablanca*, "but will give us a chance to study a different format for possible use in the 1956–1957 season."[54]

As the alternating format indicates, both companies were stalled in a holding pattern. The network was uncertain of the type of programming that it wanted the studio to supply. Should ABC continue to market the Warner Bros. name and reputation in the *Warner Bros. Presents* format, or should it request the studio to produce individual, autonomous series like *Cheyenne*, whose episodic narratives would not be framed by the studio's promotional discourse? Warners, on the other hand, was still unsure of its intentions toward television. Was the revenue from network television sufficient to justify a complete commitment to series television production? Or should Warners hedge its bet by continuing to produce a program which contained both narrative episodes and studio promotion? When it came time to renegotiate the studio's contract, neither the studio nor the network approached the bargaining talks with long-term goals. Although Kintner and Warner had agreed before the debut of *Warner Bros. Presents* to increase the studio's presence in ABC's prime-time schedule during the 1956–57 season, neither man raised the issue once the first season had concluded. Rather than exploit the success of *Cheyenne*, or lay the groundwork for other Warners series, the contract talks determined only that *Warner Bros. Presents* would be renewed in the format that had been negotiated by the conclusion of the first season. The debut season of *Warner Bros. Presents*, therefore, may have allowed Warner Bros. to cross the threshold into the television industry, but it did not signal a firm decision about the value of television production at the studio, nor certainty about the type of television text that the studio would produce.

## NOTES

1. Robert Kintner to Jack L. Warner, 12 September 1955; Jack L. Warner to Robert Kintner, 17 September 1955. Warner Bros. Archives, Department of Special Collections, Doheny Library, University of Southern California. Unless otherwise indicated, all Warner Bros. and ABC documents are from this source.

2. Kintner reported the negative reviews in New York and Los Angeles newspapers, but advised Warner to ignore them because ABC believed that unfavorable reviews had no significant effect on television audiences. Robert L. Kintner to Jack L. Warner, 14 September 1955; 28 September 1955. For examples of the negative reaction to *Warner Bros. Presents*, see "Review of *Warner Bros. Presents*," *Variety*, 21 September 1955, 35–36; "Hollywood Stubs Its Toe," *TV Guide*, 7 December 1955, 4–6.

3. Robert Kintner to Jack L. Warner, 23 September 1955.

4. Robert Kintner to Jack L. Warner, 28 September 1955.

5. Warner Bros. Pictures, Inc. and American Broadcasting Co., Contract, *Warner Bros. Presents*, 22 September 1955.

6. Benjamin Kalmenson, Testimony, *United States v. 20th Century-Fox et al.*, 31 October 1955. Warner Bros. Archive, Theatre Collection, Firestone Library, Princeton University, Princeton, New Jersey.

7. John Fiske, *Television Culture* (New York: Methuen, 1987), 13–14. Many other critics have discussed the theoretical fallacy of equating TV program and TV text, both by directing attention to the social production of meaning by television viewers and by describing the difficulty of isolating a single, discrete TV text from the endless torrent of television programming. See, for instance, Umberto Eco, "Towards a Semiotic Inquiry into the TV Message," *Working Papers in Cultural Studies* 3 (1972): 103–21; Horace

Newcomb and Paul Hirsch, "Television as a Cultural Forum," in Horace Newcomb, ed., *Television: The Critical View*, 4th ed. (New York: Oxford University Press, 1987), 455–70.

8. See Stuart Hall, "Encoding/Decoding," in Stuart Hall, Dorothy Hobson, Andrew Lowe, and Paul Willis, eds., *Culture, Media, Language* (London: Hutchinson, 1980), 128–38.

9. Jack L. Warner, Testimony, *United States v. 20th Century-Fox et al.*, 31 October 1955. Warner Bros. Archive, Princeton University; "This is Film's Cadillac Age," *Variety*, 9 February 1955, 3.

10. Warner Bros. Pictures, Inc. and American Broadcasting Co., Contract, *Warner Bros. Presents*, 22 September 1955.

11. ABC Television Network, *Warner Bros. Presents* Promotional Presentation Booklet, n.d.,c. March 1955.

12. At the time, for example, ABC Chairman Leonard Goldenson explained that his network would pursue an audience consisting primarily of "youthful families." See Herman Land, "ABC: An Evaluation," *Television Magazine*, December 1957, 94. John Fiske discusses the relations between television's modes of address and its modes of reception from a theoretical perspective, in *Television Culture*, 55–59, 72–77. A number of recent critics have argued that television spectatorship is characterized by distraction, rather than concentration. For instance, John Ellis contrasts the cinema spectator's "gaze" at the screen with the television spectator's "glance." As a result, television signifying practices are often designed to call the viewer's glance back to the TV screen, in Rick Altman's words, "to identify that which is worth looking at. . . . " See Rick Altman, "Television Sound," in Horace Newcomb, ed. *Television: The Critical View*, 4th ed. (New York: Oxford University Press, 1987), 566–84; John Ellis, *Visible Fictions* (London: Routledge & Kegan Paul, 1982), 109–72.

13. ABC, Promotional Presentation Booklet.

14. ABC-Warner Bros., Contract. Neither ABC nor Warners assumed that all three genres would be successful, and, in fact, they had considered other types of series, such as teenage romances and family comedies, before settling on those chosen.

15. Raymond Williams, *Television: Technology and Cultural Form* (New York: Schocken Books, 1974), 86–96; John Ellis, *Visible Fictions*, 112–26. For a suggestive discussion of the implications of segmentation and flow, see John Fiske, *Television Culture*, 99–105.

16. "The abc of ABC," *Forbes*, 15 June 1959, 16.

17. Robert Kintner to Jack L. Warner, 6 April 1955. The ABC programs that followed *Warner Bros. Presents* were: *The Life and Legend of Wyatt Earp, Make Room for Daddy*, and *DuPont Cavalcade Theater*.

18. For examples of the antagonism between advertisers and the major studios, see "Majors TV Plan—New Faces; But Ad Accts Want Big Stars," *Variety*, 20 April 1955, 37; Charles Sinclair, "Should Hollywood Get It For Free?" *Sponsor*, 8 August 1955, 31.

19. ABC, Promotional Presentation Booklet.

20. Robert Kintner to Jack L. Warner, 14 September 1955, 16 September 1955, 21 September 1955; Edgar Monsanto Queeny to Robert Kintner, 14 September 1955; Robert Kintner to Edgar Monsanto Queeny, 20 September 1955; Robert Kintner to Jack L. Warner, 21 September 1955; M. F. Mahoney to Robert Kintner, 7 October 1955.

21. Milton Orman to Bryan Moore, 15 November 1961.

22. John Peyser to William T. Orr, 19 October 1955.

23. Jack L. Warner to Robert Kintner, 14 October 1955.

24. Robert Kintner to Jack L. Warner, 23 September 1955.

25. William T. Orr to Richard Diggs, Roy Huggins, Jerome Robinson, Ellis St. Joseph, 30 September 1955.

26. Ibid.

27. Telegram, Robert Lewine to Monsanto, General Electric, Liggett & Myers, 27 September 1955.

28. J. English Smith to William T. Orr, 30 September 1955; Lewine, 27 September 1955.

29. Jack L. Warner to Robert Kintner, 28 September 1955.

30. Robert Kintner to Jack L. Warner, 20 September 1955; Warner to Kintner, 28 September 1955.

31. "The abc of ABC," 16; "ABC-TV in Laps of Pix Gods," *Variety*, 7 September 1955, 25.

32. "Gals Gang Up On Warner Bros. Presents," *Variety*, 28 September 1955, 31.

33. Richard Diggs to Robert Lewine, 6 October 1955, 8 October 1955. At Diggs's insistence, Lewine commissioned the network's research department to conduct a study of the audience available during the time period and the performance of the various types of programming scheduled earlier than 9:00 PM. Lewine returned a six-page report with statistics to refute all of Warners' complaints. It concluded that the program was more important than the time slot in determining audience characteristics. "The program itself will determine the audience attracted," the report stated. Donald W. Coyle to Robert Lewine, 7 November 1955.

34. Art Silver to Jack L. Warner, 11 October 1955.

35. JLW to RK, 14 October 1955; RK to JLW, 18 October 1955.

36. For instance, when the major studios wanted to caricature TV, as in the 1954 film *Bigger Than Life*, the family television set emits only a raucous assault of stampedes, cavalry charges, and gunfire from these westerns.

37. For further discussion of this topic, see Christopher Anderson, "Jesse James, The Bourgeois Bandit: The Transformation of a Cultural Hero, *Cinema Journal* 26, 1 (Fall 1986): 43–64.

38. For instance, in an article titled "Can You Tell The Difference?" *TV Guide* offered readers a "scholarly survey" comparing adult and children's westerns. See *TV Guide*, 21 September 1957, 20–23. Film industry celebrities often joked about the differences. John Wayne once distinguished the classical western from the "adult" western by explaining that an adult western was solved by talking the villain to death. Alfred Hitchcock observed that in the adult western there seemed to be no more villains—"only good guys and neurotics." See Horace Newcomb, *TV: The Most Popular Art* (New York: Anchor Books, 1974), 62; "Hitchcock Steals Show as NBC-TV Close-Circuits Its 58–59 Lineup," *Variety*, 11 September 1957, 33.

39. J. Fred MacDonald, *Who Shot the Sheriff?: The Rise and Fall of the Television Western* (New York: Praeger, 1987), 47. Throughout this critical history of TV westerns, MacDonald unquestioningly uses the distinction between "adult" and "juvenile" westerns as though these were natural categories, and not cultural constructs. To see how this distinction is replicated in another recent work, see Gary A. Yoggy, "When Television Wore Six-Guns: Cowboy Heroes on TV," in Archie P. McDonald, ed., *Shooting Stars:*

*Heroes and Heroines of Western Film* (Bloomington: Indiana University Press, 1987), 218–57.

40. For instance, during the 1950s Warners produced three distinctly different types of westerns for three different exhibition settings and different segments of the audience. The studio financed independently produced prestige westerns like *The Searchers* (1956), *Giant* (1956), and *Rio Bravo* (1958) for exhibition in first-run theatres. Warners produced its own low-budget westerns like *Fort Dobbs* (1958) and *Westbound* (1959) for second-run theatres and drive-ins. Finally, the studio produced its western television series for TV broadcast. Discussions of genre in the popular press, including the development of subcategories like the adult western, helped construct different exchange values for these films.

41. Kintner, 21 September, 23 September; Telegram, Jack L. Warner to Benjamin Kalmenson, 21 September 1955; Telegram, Robert Kintner to William M. Farrell, 27 September 1955.

42. Memo, Richard Diggs to Jack L. Warner, 28 September 1955; Memo, Richard Diggs to William T. Orr, 28 October 1955; Memo, Roy Huggins to [unnamed] Milliken, 31 October 1955.

43. "Review of *Warner Bros. Presents—Cheyenne*," *Variety*, 28 September 1955, 38; 2 November 1955, 34.

44. This comparison is skewed slightly by the fact that the competition was relatively weak until 8:00 PM.

45. Robert Kintner to Jack L. Warner, 18 October 1955; 17 November 1955.

46. Robert Kintner to William T. Orr, 27 October 1955; Robert Kintner to Jack L. Warner, 17 November 1955; Ellis St. John to William T. Orr, 22 December 1955; Robert Lewine to Jack L. Warner, 14 December 1955.

47. Paul Stewart to Gary Stevens, 24 May 1955.

48. Warner Bros.-ABC, Contract.

49. Kintner, 17 November 1955; Bryan Moore to Stephen Karnot, 27 March 1962.

50. Richard Diggs to William T. Orr, 2 December 1955.

51. Robert Kintner to Jack L. Warner, 9 December 1955; "WB to Drop *King's Row*," *Variety*, 14 December 1955, 39; William T. Orr, Deposition.

52. "Majors $2.875 Mil TV Rap," *Variety*, 1 February 1956, 37.

53. Jack Warner to Robert Kintner, 14 October 1955. Kintner responded: "It is a cardinal rule of the business that unless the emergency is unbelievable, advertisers are not let out of commitments. In addition, in view of the ratings, we would have a difficult time replacing them." Robert Kintner to Jack L. Warner, 18 October 1955.

54. Robert Kintner to Jack L. Warner, 9 December 1955.

# 9

# Desilu, *I Love Lucy*, and the Rise of Network TV

*Thomas Schatz*

Robert Saudek of the Museum of Broadcasting, looking back over a half-century of radio and television, has said that "broadcasting's bone structure was formed in the 1920s, and has never been fundamentally altered or improved upon."[1] While cable TV and the VCR boom threaten to alter—if not necessarily improve—broadcasting's "bone structure," Saudek's view of early network radio and TV has become by now commonplace among media historians. And in the most general sense, that view does indeed hold up. The genesis of network radio in the 1920s marked an unprecedented alliance of social, economic, and technological forces, establishing a "structure" which persisted into the TV age— and persists to this day in commercial television. That structure, essentially, involves national networks feeding news and entertainment programs via local stations to a mass audience which, in the process, is "delivered" to sponsors whose advertisements dominate schedules and subsidize program costs.[2]

When we move beyond generalities and look closely at the history of network broadcasting, however, Saudek's thesis is problematic, if not misleading and downright wrong-headed. The fact is that as commercial television took shape after World War II, the established "radio model" proved ill-suited to the new medium. Through an ensuing decade of struggle, negotiation, and shifting alliances, network TV gradually adjusted and effectively transformed the economic, creative, and administrative practices developed by the radio industry. With that transformation, there were significant changes in the roles, functions, and relations of power among the networks, sponsors, ad agencies, program suppliers, and the audience.

There are any number of ways in which we might trace these changes, given the convergence of forces and ever-shifting relations of power involved in TV's early development. The focus here is on the birth and decade-long rise of Desilu, an independent TV production company created by Lucille Ball and Desi Arnaz that provided much of CBS's programming during the 1950s. Desilu's 1951 flagship series, *I Love Lucy*, gave CBS its first runaway hit series and gave television a prototype for the situation comedy (the "sitcom"), a genre that by the 1960s was the programming staple of network TV.[3]

Desilu's initial success with *I Love Lucy* led to further series productions, from sitcoms to westerns and anthology dramas. In the process Desilu helped shape the institutional, technological, and economic practices in 1950s television—the shift in prime-time series production from live video out of New York to film out of Los Angeles, for instance, or the use of reruns in network programming strategies. Equally important, the CBS-Desilu alliance gives a clear indication of the networks' growing control over TV production and programming during the 1950s. Ball and Arnaz were successful enough to buy out a Hollywood studio by 1957, when Desilu was turning out more product than any other company on the West Coast, including the major movie companies. But Desilu's autonomy and authority—its so-called "independence"—steadily diminished as the economic stakes rose and the networks consolidated their control over the TV industry. By the early 1960s Desilu's role in the overall network system had changed dramatically from only a decade earlier, when television was new and virtually anything seemed possible.

## TV'S BEGINNINGS: REWORKING THE RADIO MODEL

Like dozens of other early TV series, *I Love Lucy* grew out of a successful radio program—in this case *My Favorite Wife*, a CBS radio comedy starring Lucille Ball and sponsored by Jell-O. When CBS asked Ball early in 1950 to consider doing her show as a television series, it was assumed that the series would be financed, produced, and "sold" on much the same terms as it had been on radio. According to the established radio model, national networks acted as "common carriers," feeding programs to local "affiliated" stations. Programs were actually produced by advertising agencies for sponsors who purchased "air time" from a network, specifying a slot on the network schedule when both the program and its ads were broadcast. Those local stations wishing to produce their own programs and deal with area merchants for ad revenues could remain independent from network affiliation, as did over half the 10,000 or so radio stations in the United States by 1950.

Even as early as 1950, however, when CBS proposed the new TV series to Ball, it was becoming obvious that there would be problems adapting the radio model to television. The major drawbacks were economic. The enormous cost and technological complexity of TV production prevented most local stations from producing their own programs with any real hope of competing with affiliated stations carrying network-fed programming. Because radio was relatively easy and inexpensive to produce, the majority of local stations throughout the country could—and in fact did—remain independent of the networks. TV stations could ill afford such a strategy; indeed, they couldn't afford *not* to affiliate with a national network, given the high production values and obvious audience appeal of early network programming. During TV's earliest years, fewer than 2 percent of local stations remained independent from the national networks. And because virtually all local TV stations were network affiliates, American television emerged literally overnight as a genuine *mass* medium, with far fewer stations (than radio) competing for portions of a truly national audience and thus providing sponsors with an unprecedented access to the American consumer.

In TV's early years, of course, there was still no telling just how massive a medium television might be. This was due not only to the uncertainties of an emergent industry but also to a government-imposed "freeze" on its development. TV's growth was stalled in October 1948 by the FCC, which suspended the licensing of new stations until certain technical and organizational wrinkles could be ironed out. That froze the number of licensed stations nationwide at 108, all of which were affiliated with major networks. NBC had 63 affiliates, CBS had 30, and the ever struggling ABC had 15.[4] The freeze was expected to be brief but it dragged on until 1952, and it wasn't until 1953 that the "TV boom" hit the country in full force. While the freeze slowed TV's penetration, it did provide what historian Erik Barnouw termed a "laboratory period" for the industry, "a priceless opportunity for testing and observing" various program types and trends. It became obvious during the freeze that TV, like radio, would rely heavily on a limited repertoire of program formulas.

When the A. C. Nielsen company began measuring audiences and rating TV programs in 1950, its numbers indicated how genre-bound the medium was. They also showed how heavily TV's genres were keyed to certain East Coast entertainment forms, particularly the "culture industries" based in and around New York City—not only radio and advertising, but also theater, vaudeville, music, and publishing. Not surprisingly, most of TV's early program formulas were lifted directly from radio, a process that was accelerated by the so-called "talent raids" of the late 1940s, which attracted radio stars with the promise of higher salaries, tax breaks, and more widespread exposure. Of the top twenty programs on network TV in 1950–51, all were produced live in New York; six were variety shows with roots in radio and vaudeville, seven were anthology dramas which tapped into New York's theatrical talent, and two were comedy-dramas adapted from radio. There also were three crime dramas, two of which were based on radio series, a sports program emanating primarily from New York's Madison Square Garden, and both a quiz show and a talent show broadcast simultaneously to radio and TV audiences.

When CBS suggested moving *My Favorite Wife* to its TV network in 1950, Ball was enthusiastic about the idea but only on certain conditions. She was then living in the Los Angeles area and balked at doing the show from New York City. Ball was expecting her first child and, nearing age 40, had no desire to commute or relocate for the series. She suggested that the series be broadcast live from the West Coast and that she costar with her husband and business manager, Desi Arnaz, an actor and popular bandleader in the L.A. area (with a successful radio show of his own). CBS balked and soon dropped plans for the TV series, but by now Ball and Arnaz were intrigued by the idea of costarring in a TV series. They pursued the venture on their own, engaging Bob Carroll and Madelyn Pugh, two of the writers on Ball's radio series, to create a few vaudeville-type sketches wherein Ball and Arnaz essentially played themselves. These were polished into a stage act which the couple took on a cross-country tour during the summer of 1950.

A successful stage tour (and Ball's continued obstinacy) won over William Paley, CBS board chairman, and the network agreed to a series pilot produced on the West Coast costarring Ball and Arnaz. Writer Jess Oppenheimer came aboard at this point, and together with Ball and Arnaz transformed the stage act into the domestic comedy format. Arnaz would play a Cuban bandleader, Ricky Ricardo, with Ball as his scatter-brained and star-struck housewife, Lucy. Sketching out future episodes, they incorporated the characters of Fred and Ethel Mertz as comic foils and coconspirators with Ricky and Lucy in their ongoing "battle of the sexes." The series pilot was shot early in 1951 live on video in CBS's West Coast facility before a studio audience. (Actually all video was live until the marketing of videotape in 1957.) Films taken directly from the video monitors—called "kinescopes"—were sent back to New York, along with story outlines for future episodes.

CBS was pleased with the results and within days had sold the series to Philip Morris through their ad agency, the Biow Company. Philip Morris agreed to produce the entire season's slate of 39 episodes at $19,500 per episode, and secured the 9:00 PM Monday slot from CBS. But still there were problems to be worked out over the logistics of actual production. Milton Biow, agency president, insisted that the series be done in the CBS studio in New York, where the agency could supervise production and exploit the more desirable time frame (especially since the vast majority of viewers lived in the eastern time zone). Biow also wanted the show produced with CBS's superior video production facilities. Arnaz, however, wanted creative control of the series as executive producer, which he thought would come only if the series were produced on film in Los Angeles.

That led to further negotiations between Arnaz, the network, and the ad agency, negotiations that affected the emergent TV industry on various fronts. Biow agreed to Arnaz's plan, but CBS was adamant about maintaining the live-audience dimension of the pilot. Arnaz assured CBS that they could "stage it as a play" which could be shot "simultaneously with three or four 35mm motion-picture cameras."[5] That pushed the budget up another $5,000 to $24,500 per episode—still a bargain, considering feature film budgets were then pushing beyond the million-dollar mark. CBS and Philip Morris agreed to cover $4,000 of the budget increase, but Ball and Arnaz would have to come up with the rest out of their salaries. Arnaz agreed, but only if CBS would let Desilu have full ownership of the series after its initial network showing, instead of the original agreement of a fifty-fifty split between CBS and Desilu.

Incredibly enough, CBS agreed. "Nobody was giving much thought to residuals in those days," Arnaz later recalled, "or what a film library would be worth in the future." Arnaz claimed that demanding full ownership was something of a whim, and that his primary motivation for doing the series on film had more to do with creative control and superior production values: "I just knew we could do a better show on film. Lucy would be photographed better and whatever mistakes were made even during filming could be corrected later."[6]

The network's willingness to relinquish ownership of the series would cost CBS millions over the next few years, and it is an apt indication of how little the networks understood the financial stakes and profit potential of TV series production. It also indicates a remarkable degree of flexibility and cooperation between ad agency, network, and talent in the production process. This was clearly a period of experimentation and uncertainty, before the standardization of that process would severely restrict such freedom. Only during such a period, in fact, could the Hollywood film industry have made such inroads into the network production process. The governing perception has been that the film and TV industries were bitter antagonists in the early 1950s. Actually, such hostility was evinced only by the largest movie studios, the group of surviving "major" studios: Paramount, Warner Bros., MGM, and 20th Century-Fox. These were the film companies whose massive production facilities, bloated studio overhead, and global distribution and exhibition arms rendered them most vulnerable to the emerging television industry. Not so the smaller studios and independent filmmakers, which welcomed this new medium with its insatiable appetite for product.

Even a cursory glance at the trade journals of both the film and television industries at the time of Desilu's creation indicates how openly the Hollywood film industry embraced the new medium and converted to "telefilm" production. A story in the September 10, 1951, issue of *Broadcasting*, for example, under the headline "Film in the Future—as Television's Horizons Expand," reported that at least 75 independent telefilm units were in operation in the Los Angeles area, and that some 25 of these companies had sold 40 series to the networks for the 1951–52 season at an average cost of $14,000 per episode.[7] Most telefilm series production was in the B-western category, with series like *Wild Bill Hickok, The Lone Ranger, The Cisco Kid,* and *Gene Autry* already in production. The article also reported that some 780 hours of telefilm material had been produced over the past year, almost the exact equivalent of the number of hours of feature films and short subjects produced for the movie industry. "How far the major networks will go in the way of making filmed programs for television is yet to be seen," concluded the article. "The situation, instead of becoming clearer each week, simply becomes more muddled."

Hollywood's leading trade paper, *Variety,* also charted the film industry's incursions into television. An article that appeared on December 12, 1951, typified the growing sentiment at the time that telefilm production might replace Hollywood's B-movie output, which was tapering off during the postwar era. Paramount production chief Y. Frank Freeman and long-time independent movie producer Hal Roach were reported as being in agreement that "formula pictures are on their way out of the major film lots" in Hollywood. Paramount's Freeman "pronounced the death knell of low-cost B production," while Roach "predicted that motion picture and television are destined to complement each other with the major studios dropping B pictures in favor of telepic programs."[8]

*Variety* also noted that with each passing month, the shift to telefilm production was more evident. A January 9, 1952, article with a typical *Variety* headline, "Vidpix Weed Out Shoestringers," described "the gradual but definite stabilization" of Hollywood-based telefilm production, "to the point where 80-odd vidfilm companies existing in these parts early in 1951 have boiled down to around 20 financially stable outfits."[9] Much of this stability was due to the recent entry "into the telepix field of motion-picture companies such as Republic, Universal-International, and Monogram." The article concluded on a telling note: "more and more sponsors . . . put their coin into vidfilm, apparently realizing that in a piece of negative [film] they retained continued marketable merchandise."

The major studios like Paramount and Warners would not come around to telefilm production for several more years, but second-rank companies like Universal and Republic were ideally suited to telefilm production, given their orientation toward efficient, low-budget, formula-based filmmaking. In fact the January 23, 1952, issue of *Variety*, in its weekly report on "TV Films in Production," lists Republic studios as providing facilities and personnel for Jack Webb's independent production company, Mark VII Productions, in the filming of a "half-hour adventure telepic."[10] That series, of course, was *Dragnet*, whose location shooting in and around Los Angeles and careful attention to the details, jargon, and ennui of day-to-day police work would bring a new level of "realism" to the genre, and one that could only be captured on film. *Dragnet's* impact on the urban crime genre was significant, but nowhere that of *I Love Lucy*, which shaped the style, the technique, the veritable "grammar" of the sitcom. And beyond the series' impact on the genre, there was Desilu itself, which affected the institutional, economic, and even the technological practices in the TV industry.

## *I LOVE LUCY* AND DESILU'S EARLY ASCENT

Producing *I Love Lucy* on film was clearly the principal challenge for Arnaz and company, and not only for technological reasons. There was the ad agency's insistence that the series have top production values, as well as CBS's demand that the show be done before a live audience. Unlike a crime drama or western, sitcom production allowed for no "second unit" work or the incorporation of "stock footage." What's more, for such a production to engage a live audience, it would have to be enacted "in continuity" and shot in "real time." Each episode would have to be filmed as if it were a stage play, without breaks between each separate shot to move the camera and relight the scene, as is done under conventional filmmaking conditions.

Arnaz realized that if he could economize on camera setups he could reduce the amount of time spent on production and thus reduce the budget. The demands of TV scheduling meant that each series segment had to be written, rehearsed, and shot in the span of a week, as opposed to even the cheapest and quickest of B movies, which would cost upwards of $250,000 and were produced in four to six weeks. Arnaz turned for assistance to Hollywood cinematographer Karl Freund, who had worked with Ball at MGM in the early 1940s. Freund was among the industry's acknowledged pioneers in lighting and camera work, and was noted for creative, economical solutions to difficult technical or artistic problems. He was easing into retirement in 1951, but when approached by Ball and Arnaz, Freund agreed to work (at union scale) as director of cinematography on the series.

Freund quickly convinced Arnaz that the series should be shot not on a theater stage but on a "sound stage" in a film studio, which would ease the problems of lighting and camera synchronization. Editing presented a more complex problem, which was solved by interlocking three Moviola editing machines. As Ball recalls, "One night [Freund] brought us to his house in the valley and showed us the system he'd invented for us, one that could film simultaneously on three cameras and then, when the show was over and the film was developed, you could sit in the cutting room and his machine played back all three shots simultaneously, so you could cut from one shot to another."[11]

By then Arnaz had secured Stage 2 from the near-bankrupt General Services Studio, a site large enough to accommodate Freund's three-camera system and also CBS's requirement of a studio audience. The network put up an additional $50,000 to "remodel" the studio, which entailed removing a wall and adding fire exits and bleachers for about 300 spectators. As amenable as CBS was in this regard, though, the network was fairly uncooperative in other areas, particularly the casting of William Frawley, an unemployed, alcoholic character actor, in the role of Fred Mertz. But Arnaz's contract as executive producer gave him complete creative control, and he took CBS no more seriously in this instance than when the network balked at Arnaz himself playing Lucy's TV husband.

*I Love Lucy* premiered on October 15, 1951, and was an immediate hit. Clearly the economy of production design—the limited sets and locales, the four-character constellation, the repetitive plot structure of each episode—did not undermine the show's appeal. On the contrary, the very simplicity and formulaic nature of *I Love Lucy* was essential to its success, particularly in the way it concentrated the entire narrative enterprise on Ball's hare-brained, hustling, mock-heroic housewife, the inimitable (though much imitated) Lucy Ricardo.

Ball's character was the source of conflict and comedy in each series installment, and her chronic domestic anarchy clearly struck a chord for the millions of TV viewers caught up in America's postwar baby/family/housing boom.

After modest success as a movie comedienne, Ball was quite suddenly America's top screen star. *I Love Lucy* also gave CBS, then battling NBC for industry dominance, a potent weapon—a low-cost, high-yield series to challenge NBC's costly and widely acclaimed comedy-variety hits, particularly Milton Berle's *Texaco Star Theater* and Sid Caesar and Imogene Coca's *Your Show of Shows*. In early 1952, *I Love Lucy* overtook *Texaco Star Theater* as TV's top-rated show, becoming the barometer of the new medium's growing popularity. In late April 1952, the American Research Bureau (ARB) announced that *I Love Lucy* was the first television program to reach 10 million homes, and by the end of its first season, the series was regularly drawing viewers in two-thirds of America's television homes. A review of the 1951–52 TV season published in *Variety* reported that the combined Nielsen-Trendex-ARB figures "offer a revealing story of changing patterns in television and audience viewing habits."[12] The most significant trends, according to *Variety's* George Rosen, were "the end of the 'Milton Berle Era' of TV leadership" and "the virtual disappearance of dramatic programming fare from top ten recognition." These live New York-based programs were being displaced by other genres, reported Rosen, who noted in particular "the ascendency of the situation comedy, which finds CBS moving into a new sphere of importance as 'I Love Lucy' sets the leadership pace on all three ratings services."

During that first season, Arnaz proved not only that he could deliver a hit series, but one produced economically, efficiently, and with solid production values. The 39 episodes in *I Love Lucy's* first season, all told, came in only $9,500 over budget—at $24,750 per segment rather than the budgeted $24,000.[13] This included Desilu's purchase of four "crab dollies" to facilitate camera movement and two interlocked editing machines, all of which it would use for future production. The production efficiency extended into scheduling as well, as Arnaz and company soon cut their actual studio requirement to only two days per week: for camera rehearsals on Thursday and Friday, and then shooting (before the live audience) Friday evenings.

As this "system" was refined, Arnaz realized that he could expand Desilu's output within the existing General Services Studio setup. He had been approached by Eve Arden, whose radio sitcom *Our Miss Brooks* was being considered for CBS-TV, and he decided that Desilu could take on another series. Arnaz's decision to produce the series rankled CBS, which still had serious reservations about telefilm production.

Arnaz later recalled:

The reason they were against film, was that the more shows done on film instead of live, the more power and control they would lose. If a show was live, independent local stations wanting that show had to become an affiliate of the network that was televising it. . . .

But with film, the local independent stations could make direct deals with the producers. That's how syndication started.[14]

Still, the network brass let Arnaz proceed with *Our Miss Brooks* as a telefilm series—a clear indication of Desilu's leverage over CBS due to *I Love Lucy*'s success.

In mid-1952 when *Our Miss Brooks* went into production, TV was just coming out of the freeze and neither the networks, ad agencies, local stations, nor independent production companies had any clear idea what lay ahead for commercial television. Indeed, no one was quite sure to what extent the public at large would buy into the new medium once the freeze was lifted. Many feared that early TV's major-market skew was giving the industry an altogether unrealistic picture of the medium's overall appeal. (According to *Broadcasting* magazine, the 108 TV stations that had been licensed by the time *I Love Lucy* premiered in October 1951 were situated in only 63 markets nationwide, serving a total of 13,598,000 TV sets. Over 6 million of those sets were in only five cities: New York [2.5 million sets], Los Angeles [1 million], Chicago [950,000], Philadelphia [883,000], and Boston [766,000].)[15]

When the FCC lifted its licensing restrictions late in 1952, any doubts about TV's post-freeze development quickly vanished. Within three years the number of television stations quadrupled to well over 400, and the proportion of television-equipped households nationwide climbed from a mid-freeze figure of 12 percent to 67 percent by June 1955 and 83 percent by January 1958.[16] With this explosion in audience size, the financial stakes for the networks, sponsors, ad agencies, and production companies rose accordingly. "Radio had always been profitable," wrote David Halberstam in *The Powers That Be*, "but television profits were staggering." Halberstam was particularly impressed by the phenomenal growth of CBS.

In 1953, television reached 21 million American homes and CBS income after taxes reached $8.9 million; by 1954, the year that CBS, by virtue of television, became *the largest advertising medium in the world*, the net income was $11.4 million; by 1957, 42 million homes had television and the profits after taxes reached $22.2 million. It was a constantly ascending curve."[17]

This growing profit potential steadily pushed up production costs as network competition for affiliates and viewers grew more intense. Not surprisingly, sponsors found it difficult to cover the production costs for an entire series, and so the single-sponsored network series gradually disappeared during the post-freeze '50s. At the same time, there emerged a new brand of network executive: the programming chief. "Television programmers have no direct antecedents in radio," points out Laurence Bergreen, "where ad agencies assumed the burdens of production. This responsibility remained with ad agencies until the anticipated cost, complexity, and risk of television forced them to yield programming power to the networks, which for the most part served as common carriers."[18] The networks coveted this power, of course, since controlling individual programming decisions meant they could design the overall *schedule* to attract the maximum number of viewers and thus maximize network profits.

The most important of this new breed of network programmer was Sylvester L. "Pat" Weaver, a former adman whom NBC chairman David Sarnoff promoted to network presidency in 1953 to chart the network's post-freeze destiny. Weaver was quoted in an October 1954 *New Yorker* profile as saying that when he began his tenure as NBC president, "the programming just had no direction. Programs landed next to each other by mere chance, with each agency building its show in a way that was aimed at nothing more than keeping the client happy."[19] Weaver was intent on developing a more coherent, integrated schedule. He began by reorganizing the prime-time offerings, slotting comedies early when children were viewing and scheduling drama later in the evening for older viewers. He emphasized New York-originated programs, from comedy-variety series like *Your Show of Shows* to "spectaculars" (what are now termed "specials") like *Peter Pan*. Outside of prime time he developed an early morning news magazine, *Today*, and a late-night variety program, *The Tonight Show*. As Weaver recalled years later, "in 1955 I controlled almost all major programming decisions at NBC, for both daytime and prime time. From 'Today' . . . to 'The Tonight Show,' we had taken control from the ad agency."[20]

Looking back, what distinguishes Weaver's network-originated schedule and what undoubtedly accounts for much of NBC's early reputation as TV's "prestige" network, was the network's reliance on New York-based live programming. Weaver did schedule a few half-hour telefilm series—urban crime dramas like *Dragnet* and sitcoms like *The Life of Riley*—but still NBC relied much less on telefilm formulas than on live programs out of New York. Both ABC and CBS, meanwhile, were intensifying their telefilm schedules, and both were relying on Desilu as a program supplier. In 1953, *Our Miss Brooks* climbed to number 14 in the Nielsen ratings and Desilu, on the strength of production deals with Loretta Young, Ray Bolger, Danny Thomas, and Jack Benny, vacated the General Services Studio and leased six sound stages in L.A.'s Motion Picture Center. All were converted into Desilu's distinctive theater-audience studios.

The year 1953 also saw Desilu initiate production on a series with its own capital. CBS wanted to move its radio series, *December Bride*, to TV, but without radio star Spring Byington in the lead. CBS co-owned the series with its writer-producer, Parke Levy, who wanted Byington for the TV series lead. When negotiations reached an impasse, CBS let its option lapse and Desilu bought the network's share of the program. Arnaz produced the series for General Foods, which sold it to CBS. Board chairman William Paley was furious after seeing the pilot for *December Bride*, when he learned that CBS had let the series go. Paley personally entered negotiations with Arnaz, who demonstrated his own scheduling savvy. Arnaz gave CBS one-quarter ownership of the series in exchange for the 9:30 time slot on Monday evenings—immediately after *I Love*

*Lucy.*[21] That blockbuster lead-in ensured the success of Desilu's new series, which debuted in April 1954 and finished the season at number eleven in the ratings. Over the next two seasons, *I Love Lucy* and *December Bride* were TV's two most successful sitcoms. Desilu, meanwhile, steadily increased its overall output. In 1953 alone the company produced 229 half-hour series episodes, the equivalent of nearly 100 feature films. That output increased in 1954, the year that Desilu purchased controlling interest in the Motion Picture Center.

Clearly Desilu was fast becoming a major industry power—and something of a threat to CBS's programming control. But the network had been careful to hedge its bets against the potential power of Desilu and other independent producers. One hedge was to expand its own production operations, which CBS did quite dramatically with the construction of "Television City" in Los Angeles in 1952. CBS also began buying into independent production companies if, like Desilu, they wished to become steady suppliers of network programming. Before signing a new two-year contract for *I Love Lucy* after the first season, the network bought one-quarter ownership of Desilu for $1 million. What's more, the network itself went into syndication. Early in 1952, CBS-TV Sales was created as a distribution company and a separate entity from the network. Its creation was reported in *Variety* on February 13, when CBS announced that it "will distribute films produced either by the web [the network] itself or by indie producers."[22] Thus CBS's syndication company, like the one created by NBC in 1951, would sell both "off-network" shows ("reruns") and "first-run" shows, those never offered on network schedules but sold directly to local stations.

The importance of syndication was becoming more evident with each passing TV season, not only as a scheduling strategy but also as a means of attracting new affiliates and of appeasing those already on line. CBS initiated certain "incentive plans" in the summer of 1952 involving discounted telefilm offerings and "rebate" periods extending from early July through late August. *Broadcasting* reported in March 1953 that NBC-TV, "which offered no special inducement concessions last year, currently is considering the question."[23] The network was definitely set, though, to follow "the precedent set last year by *Dragnet* and *The Groucho Marx Show*, wherein advertisers repeated as summer fare, the best programs of the winter season." NBC's summer reruns in 1953 would include *I Married Joan* and another sitcom, *My Hero* (with Bob Cummings), while CBS planned to rebroadcast *Our Miss Brooks* and *Four Star Playhouse*, an anthology drama produced by Dick Powell. "Since all these shows are on film," *Broadcasting* reported, "the production costs involved will be negligible."

A hit series like *I Love Lucy* was crucial to such a strategy, but Arnaz decided to withhold Desilu's wholly owned series from summer reruns. Instead Desilu supplied *My Little Margie*, another Philip Morris-Desilu production, which could be test marketed by CBS during the summer months. By late summer, with the post-freeze boom well under way, the networks all reported profitable summer rerun schedules and announced plans to further reduce production contracts, virtually eliminating 52-week deals and reducing many 39-week contracts to 30 weeks as the term "summer" took on ever broader connotations. The surplus value of telefilm series extended far beyond the summer months, of course. When a series' life span reached approximately 100 episodes, it could be "stripped" for off-network syndication. Eventually the FCC would restrict network ownership of both TV series and syndication companies, but during the mid-to-late 1950s all three networks were hell-bent on purchasing their most successful series to reap the benefits of syndication.

Not surprisingly, CBS paid dearly for the syndication rights to Desilu's flagship series. Early in 1955 the network signed a new two-year contract with Desilu for another 52 episodes of *I Love Lucy*; the network paid Ball and Arnaz an additional $4.5 million for outright ownership of all 179 of the series episodes, including those of the next two seasons. CBS also bought Desilu's share of *December Bride* for another half-million dollars. That gave the network part ownership of Desilu's two most successful series, though *I Love Lucy* and *December Bride* represented only a fraction of the company's output. In all, that output for the next two seasons would total 691 half-hour series segments, making Desilu the most productive independent in the industry and the principal supplier of CBS's prime-time programming.

## EXPANSION, DIVERSIFICATION, AND THE LOSS OF "INDEPENDENCE"

The new CBS-Desilu pact typified all three networks' growing inclination to "cooperate" with "outside sources" in developing series for their schedules. By now the networks recognized the need to control programming in order to maximize their audience base and thus their revenues. But the networks also were learning that to control programming, they did not necessarily have to produce or even to own their programs. There were clearly some very good reasons for the networks to minimize their own production efforts. One was the financial risks involved in TV series production, particularly during prime time when the costs and thus the stakes were highest. Another was the federal government's antitrust posture. The Justice Department and the courts had recently dismantled the movie industry's integrated production-distribution-exhibition system, and so the networks were well aware of the need to restrain their quest for control of TV's production and dissemination.

Thus the reliance on independent companies like Desilu, which, in fact, CBS President Frank Stanton outlined in some detail for the U.S. Senate in June 1956, responding to an antitrust investigation of the TV industry.[24] Stanton reported that CBS owned 29 studios (22 in New York, 2 in Chicago, and 5 in Los Angeles), of which only 5 were equipped for telefilm production. For the week ending April 7, 1956, CBS delivered to its affiliates a total of 72 3/4 "sponsored broadcast hours," of which 55 3/4 hours were live video and 17 hours were on telefilm. To blunt any accusations of monopoly control, CBS pointed out that only 23 percent of those hours were produced by the network (down from 39 percent in 1954). One half of CBS's April 1956 broadcast hours were "produced entirely by 38 outside producers with whom CBS Television has no direct connection."[25] The remaining 27 percent were produced by eight outside outfits "in association with" the network. This latter group included Desilu, the only outside company in which CBS had an actual "financial interest."

What the report did not point out, however, was that all the telefilm hours were for prime-time series and were produced by outside sources, while CBS itself produced live programs such as news shows, game shows, and soap operas. CBS was not alone in this practice. By the 1956–57 season all three networks were farming out virtually all prime-time episodic series programming—whether sitcom or western, police drama or adventure series—to independent telefilm producers. This practice was on the increase due to yet another key factor in telefilm production: the entry of the major Hollywood studios. As was already noted, the lesser film production companies had been producing telefilm series since TV's earliest years. It wasn't until ABC signed Walt Disney Productions for *Disneyland* in 1954 and Warner Bros. for *Warner Brothers Presents* in 1955, however, that the wholesale shift by Hollywood's established powers to TV series production began. Within another year MGM, 20th Century-Fox, and Paramount also joined the fray and began producing telefilm series.[26]

Not surprisingly, this incursion by the Hollywood majors had considerable impact both on network programming and on L.A.-based telefilm series production. The major studios specialized in hour-long series with superior production values, often shot on location and done in the time-consuming "one-camera style" used for motion picture production. Thus production costs steadily climbed, to a point where "deficit financing" became standard operating procedure in telefilm series production. In other words, production companies were willing to take a loss on the initial run of a series, expecting to turn a profit once the series went into syndication. The studios were able to cover those initial losses in one of two ways: via revenues from current movie hits, or via the sale of their old movies to TV syndicators. The smaller or weaker telefilm production outfits simply could not compete at this level, of course, and many were either swallowed up or forced out of business. The stronger independent companies, meanwhile, had little choice but to up the ante and compete at the major studios' level.

No independent was stronger than Desilu, which continued to thrive during this transformation although Arnaz was well aware that the stakes were changing rapidly. During the mid-to-late 1950s, according to Arnaz, "the economics of the television business began to get ridiculously bad. I put the blame for that squarely on all the motion-picture studios. When they finally decided to enter television, they would sell a series for much less than they knew it would cost them, just in order to sell it."[27] Still, Desilu not only held its own but continued to expand. For the duration of the two-year pact signed with CBS in 1955, Arnaz and company solidified their position as top independent producer, with Desilu's profits climbing from $675,000, in April 1956 to $3,183,000 a year later.

That surge enabled Desilu to compete more directly with the majors. In September 1957 Arnaz paid $6.15 million for RKO, the Hollywood studio where both he and Ball had been employed as contract players two decades earlier.[28] RKO, once a major studio power, had suffered a severe postwar slump under the mismanagement of Howard Hughes before changing hands several times in the 1950s. By the time Desilu bought RKO, much of its real estate holdings (particularly its theaters) and virtually all of its library of feature films and shorts had been siphoned off. But Desilu's primary interest was in RKO's production facilities, both its sound stages and the "back lot," which were needed as Desilu expanded from sitcom production into action-adventure series—westerns like *Jim Bowie* and *The Sheriff of Cochise*, and even an ambitious urban-crime series, *The Untouchables*, which Desilu had on the production docket for ABC in 1958.

With the purchase of RKO and expanded production operation, Ball and Arnaz were hailed as the "new moguls" in Hollywood's television era. A telling irony at this point was the steady dissolution of the Ball-Arnaz marriage and the decision at Desilu to discontinue *I Love Lucy* as a weekly series after the 1956–57 season, despite its number-one Nielsen rating. Both Arnaz and Ball were looking in different professional directions—Arnaz for other telefilm ventures and Ball for feature film and stage roles. CBS kept *I Love Lucy* on its prime-time schedule by rerunning old episodes, but the series' popularity quickly fell off. It was bolstered somewhat by a succession of Arnaz-produced hour-long specials, *The Lucille Ball-Desi Arnaz Show*, usually featuring the Ricardos and the Mertzes in some exotic locale.

Yet another irony in the late 1950s was Arnaz's growing disdain for the sitcom. Having reached the higher echelons of independent television production, Arnaz now wanted very badly to experiment with different programming forms and felt that he'd earned the right to do so. Bucking the odds and the system he'd helped to shape, Arnaz sent two anthology drama series into production in the late 1950s: *Fountain of Youth* in 1957 and *Desilu Playhouse* in 1958. But this time Arnaz found the network much less receptive. In fact, with *Fountain of Youth*, whose pilot boasted the considerable creative energies of Orson Welles, the networks refused even to pitch the series to either public or sponsor. This marked a curious reversal of the network's role back in 1951, when CBS had successfully pitched *I Love Lucy* to Philip Morris and had given Arnaz and Ball free rein in developing the series. Now CBS was calling the shots and was less inclined to take such efforts or such risks. Hubbell Robinson, CBS programming chief, told Arnaz he doubted the public would "understand" the program, and Robinson later confided to a TV critic, "I think that Orson Welles would set television back twenty years."[29] Eventually all three networks rejected *Fountain of Youth* in 1957, deeming it too innovative and sophisticated for the general audience. Only a last-minute cancellation at NBC put Welles's pilot on *Colgate*

*Theater* in 1958, where it won widespread critical praise and a prestigious Peabody Award; but still it wasn't picked up as a series.

In a certain sense, Desilu had become its own worst enemy, refining both the programming formulas and efficient production techniques, the narrative and material "economies" which had become so ingrained in TV series production that they restricted certain deviations from the norm. These constraints were becoming even more pronounced in the late 1950s with TV's gradual shift toward multiple sponsors on series, which meant shows had to be designed not only to attract the maximum number of viewers but a range of sponsors as well. And as Arnaz knew when he produced *Fountain of Youth* and *Desilu Playhouse,* anthology dramas hardly drew the numbers of viewers or provided the kind of context that sponsors wanted for their commercial messages. As TV historian Erik Barnouw points out, the decline of the anthology drama, the rise of the telefilm series, and the increasing commercialization of television were closely interrelated. In Barnouw's words:

The anthology form survived on film but was eclipsed by filmed episodic series of upbeat decor, preferred by most sponsors. Identification with a continuing, attractive actor had merchandising possibilities, and some actors were willing to do commercials. Above all, the series *formula* offered security: each program was a variation on an approved ritual. Solutions, as in commercials, could be clear cut.[30]

This was scarcely new to Arnaz and company, but relearning that lesson after pioneering telefilm series production came hard—and it cost the company dearly. When Desilu went public in 1958, it reported assets of $14.9 million, but its profits for the year had fallen to $75,000. Things went a bit better the following year, with Arnaz overseeing the production of *Desilu Playhouse* along with 25 other series at the refurbished RKO studio. Arnaz reported to the stockholders in a July 1959 meeting that Desilu's various series and specials during the 1958–59 season had generated $20.4 million in gross revenues; the net profits for that period were $250,000.[31]

By then *I Love Lucy* had been out of production for two seasons, but Desilu's flagship series was still its biggest draw. CBS was eager to get Lucy back into a weekly series but Ball still wanted to pursue stage and feature film work. The old cast of Ball, Arnaz, Frawley, and Vance did reconvene for a summer replacement series, *Lucy in Connecticut,* which aired from July through September 1960, but by then the growing strain on the Ball-Arnaz marriage had already taken its toll. The couple hadn't been living together since late 1959, and Ball had filed for divorce. The divorce was granted on May 4, 1960, and when the *Lucy* foursome filmed the summer replacement series, Arnaz already had agreed to step down as president of Desilu. He stayed on long enough to launch Ball's new series, *The Lucy Show,* which debuted in the fall of 1962 and immediately established itself as a prime mover in CBS's remarkable sitcom surge during the

1960s. With her new show in production, Ball bought out Arnaz for $2.5 million and took over as president of Desilu.

## EPILOGUE: THE MACHINERY OF THE INDUSTRY

Despite the success of *The Lucy Show* throughout the 1960s, Desilu steadily declined as an industry power. Losing Arnaz was a factor in that decline, of course, particularly in terms of Desilu's interaction with the networks. CBS insider Robert Metz recalls in his network history, *CBS: Reflections in a Bloodshot Eye*, that Arnaz "had always done the negotiating" with the network, and had been "both resourceful and tough" in staking out his company's position. Without Arnaz "to keep CBS at bay," there was a severe downturn in Desilu's innovation and output.[32] Metz's point is well taken, but actually the networks did little "negotiating" with *any* of their outside program suppliers during the early 1960s, a period that saw the networks consolidate their control of the commercial TV industry.

The catalyst for network control was the "quiz scandals" of the late 1950s. In fact, the NBC telecast of Desilu's *Fountain of Youth* pilot in 1958, which had been turned down by all three networks a year before, resulted from NBC's last-minute cancellation of *Dotto*, a high-stakes quiz show implicated in the industrywide "fixing" of such series by their sponsors. The quiz scandals broke wide open in 1959 with a congressional investigation, giving the networks a rationale for taking over virtually all programming and production decisions. CBS's Frank Stanton, for example, responded to the scandals by asserting, "the American people hold the networks responsible for what appears on their schedules. From now on *we* will decide not only *what* appears but *how*."[33]

The networks were particularly aggressive in taking control of prime time. They still relied on outside producers for up to 80 percent of prime-time programming in the 1960s, but such bona fide independent TV production as documentary news specials and first-run syndicated series virtually disappeared from prime time after the scandals. In 1960, all three networks adopted a policy of in-house news and documentary production; they also pressured affiliates to accept their full prime-time schedules, which forced the first-run syndicated series out of mainstream production. Back in 1956 some 30 syndicated series ran during prime time; in 1963 there were only three and by 1965 there were none. What's more, the sponsor-initiated pilot and the single-sponsor series, once so essential to prime time, were phased out in the early 1960s as the multiple-sponsored series became the standard. This diminished the sponsor's authority and all but eliminated the ad agency from the production and programming process.

By the mid-1960s, the networks had a lock on TV programming and Hollywood's "creative community," from the studio powers to the struggling independents, were relegated to mere subcontractor status. TV's penetration was well over 90 percent of American households, and network executives coined terms like "least objectionable programming" and "lowest common denominator'' in their tireless efforts to maximize audience shares and revenues. Not surprisingly, programming strategies grew increasingly conservative and predictable as the experimentation and innovation of the 1950s gave way to standard operating procedure. The network system became so monolithic and inflexible during the 1960s, in fact, that by decade's end Les Brown, a leading TV critic and historian, argued that no individual, not even a network's chief executive, had any real power to affect the system. ''The president of a network,'' wrote Brown in *Televi$ion: The Business Behind the Box,* ''can buy a show and set operating policies, but he is powerless to alter the machinery of the industry.''[34]

Quite a change from the 1950s, when the ''machinery'' of radio broadcasting was retooled and redesigned for the Television Age. The result was nothing less than a cultural transformation, a unique convergence of social, economic, and technological forces that forever changed the American experience. Those changes were scarcely arbitrary, nor were they predetermined and inevitable. Once the established radio model proved inadequate, there were any number of directions the TV industry might have taken. The network-controlled system of the 1960s resulted not only from the interplay of ''larger'' cultural forces, but also from the ideas and efforts of individuals like Sarnoff and Paley, Stanton and Weaver, Ball and Arnaz—men and women who suffered choices, took risks, and made a difference. Their individual contributions can only be gauged in terms of a larger design, of course, as factors in a complex cultural and industrial equation. And in factoring that equation, few independent producers or production companies figure as heavily as Lucille Ball, Desi Arnaz, and Desilu. They provided the nascent industry with its biggest star and most successful series, with a blueprint for its most pervasive genre and production format, and with a model for the independent television production company that persists, like those perpetual reruns of *I Love Lucy,* to the present day.

## NOTES

1. Quoted in Laurence Bergreen, *Look Now, Pay Later* (New York: Doubleday and Co., 1980), p. 6.

2. For general historical treatments of the network television industry, see Erik Barnouw, *Tube of Plenty: The Evolution of American Television* (New York: Oxford University Press, 1975).

3. For an overview of the creation of *I Love Lucy* and the general development of Desilu, see Barnouw, *Tube of Plenty*; Rick Mitz, *The Great TV Sitcom Book* (New York: Richard Marek Publishers, 1980); Bart Andrews and Thomas J. Watson, *Loving Lucy* (New York: St. Martin's Press, 1980); Tim Brooks and Earle Marsh, *The Complete Directory to Prime-Time Network TV Shows,* revised ed. (New York: Ballantine Books, 1981). The Nielsen figures here and elsewhere are also culled from Brooks and Marsh, pp. 922–31.

4. Christopher H. Sterling and Timothy R. Haight, *The Mass Media: Aspen Institute Guide to Communication Industry Trends* (New York: Praeger, 1978), p. 47.

5. Desi Arnaz, *A Book* (New York: William Morrow and Company, 1976), p. 202.

6. Ibid., p. 203.

7. Dave Glickman, "Film in the Future—As Television's Horizons Expand," *Broadcasting* (September 10, 1951), p. 79.

8. "Freeman, Roach See Upped Quality, No 'B' Pix in Industry Future; TV Forecast as New Cradle of Talent," *Variety* (December 12, 1951), p. 5.

9. Dave Kaufman, "Vidpix Weed Out Shoestringers," *Variety* (January 9, 1952), p. 1.

10. "TV Films in Production," *Variety* (January 23, 1952), p. 28.

11. Quoted in Max Wilk, *The Golden Age of Television* (New York: Delacorte Press, 1976), p. 252.

12. George Rosen, "TV's Changing 'Best Bet' Lineup," *Variety* (June 4, 1952), p. 25.

13. Mitz, *Great TV Sitcom Book*, p. 43; Arnaz, *A Book*, pp. 228–31.

14. Arnaz, *A Book*, p. 272.

15. *Broadcasting* (October 8, 1951), p. 82.

16. Sterling and Haight, *The Mass Media*, p. 68.

17. David Halberstam, *The Powers That Be* (New York: Dell Publishing Co., 1979), p. 579.

18. Bergreen, *Look Now*, p. 178.

19. Quoted in ibid., p. 189.

20. Pat Weaver in a book review of Bedell's *Up the Tube*, which appeared in *American Film* (December 1981), p. 81.

21. Arnaz, *A Book*, p. 279.

22. "CBS Sets up Vidpix Syndication Unit; Webs Move into 'Local Time' Picture" *Variety* (February 13, 1952), p. 2..

23. "Repeats, Discounts in Summer Plans," *Broadcasting* (March 2, 1953), p. 28.

24. *Network Practices*: Memorandum Supplementing Statement of Frank Stanton, President, Columbia Broadcasting System, Inc., Prepared for the Senate Committee on Interstate and Foreign Commerce by the Columbia Broadcasting System, Inc., June 1956.

25. Ibid., pp. 32, 58–59.

26. For detailed treatment of the Hollywood studios' shift to telefilm production, see the special issue of *Quarterly Review of Film Studies* (Summer 1984) devoted to the subject, especially Robert Vianello, "The Rise of the Telefilm and the Networks' Hegemony Over the Motion Picture Industry" and Douglas Gomery, "Failed Opportunities: The Integration of the U.S. Motion Picture and Television Industries." See also Christopher Anderson, "Hollywood TV: The Role of Television in the Transformation of the Studio System" (Ph.D. diss., University of Texas at Austin, 1988).

27. Arnaz, *A Book*, pp. 308–9.

28. Figures on 1957–58 season taken from: "The New Tycoon," *Time* (April 7, 1958), p. 69; Cecelia Ager, "Desilu, or from Gags to Riches," *The New York Times Magazine* (April 20, 1958), p. 32; and "There's No Business Like Show Business: Desilu Productions Inc.," *Business Week* (November 22, 1958), p. 98.

29. Robinson quoted in Richard Austin Smith, "TV: The Light That Failed," *Fortune* (December 1958), p. 166.

30. Barnouw, *Tube of Plenty*, p. 166.

31. Arnaz, *A Book*, p. 311.

32. Robert Metz, *CBS: Reflections in a Bloodshot Eye* (Chicago: Playboy Press, 1975), p. 193.

33. Quoted in A. Frank Reel, *The Networks: How They Stole the Show* (New York: Scribner's, 1979), pp. 69–70.

34. Les Brown, *Televi$ion: The Business Behind the Box* (New York: Harcourt Brace and Jovanovich, 1971), p. 4.

# 10

# The Screen Gems Division of Columbia Pictures: Twenty-Five Years of Prime-Time Storytelling

*David Marc*

Novels are written by authors; films are shot by directors; and of course only God can make a tree. But who creates a TV program? In television's early days, the only people who seemed to be asking that question were members of the House Un-American Activities Committee and their close friends. Perhaps the question never occurred to most viewers because television seemed more like a medium for conveying other arts than an art itself. Comedy-variety stars like Milton Berle and Red Skelton offered home-delivered "vaudeville." You could "attend a play" in your own living room on *Ford Theater* or *Playhouse 90*. By 1961 you could even "go to the movies" in your underwear with *NBC's Saturday Night at the Movies*. But what about the bread and butter of televiewing—the weekly continuing narrative series? Was *Route 66* a movie? Was *Father Knows Best* a play? Was *Burns and Allen* vaudeville?

There were only a few exceptions to the general anonymity of TV series authorship before the 1970s. Jack Webb had taken advantage of his visibility as a star to leave his personal production mark on *Dragnet*. Each episode of *The Honeymooners* ended with the full-screen credit, "Entire Production Supervised by Jackie Gleason," as if anyone could still harbor doubts after seeing it. A viewer could always tell a Quinn Martin show, such as *The Fugitive* or *The FBI*, because QM series were the only ones that had "Acts" and "Epilogues." But otherwise, there were only the credits to consult, and even if they were spinning

This chapter first appeared in The Museum of Broadcasting's exhibition catalogue *Columbia Pictures Television: The Studio on the Creative Process*. © 1987 The Museum of Broadcasting. All Rights Reserved.

by slowly enough to actually read, what in the world was the difference between an associate producer and an executive producer, anyway?

It was not until the sitcom renaissance of the early 1970s that it became widely acknowledged that television series don't just materialize from thin air. Producers such as Norman Lear, Larry Gelbart, and Garry Marshall became recognized personalities with distinctive styles, values, and politics. The smudged fingers of human beings were emerging from behind the technological monolith. Studios began to establish identities as distinctive aesthetic entities. In the cases of Lear and Marshall, the auteur was the studio. But other houses, whose portfolios consisted of work by a variety of authorial figures, developed popular corporate themes and styles as well: the MTM single woman (*Mary/Rhoda/Phyllis*); the age-, sex-, and race-conscious cop shows of Spelling-Goldberg Productions (*Mod Squad, The Rookies, S.W.A.T.*); the Lorimar prime-time Sunbelt soap sagas (*Dallas, Knots Landing, Falcon Crest*), and so on.

Screen Gems, the old short films division of Harry Cohn's Columbia Pictures, had already been making and distributing television programs for some twenty years before Archie Bunker began turning Norman Lear into a household name. Columbia's corporate logo—the Muse of the New World lifting her beacon—was familiar to television viewers long before the Warner Bros. family shield or the Universal portrait of planet Earth became part of everyday homescreen iconology. But while the studio's success in television was coveted by its competitors, Screen Gems never developed the kind of public identity that would prepare a future generation of TV viewers for a promo such as "From the folks who gave you *Hill Street Blues*...."

Early on, Screen Gems made use of the Columbia soundstages and backlots to fill the often static air of pioneer TV with a slew of syndicated adventure series. *Jungle Jim* (1955) brought back the Tarzan of the Great Depression, Johnny Weissmuller, this time as a great white hunter decked out in a safari suit to cover the coming of age. Alan Hale, Jr. starred as *Casey Jones* (1958), the legendary engineer at the throttle of the Midwest & Central Railroad's Cannonball Express; two decades later he would take the helm of the ill-fated *SS Minnow* as the skipper on *Gilligan's Island*. The most popular of the Screen Gems early adventures was probably *Wild Bill Hickok* (1951–58), one of TV's first hit westerns. Producers William F. Brady and Wesley Barry had taken the form of the old Hollywood Saturday afternoon movie serial, honed the sharp edges of the breathless serial finish into smooth little episodic climaxes, and found a market for 113 twenty-four minute telefilms. Though the plots of the show fade into the telefluvia, the image of the show's signature montage endures: Sheriff Hickok (Guy Madison), a handsome, sleek guy on a handsome, sleek horse, rides by in overdrive as his erstwhile endomorphic companion Jingles (Andy Devine) gallops after him yelling, "Hey, Wild Bill, wait for me!" The half-hour western was in color for the privileged few.

Two early Screen Gems network series, *The Adventures of Rin Tin Tin* (ABC,

1954–59) and *Circus Boy* (NBC, 1956–57; ABC, 1957–58), were of a piece, each the story of an orphaned boy who is adopted and given nurture by an all-male vocational extended family. On *Rin Tin Tin*, Rusty (Lee Aaker), is the ward of a post-Civil War Army platoon stationed somewhere in the southwest. Parental authority is shared by two archetypal American masculinity figures: Lt. Rip Masters (James Brown) who, as an officer, gentleman, and matinee idol, provides Rusty with a genteel model for development; and Sgt. Biff O'Hara (Joe Sawyer), a crusty, emotional, all-too-human noncom from whom the boy gains character and the common touch. Rusty's greatest teacher, however, is Rin Tin Tin, a German shepherd who outstrips even human adults in his ability to distinguish right from wrong.

In *Circus Boy*, Rusty became Corky (Mickey Braddock, a.k.a. Dolenz). The owner of the circus, Big Tim Champion (Robert Lowery), was his upscale father-figure, while Joey the clown (Noah Beery, Jr.) provided him with proletarian understanding and pathos. Even Rinny was conceptually cloned. Just as Rusty took care of his dog, who in turn took care of him, Corky was waterboy to Bimbo the elephant. If Rinny could race back to the fort to get help when Rusty was stuck out alone with a broken leg and no water in the desert, Bimbo could pull fallen trees off Corky's legs or even scare off anti-circus rednecks. Both series eschewed the televisual norms of the pastoral suburban 1950s family, offering children visions of adventurous lives in exotic settings, freed from the constraints of mom and dad (especially mom; neither of these shows had a single female regular).

Herbert B. "Bert" Leonard had produced both *Rin Tin Tin* (with Norman Blackburn) and *Circus Boy* (with Fred Briskin). But among Leonard's portfolio of male-bonding epics, the most famous remains *Route 66* (CBS, 1960–64). Premiering just three years after the long-suppressed publication of Jack Kerouac's *On The Road*, *Route 66* was arguably prime-time's first acknowledgment that somewhere out there beyond the housing tract horizon there just might be a bit of what Allen Ginsberg had recently called "the lost America of love." Tod Stiles (Marty Milner) and Buz Murdock (George Maharis), sitting pretty in their fully loaded Corvette, were a couple of pretty tepid hipsters to be sure. But at least they were post-pubescent, single, and ready to rock and roll. Eros was a subtler thing on television before the end of pre-cable/VCR innocence.

Tod (blond) was a rich kid who had lost his money; Buz (dark) was a slum kid who never had any. Together, they cruised the great Whitmanian transcontinental highway. Where were they going? Wherever the action was! Destinationless! Dean Moriarty, however, had nothing to worry about. Like most TV heroes, Tod and Buz seemed to get more kicks out of doing *the right thing* than out of satisfying the craven needs of their organic selves. The tanktowns were littered with a million American dreams: beautiful but confused women; promising but confused young people; proud but confused ordinary folks. During the final season of *Route 66*, with George Maharis suffering from hepatitis, Linc

Case (Glenn Corbett), television's first Vietnam veteran (1963!), took Buz's seat in the 'vette. *Route 66* never hit Nielsen's top 25 during its four-year production run, though it is currently enjoying a national syndication vogue.

*Naked City* (ABC, 1960–63) was yet another Bert Leonard production and it too was a self-consciously "different" kind of action series with "adult" overtones. If *Route 66* had been upbeat, adventurous, and western, *Naked City* was gritty, nervous, and Northeast Corridor. If *Route 66* had telemutated Kerouac and the Beats into prime-time material, *Naked City* performed a similarly haunting experiment on Elia Kazan and liberal-anticommunist social realism. ("There are eight million stories in the Naked City . . . ").

Detective Adam Flint (Paul Burke) is the center of viewer identification. A nattily dressed amalgam of collegiate idealism and street savvy, Adam is the WASP persona for each episode's stark walk through New York's ethnic Disneyland. His boss, Lt. Mike Parker (Horace McMahon), makes noises like an old-fashioned law-and-order cop, but when the chips are down he throws away the book and lets Adam follow his socially concerned impulses. Those impulses are often stimulated in Adam by his quasi-bohemian girlfriend, Libby (an appropriate name for the first female regular to appear in a Leonard series). Like *Route 66, Naked City*'s viewership was loyal, but never large enough to boost it into a top ratings position.

The studio, however, was not without its share of bona fide Nielsen successes. The first Screen Gems production to hit the top ten had been *Ford Theatre* (various; 1949–57), which finished number seven in 1953–54. A dramatic anthology, the show's schedule of hour-long plays that same season included "First Born," starring Ronald Reagan and his wife Nancy (Davis) Reagan in their initial joint professional billing. Though *Ford Theatre* was pretty much forgotten after the death of anthology drama in the late 1950s, Screen Gems's other big ratings ace of the decade was a sitcom that not only scored big in the numbers, but would go on to become eternally identified with the very weltanschauung of television in the 1950s: *Father Knows Best* (various; 1954–60).

Along with a handful of similarly styled sitcoms—*Donna Reed, Ozzie and Harriet, The Trouble with Father* et al.—*Father Knows Best* strikes at the etiological heart of domestic situation comedy. It offered Depression-born, warweary Americans a vision of peaceful, prosperous suburban life centering on stable, nuclear family structure. The economic, political, and social travail of the past two decades were left behind by Jim Anderson and his family for a brave new teleworld in which modern technology was found to be utterly compatible with traditional values:

Once upon a time, in America, there was a family—a husband and wife raising children. This family was white and had a name that bespoke Anglo-Saxon ancestry and Protestant religious affiliation. Surprisingly enough, the darndest things happened to them. Each week a child—a little citizen-in-training—would encounter some ethical crisis or moral dilemma smack in the middle of this otherwise relentlessly normal state of affairs: Mischievous Bud overspends his allowance on a new set of hubcaps; high-strung Betty just can't stand the way the new girl at school is getting all the attention, Tomboy Kathy messes up her good Sunday dress playing baseball. Margaret—a housewife, a mother, and proud of it—cooks, cleans, and rears children without ever even having to change her dress. Jim, insurance agent and paterfamilias extraordinarie, is only too ready for any contingency with an appropriate moral tautology. Jokes? Not too many knee-slappers. Pathos? The sky was the limit. In the spring of 1960, *Father Knows Best* took itself out of production even though the show had finished number six for the season. Robert Young had simply tired of the project. The show's popularity was so great, however, that reruns continued to air on prime-time network television for the next three years.

Eugene Rodney's *Father Knows Best* was probably the biggest single hit ever to come out of Screen Gems. But if the work of any of the studio's producers can be said to characterize the Screen Gems oeuvre as a whole, it is probably the string of popular sitcoms produced by Harry Ackerman during the 1960s. A Dartmouth graduate, Ackerman became vice president of Screen Gems in 1958 and served as executive producer for a spate of hits that included *Dennis the Menace* (CBS, 1959–63); *Hazel* (CBS, 1961–66); *The Farmer's Daughter* (ABC, 1963–66); *Bewitched* (ABC, 1964–72); and *The Flying Nun* (ABC, 1967–70). The Ackerman sitcoms were played much more broadly than shows like *Father Knows Best* or *Donna Reed*, offering generous doses of relief from the relentless didacticism of the gothic family sagas. Jokes, pratfalls, and even some pie-in-the-face mingled freely with ethical instruction.

Dennis the Menace (Jay North), whose wardrobe consisted exclusively of overalls years before SoHo was a twinkle in a real estate developer's eye, drives the grumpy Mr. Wilson (Joseph Kearns; after his death, Gale Gordon) to an early grave with his well-meaning pranks. Hazel (Shirley Booth), also based on a comic strip, bullies the bourgeois Baxters with her instinctual working-class wisdom. Mr. B. is so pig-headed. Mrs. B. is so helpless on her own. Little Harold can hardly survive the ineptitude of such parents. Hazel was more than just a maid. *The Farmer's Daughter*, adapted from the 1947 film starring Loretta Young, also deals with the servant issue. Katie (Inger Stevens), the daughter of Swedish immigrant Minnesota farmers, holds down a job in Georgetown as nanny to the children of a congressman (William Windom), marrying him in the show's final season.

While these first three sitcoms paid some homage to the notion of probability, Ackerman's next two efforts cut all ties to Sir Isaac Newton and his ilk. In *Bewitched*, the power of American women takes on a new dimension—or perhaps reassumes an old one. Samantha Stevens (Elizabeth Montgomery) is a witch, a female figure of American legend that has been an obsession of the national imagination since the first boatloads of European settlers started arriving in Massachusetts Bay (see Nathaniel Hawthorne). Though possessed of magical powers, Samantha agrees to give up her special gifts for the life of a Margaret Anderson-type suburban housewife. She is persuaded to do this by her husband

Darren (Dick York; later Dick Sargent), a Madison Avenue executive, who is determined to keep her locked away safely at home. In *I Love Lucy*, a sitcom to which *Bewitched* owes much, Ricky had simply forbidden Lucy from pursuing her dreams of a show business career. Darren, however, is even crueler. In episode after episode, he expects Samantha to entertain business contacts at home, but forbids her from using her magical powers. Though she can prepare an elaborate banquet with one short spell (usually a single rhyming couplet and a twitch of the nose), Darren demands that Samantha slave over a hot stove all day just to satisfy his incorrigibly puritanical vision of marriage.

A smash hit, *Bewitched* inspired a subgenre that was dominated by Screen Gems productions. Producer Sidney Sheldon's *I Dream of Jeannie* (NBC, 1965–70) abandoned the strict family structure of *Bewitched*, this time depicting the supernaturally powerful but emotionally vulnerable woman as a scantily-clad genie (Barbara Eden) waiting in a bottle at the beck and call of her bachelor/astronaut/master (Larry Hagman). In Ackerman's *The Flying Nun* (ABC, 1967–70), the witchcraft metaphor was traded in for an ambiguous mixture of physics and religion: Did Sister Bertrille (Sally Field) fly through the air by virtue of her slight build and aerodynamic habit, or was the Prime Mover intervening directly to carry her aloft? *The Girl With Something Extra* (NBC, 1973–74) takes Sally Field out of the convent and gives her para-normal psychological powers. She reprises Samantha's wedding night announcement to Darren by letting John Davidson know that she is plagued with the zany gift (or is it a curse?) of E.S.P. In all of these shows, women possess mysterious powers that defy male reason. The prognosis: They must be controlled.

The magicoms that Screen Gems made during the 1960s were very much products of their time. When Agnes Moorehead wasn't turning Dick York into a barnyard animal, Sister Bertrille might be seen at 30,000 feet over San Juan. Traditionalists such as Gladys Kravitz and Major Bellows could only stand by in amazement, their mouths wide open. It was as if someone had slipped the uptight old sitcom a sugarcube of LSD.

Another Screen Gems response to the 1960s was to try to synthesize top forty music with situation comedy in sitcoms such as Bob Rafelson and Bert Schneider's *The Monkees* (NBC, 1966–68) and Paul Junger Witt's *The Partridge Family* (ABC, 1970–74). Taking its inspiration from the Beatles' 1965 film, *A Hard Day's Night, The Monkees* presented the rock group as an eternally adolescent all-male commune and slapstick troupe. Though the series lasted only two years, a mechanism for marketing top forty songs in prime time had been discovered. Bobby Sherman songs were promoted this way in *Here Come the Brides* (ABC, 1968–70), which starred Sherman and pre-Hutch David Soul. The method was again put to lucrative use in *The Partridge Family* in which Shirley Jones and David Cassidy costar as mother/keyboard player and son/lead singer in a futuristic vision of the nuclear-family-as-pop-group.

While Screen Gems had for the most part avoided the political turmoil of the

1960s with these magicoms and musicoms, the studio did eventually make at least one half-hearted effort at post-Norman Lear social consciousness. *Bridget Loves Bernie* (CBS, 1972–73) was the story of a Jewish-Gentile marriage in the lighthearted tradition of *Abie's Irish Rose*. The show did well enough in the ratings, but was cancelled after only one season, primarily because of the protests of Jewish groups over what was seen as a valorization of mixed marriage.

In the mid–1970s, its sitcom salad days coming to a close, Screen Gems found a measure of success in its old action-adventure roots with producer David Gerber's *Police Story* (NBC, 1973–77). Gerber, along with rival producer Aaron Spelling, did much to reinvent the mythology of TV crime. With the coded banter of the police radio crackling on the soundtrack, with the glare of flashing red strobe lights spinning from the tops of black-and-white units, Gerber cops confronted inner city decay with an unbeatable combination of high-tech equipment and good old-fashioned police work. Conceived of as a modular series that would act as an anthological umbrella for several series-within-a-series, *Police Story* gradually spawned its share of spin-offs. The most successful of these was *Police Woman* (NBC, 1974–78), starring Angie Dickinson as the tough but warm, sexy but stubborn undercover cop, Sgt. Pepper Anderson. Created by Joseph Wambaugh, a retired L.A.P.D. officer, the Gerber shows helped define the state-of-the-art in crime-show representationalism until the abrupt appearance of MTM's *Hill Street Blues* in 1981.

The critic John Cawelti has written that popular genres emerge from ongoing cycles of "convention" and "invention." The life of a commercial work depends as much on its ability to offer recognizable attractions as on its ability to offer something fresh and up-to-date. Screen Gems did yeoman's work in this regard. In shows such as *Route 66, Bewitched*, and *The Monkees*, the studio searched for a middle with something from the edge. *Hazel, Dennis the Menace*, and *The Farmer's Daughter* were attempts to adapt products with proven track records in other media (comic strips, movies) to prime-time TV form. But personally, I will remember Screen Gems not so much for any particular aesthetic vision that emerged from the thousands of hours of situation comedy and melodrama that it produced, but rather for the bits of cultural debris that fell off the edges of its image-making machinery:

Ezra Stone's *The Hathaways* (ABC, 1961–62) starred Jack Weston and Peggy Cass as a childless couple raising three chimpanzees in an otherwise painfully normal suburban-American home. With the chimps dressed in kiddie clothing and swinging from the chandeliers as Weston and Cass chase after, the sitcom aspires to a level of anthropomorphic mayhem that eclipses the capacities of J. Fred Muggs.

Harry Ackerman's *Grindl* (NBC, 1963–64) featured Imogene Coca as a sad sack female domestic, sent out each week by an employment agency to work at another impossible job for another impossible boss. A veteran of the by-then dying genre of comedy-variety, Coca made a valiant attempt at synthesizing her talents as an old-fashioned pantomime-and-banana peel specialist into a sitcom format; unfortunately she was counter-programmed against *The Ed Sullivan Show* during the British invasion.

The prescient *Occasional Wife* (NBC, 1966–67) was about a proto-yuppie bachelor who lands a job with a baby food company that requires all its executives to be married. He convinces a would-be painter who is working as a hat-check girl to move into his apartment building so she can remain on 24-hour call to play his wife for work-related occasions. In return, she receives art lessons and a pair of contact lenses.

Though Screen Gems no longer exists as such, the life of its work in American culture has not yet been fully measured. Old TV shows never die, they just go into syndication. Some of the studio's "failures" seem to have demonstrated as much staying power as its hits. *The Wackiest Ship in the Army* (NBC, 1965–66) and *Here Come the Brides* (ABC, 1968–70) have been born again in reruns on Christian cable after two dormant decades. A remake of *Gidget* (ABC, 1965–66) recently went into production at Columbia for the syndication market. What role did *Tallahassee 7000* (Syn., 1961) play in the genesis of *Miami Vice*? Can we look forward to the day when complete episodes of *Camp Runamuck* (NBC, 1965–66) will be available in videocassette so the public can finally get a look at this long-suppressed surrealist classic?

# Part IV
Individual Authorship Studies

# 11

# Rewriting Culture: A Dialogic View of Television Authorship

*Jimmie L. Reeves*

> And no man putteth new wine into old wineskins; else the new wine will burst the skins, and be spilled, and the skins will perish.
>
> But new wine must be put into fresh wineskins; and both are preserved.
>
> No man also having drunk old wine straightway desireth new: for he saith, The old is better.[1]
>
> —Luke 5: 37–39

In some circles, these three verses are known as the Parable of the Wineskins. Authorship of the parable is, of course, attributed to Jesus of Nazareth. But, as in all texts, the meaning of this allegory is dependent on contextual factors. Within the parameters of Luke's biography of Jesus, the parable is clearly meant to be interpreted as Jesus' response to harsh criticism from an influential group of religious authorities known as the Pharisees. Disturbed by Jesus' practice of mingling with social outcasts, the Pharisees publicly confronted the Nazarene with the loaded question, "Why do you eat and drink with publicans and sinners?" (Luke 5: 30). As the parable suggests, the very people whom the Pharisees despised and ostracized were, for Jesus, receptive vessels able to accommodate the new wine of his radical message. In the context of the New Testament, then, the Parable of the Wineskins was meant to illustrate how a revolutionary theology could not be contained by the attitudes and prejudices of orthodoxy.

This chapter, though, will place the parable into another context—the context of a general critique of traditionalism. Situated in this broader frame, the parable provides metaphoric commentary on the struggle that accompanies the institution of any new order of experience. In symbolizing this struggle, "old wineskins" represent the inflexibility of traditional views of the world; the image of "new wine" expresses rapidly changing cultural and material conditions; and "fresh wineskins" speak of the innovation and vitality of emerging modes of thought that are better able to accommodate the ferment of precipitous change.

Taken as a metaphor for a crisis in traditionalism, the parable provides decisive insights into the history of critical inquiry directed toward the study of television. As Booth (1987, p. 414) suggests, television criticism is unique in that it is the only body of criticism that practices *de*-preciation more than appreciation. And one of the chief grievances leveled at television echoes the Pharisees' rebuke of Jesus: The tired complaint "Why does TV have to cater to the lowest common denominator" expresses the same elitist sentiments of "Why do you eat and drink with publicans and sinners?". Clearly, traditional assumptions and attitudes regarding art and the critical enterprise are challenged by the crass commercialism and brute popularity of American television. Notions about artistic expression being the province of an individual author's personal vision are not relevant to television's collaborative production process. And standard interpretive methods that treat the isolated work as the object of critical evaluation are not able to accommodate the turbulence of television's fragmented form, nor the fundamentally derivative character of television's intertextual storytelling dynamic.

It's not at all surprising, then, that critics trained to appreciate the old wine of the high arts are almost unanimous in dismissing the aesthetic possibilities and the ideological power of television with the nostalgic lament, "The old is better." As the final line of the parable observes, "No man also having drunk old wine straightway desireth new."

## RUPTURING AN OLD WINESKIN

In attempting to fashion a new critical wineskin that is flexible enough to embrace the ferment of television, this chapter will adopt few of the assumptions underlying traditional views of authorship. In the first place, such views are based on a disavowal of the commercial that masks the economic dimensions of all taste cultures and expressive practices. As Bourdieu (1986, p. 133) forcefully argues, "the ideology of creation, which makes the author the first and last source of the value of his work" conceals the enterprise of the "cultural businessman." According to Bourdieu, art dealers, gallery owners, and publishers do much more than merely exploit "the labor of the 'creator' by trading in the 'sacred'. . . . " In fact Bourdieu considers the marketing, publishing, and staging of a work of art to be nothing less than *acts of consecration*. In this consecration, the art trader anoints a product he has "discovered" with the oil of his reputation as a man of "distinction." And, in Bourdieu's words, "the more consecrated he [the art trader] personally is, the more strongly he consecrates the work."

By indulging in the prestige and posturing of economic "disinterestedness," the legitimate artist is also implicated in the ongoing hypocrisies of the legitimate art business. Such feigned disinterestedness is only plausible because, after all, the art trader acts as a mediating agent who both links the artist to and screens the artist from the market. According to Bourdieu (1986, p. 136) the pretenses of this producer-trader relationship are, in part, sustained by a curious double bind: artists "cannot even denounce the exploitation they suffer without confessing their own self-interested motives." Ultimately then, Bourdieu sees the makers and marketers of works of art as "adversaries in collusion":

[E]ach abide by the same law which demands the repression of direct manifestations of personal interest, at least in its overtly "economic" form, and which has every appearance of transcendence although it is only the product of the cross-censorship weighing more or less equally on each of those who impose it on all the others (1986, p. 136).

Blind to and blinded by this "cross-censorship," the legitimate art establishment perpetuates the affectations of what Newcomb and Alley (1983, p. 37) term a "historically grounded class-bias." According to Newcomb and Alley, this bias tends to value the work of art "not only for its innovative vision, but for its sheer difference":

With other Western societies we have, since the Renaissance, distinctly valorized the innovative, the daring, the non-traditional, the "unique." The presence of these qualities rests, in turn, on our willingness to grant the artist something like "freedom" or "individuality." The autonomy of the artist is viewed as the source of creativity, and without it, "true" art is deemed impossible (1983, p. 35).

Of course, "individuality" and artistic "freedom," like "sovereign ego" and "private property," are relatively new concepts in the history of ideas—concepts that are closely linked to the rise of individualism and capitalism.

However, a more ancient notion of art is expressed in the ornaments adorning the Pharaoh's sarcophagus, or the psalms guiding the thoughts of the Israelites, or the totem poles ordering the gods of the Haida Indians. Here, the aesthetic object is understood to project the ideals and values of the community, not the vision and aspiration of an individual. In individualizing authorship, traditional criticism fails to recognize that even the most inaccessible piece of modernist fiction has some of the same adorning, guiding, and ordering properties of pre-Renaissance and pre-industrial art. For, as Bourdieu (1984, p. 56, 57) demonstrates, high art and the aesthetic sense essentially operate as *class definers* in contemporary technocracies:

The most intolerable thing for those who regard themselves as possessors of legitimate culture is the sacrilegious reuniting of tastes which taste dictates shall be separated. This means that the games of artists and aesthetes and their struggles for the monopoly of artistic legitimacy are less innocent than they seem. At stake in every struggle over art there is also an imposition of an art of living, i.e., the transmutation of an arbitrary way of living into the legitimate way of life which casts every other way of living into arbitrariness.

Ultimately, in legitimating an "arbitrary way of living," traditional views of authorship adopt what Allen and Gomery (1985) identify as the "great man" theory of history—"the belief that history is made by the inspired acts of outstanding individuals, whose genius transcends the normal constraints of historical context." Of course, in the West, aesthetic histories based on the "great man" theory are principally written by privileged white men, tend to celebrate "masterpieces" made by privileged white men, and usually uphold the "arbitrary ways of living" valued by privileged white men.

Based on a denial of the economic and contaminated by an elitist bias, the "great man" view of authorship has dire interpretive consequences. Like Judge Robert Bork's interpretive approach to the U.S. Constitution, traditional notions of authorship tend to reduce meaning to a matter of "original intent." In privileging authorial intention, such approaches endorse a static view of the communication process that isolates the message-product from the flow of history and treats meaning as a frozen asset that is somehow deposited in the work by its creator. However, as Bakhtin (1981), Newcomb (1984), Fiske (1987a, 1987b), and other critical scholars argue, human communication is much more complicated than a series of monologues articulated by self-determined individuals. Rather than approach meaning solely in terms of original intent, these scholars see the text as an arena for symbolic and political contestation. And in this contestation, meaning emerges from a multidimensional struggle: between writing and reading; between text and context; between "Us" and "Other"; between said and unsaid; between known and unknown; between domination and resistance; between revulsion and relevance; between estrangement and pleasure.

## FASHIONING A NEW WINESKIN

In trying to make sense of what Allen (1987b, p. 4) calls "the circumscribed role of the author," I hope to elaborate a theory of cultural production that emphasizes the dynamic operation of "rewriting" in television's storytelling process. This emphasis is, in part, an acknowledgment of the logistical, intellectual, and creative demands of TV's assembly-line storytelling. The brutal time constraints of this assembly line force the creative staff of most TV series to work on several episodes, in various stages of completion, at the same time. In other words, in series television, rewriting is an overlapping cyclic process that requires the precise coordination of a community of creators in an efficient routine. And, as Anderson observes:

[I]t is no wonder that these stories develop through formulaic repetition and the invocation of references, stereotypes and cliches.... This is necessarily the way in which popular culture works. Meaning develops according to a delicate operation of similarity and difference. In this process, a single story gains significance both through its identity with the stories that precede it and through its disruption of these stories (1987, p. 119).

In this "delicate operation of similarity and difference," rewriting acts as a *generative ritual* that insures each episode of a series is faithful to narrative patterns established in previous episodes. From the earliest moments of scripting, the rewriting conforms to the age-old imperative that the show, indeed, must go on. And elsewhere (Reeves, 1988), in an analysis of preproduction documents associated with the making of a single episode of *Newhart*, I have demonstrated how the necessity to rewrite the series activates, informs, directs, and inhibits every stage of creative collaboration.

But, here, the accent is placed on a different level of rewriting—the rewriting of generic conventions into the chain of texts collectively known as the "TV series." Following Newcomb and Alley, this chapter proposes that it is at the level of series creation that questions of authorship become a pertinent critical concern. Of course, at this level of discourse, the dominant creative force is the television producer.

Because of the scale of series production, television producers can ill afford to indulge in the pretenses of the "legitimate" art business. Rather than wear the "legitimate" artist's mask of "disinterestedness," rather than engage in a ritual disavowal of economic interest, television producers combine the role of the narrative artist with that of the trader in cultural goods. And as storytellers who cut deals, watch the bottom line, and live and die by the ratings, television producers are actively engaged as interpreters of the culture. When devising a new series or revamping an old one, they take their place beside advertising agents and fashion designers as what Sahlins calls "hucksters of the symbol."[2] In Sahlins' words:

In the nervous system of the American economy, theirs is the synaptic function. It is their role to be sensitive to the latent correspondences in the cultural order whose conjunction in a product symbol may spell mercantile success (1976, p. 217).

This chapter proposes that the spirit of rewriting provides the synaptic spark that brings these "latent correspondences in the cultural order" to life. For, as hucksters of the symbol, television producers are engaged in an ongoing revision of the American way—a revision that translates the conflicts and contradictions of modern life into terms that are comprehensible and forms that are meaningful to a vast, heterogeneous audience.

In sketching out a "dialogic view of authorship," I aim to underscore the *open orientation* of this rewriting of culture. For the work of television producers is not simply directed toward the series at hand. Instead, they must always take into account the force of other texts (i.e., previous texts, competing texts, future texts) and other contexts (i.e., the production budget, the legal climate, the ratings). On television, this open orientation is responsible for both the conventional and the innovative.

Of course, the sector of conventional storytelling demands a central place in television studies. Like burial charms, sacred psalms, or totem poles, conventional series deserve to be interpreted as documents that give concrete form to widely held values and beliefs. In fact, some of the most provocative scholarly television criticism has centered around the careful analysis of such conventional programming as *The Love Boat* (Schwichtenberg, 1987), *Guiding Light* (Allen, 1987a), and *The A-Team* (Fiske, 1987a, 1987b).

To account for changes in the operation and evolution of television's system of stories, studies investigating narrative innovation have generally placed authorship in a more prominent position on the critical agenda. In the first decade of television, this innovation was directed toward adapting popular story formulas from film and radio to the formal, economic, scheduling, and ideological constraints of a new and evolving storytelling system. During this formative stage, Jack Webb's work on *Dragnet* serves as a particularly cogent example of early generic adaptation that would have a lasting influence on the future of television. In Marc's words:

*Dragnet* was not merely a hit. It was an ideology, a "look," and an object of satire that made it a household word even in households that did not necessarily tune into it. It was TV's first big crimeshow money-maker, drawing serious network attention—and cash— to the genre. . . . Webb had moved the TV crimeshow from the thin artifice of tiny New York studios (most were hastily converted radio facilities) to the cavernous sound stages and spacious boulevards of Hollywood. Webb's purchase of an old Republic Pictures studio lot in North Hollywood, where he constructed a new TV production complex, was a sign of the times. Cop, car, criminal, and camera would not be separated again (1984, p. 74).

As Marc, Newcomb (1974), and other television scholars have demonstrated, this early generic translation/adaptation/innovation is also apparent in such classic TV fare as *I Love Lucy, Gunsmoke*, and *Perry Mason*.

Later, the innovation would primarily be directed toward refining the formulas which survived and thrived on the new medium. Consider, here, the corporate authorship of MTM. With series like *The Mary Tyler Moore Show, Rhoda*, and *The Bob Newhart Show*, MTM literally rewrote the situation comedy formula to accommodate more complex characters. As Feuer (1987, p. 55) puts it:

"Character ensembles," "motivation," "a set of little epiphanies," have transformed the problem/solution format of the sitcom into a far more psychological and episodic formula in which—in the hand of MTM—the situation itself becomes the pretext for the revelation of character.

This refinement of genre is also evident in the work of Richard Levinson and William Link (*Columbo*), Larry Gelbart (*M\*A\*S\*H*), and Danny Arnold (*Barney Miller*).

In the last decade—in part because of television's maturation as a storytelling system and the parallel maturation of the "television generation"—innovation has often resulted in talented producers exploring and blurring generic boundaries. Steven Bochco and Michael Kozoll did this with *Hill Street Blues*, enriching the cop show formula with the humor of the dark comedy and the tangled relationships of the soap opera. But more recently, this generic blurring is evident in a group of shows that labor under the label of "dramedy": *Frank's Place, The Days and Nights of Molly Dodd, The "Slap" Maxwell Story*, and *The Wonder Years*.

Although the shows are profoundly different from each other, they do share certain common features: all, admittedly, integrate moments of poignance into a comedic framework; all are shot film style; none use a laugh track. And in *Electronic Media*'s semi-annual poll of newspaper critics, all of the so-called "dramedies" placed in the top ten (1988, p. 18).[3] The audience, though, has not been as enthusiastic. Because of low ratings, *Molly Dodd, "Slap" Maxwell*, and *Frank's Place* vanished from prime-time network television after only one season.

*The Wonder Years*, though, is another story. ABC gave *The Wonder Years* an early boost by running it as a mid-season replacement that premiered immediately following the network's broadcast of the 1988 Superbowl. This auspicious beginning was certainly a contributing factor in making *The Wonder Years* the only one of the four celebrated "dramedies" to attract a consistently large audience. Primarily because of this commercial success, I will use *The Wonder Years* to further illustrate the dialogic character of television authorship.

## ANALYZING THE FERMENT OF NEW WINE

To understand how a show like *The Wonder Years* gets developed, we first have to consider the economic context of the major broadcast networks in the 1980s. Thanks to the most extreme shift in the structure of the American communication complex since the 1950s, the dominance of the three-network oligopoly that television inherited from radio has been severely and swiftly undermined by new forces in the marketplace. Just over ten years ago, 91 percent of TV's prime-time audience watched programs broadcast on the three national networks (Stevenson, 1985). But at that time, only a little over 17 percent of America's TV homes were wired into a cable system (Sterling and Kittross, 1978, p. 536) and the domestic VCR was still too expensive for most medium-income families. By 1985, cable had penetrated 46 percent of America's households, 30 percent owned VCRs (Miller, 1986, p. 16), and the major networks' combined share of the prime-time audience had slipped to 73 percent. Ironically, during this period of decline for the networks, Americans devoted even more time to television—the average family's weekly consumption increased from 47 hours and 47 minutes in 1982 to 49 hours and 58 minutes in 1984 (Stevenson, 1985).

To grab a share of the growing mass and shrinking particular audience, ABC has instituted a programming strategy that involves targeting specific age and generational groups. And one of the prime groups that is especially attractive to both ABC and its advertisers is the first television generation—the infamous baby boomers. *Moonlighting, thirtysomething,* and *The Wonder Years* are all shows that form the programming base for ABC's strategy.

But, where yuppie sagas like *thirtysomething* look at baby boomers booming in the Reagan-Bush era, *The Wonder Years* takes a different perspective. Significantly, the show's coproducers (Neal Marlens and Carol Black) are very self-conscious about this difference. Their self-consciousness was, in fact, the subject of a newspaper article appearing on the front page of the *Los Angeles Times*:

Even though some in the TV industry have jokingly called "The Wonder Years" "twelve-something" or "The Little Chill," Marlens said the show views the world with 12-year-old wonder rather than the disillusionment of radicals who have reluctantly entered the Establishment.

"We saw that a lot of the shows that seemed to be made by yuppies, baby boomers, people in their mid-30s to mid-40s, seemed to be so directly and literally about contemporary life," Marlens said. "I think that there's some value in that, but it's also real dangerous. It's like looking in a mirror, which is not necessarily the best way to get a perspective on yourself" (Haithman, 1988, pp. 1, 24).

Beyond being made for and about the television generation, *The Wonder Years* is also made by members of that generation: Marlens and Black are both in their early thirties.[4] And their familiarity with the television experience is evidenced by the savvy references to television history that enrich the series. Indeed, in combining a two-syllable, emotionally charged adjective (Wonder) with a one-syllable time designator (Years), the very title of the series acknowledges the influence of *Happy Days*. Where *Happy Days* examined the banal problems of middle-class family life in the 1950s, *The Wonder Years* centers on a suburban family caught up in the turmoil of the 1960s.

And *The Wonder Years* invokes the history of situation comedy in other meaningful ways. Like *Leave it to Beaver*, the organizing sensibility in the series is the youngest member of the family, a 12-year-old named Kevin Arnold (Fred Savage). And his older brother, Wayne (Jason Hervey), is Wally Cleaver with Eddie Haskell's horns. Providing much of the humor of the series, Kevin and Wayne's sibling rivalry is established in the early moments of the pilot when the voice-over narration of an adult Kevin tells us: " . . . years later, when we were both adults, we finally got to know and understand each other, and Wayne explained that, basically, he just deeply regretted the fact that I was born, and he wanted me to feel the same way."

Voice-over narration, of course, is not a standard feature of the sitcom. And, the voice of the adult Kevin speaks to the show's status as a generic hybrid. In addition to triggering memories of other situation comedies, *The Wonder Years* also resonates with *The Waltons*, a family drama set in the 1930s. The narration of John Boy Walton reminiscing about those bygone days contributed to what

Newcomb (1987) has appraised as *The Waltons'* profound sense of "intimacy, continuity, and history." While the voice-over narration on *The Wonder Years* is often used for comedic effect, providing ironic commentary on the action, it also frequently accomplishes the aesthetic effects valued by Newcomb.

The sense of history aroused by the voice-over is further stimulated by the show's frequent use of pop music of the era. In an early episode, for instance, "Black Bird"—the Beatles' acoustical dirge—enhances the pathos of one of Kevin's many disappointments on the path to adulthood. And Marlens and Black did not commission a theme song for *The Wonder Years*. Instead, a hit tune like Joe Cocker's rendition of "I Get By With a Little Help from My Friends" plays as the opening credits appear under nostalgia-inducing "home movies" of *The Wonder Years'* family.

For me (because of my dual status as a baby-boomer and a son), the most moving episode of the first season explored Kevin's relationship with his father. In my analysis of this episode, I intend to demonstrate how Marlens and Black rely on viewer familiarity with the television experience—and how this reliance, in turn, enables them to fashion a relatively compelling commentary on contemporary suburban life.

Interestingly, television plays a prominent and humorous role in disclosing the premise of the story. In fact, the episode opens with a close up of an ancient, black-and-white set exhibiting a nature documentary. As a large gorilla moves through a forest, the documentary's narrator explains, "The male enters a hostile environment to find sustenance. He returns after an unsuccessful foray, aggressive and unpredictable." At this time, a wide shot reveals that the TV is located in the Arnold kitchen and is being watched by Kevin, Wayne, and their mother, Norma (Alley Mills). We continue to hear the documentary's narrator, but now he seems to be describing the action of the Arnold family. Offscreen, a barking dog and screeching tires signal the homecoming of Jack Arnold (Dan Lauria). As Norma rushes to the kitchen window, the docu-narrator continues with bland scientific detachment: "Notice the reaction of the startled mother and her offspring as they begin to sense the presence of the male." Norma, on reading Jack's mood, issues a warning to the brothers: "Your father's had a bad day at work, so no noise." Kevin and Wayne exchange knowing looks as the despondent father enters through the kitchen door. Norma greets him with a neutral, "Hi, hon. How's work?" Without acknowledging the existence of Kevin and Wayne, Jack moves quickly through the kitchen, grunting "Work's work" as he exits into the living room. The close-up of the TV reappears, showing young gorillas scurrying into the undergrowth as the docu-narrator observes: "The irritable male gives out unmistakable signals that tell the young to keep their distance." Cutting back to a wide-shot of the kitchen, the screen shows Norma and her boys react with fear to Jack's offscreen slamming of a door. Finally, after the boys flee the house to go play catch, the introductory scene ends with another shot of the television, now showing an angry gorilla beating its chest.

The clever construction of this opening sequence speaks not only to the wit of *The Wonder Years*, but also to its deviation from the norms of domestic comedy. Jack Arnold represents a significant rewriting of the benign TV father regulating such conventional shows as *Leave it to Beaver, Happy Days*, and *The Cosby Show*. As a stern disciplinarian who has trouble communicating with his spouse and children, Jack is one TV father who, very often, doesn't "know best." Unlike the fatherly lawyers, obstetrician-gynecologists, and briefcase-carrying businessmen of other domestic comedies, Jack is a mid-level manager who is frustrated by the pressure and drudgery of his job.

Viewers discover, in voice-over narration immediately following the opening scene, that Jack copes with this frustration in two ways:

When my father had a bad day at work, he'd just sit in the dark by himself and watch TV. We learned early on that this was a danger signal and we adapted our behavior accordingly. And when he had a really bad day, I'm talking about a very not-good day, he had this telescope and he'd go out in the back yard and just look through it for hours.

Ultimately, the star gazing will be a device that helps soften and humanize Jack's character.

Jack's television viewing, though, is presented as something that separates him from his family. For instance, a turning point in the story occurs when Kevin interrupts Jack while he watches the sports news. Curious about Jack's work and not understanding what it means to manage "distribution and product support services," Kevin asks Jack what he "does all day." Miffed because Kevin causes him to lose track of the day's baseball scores, Jack snarls, "Shovel other people's crap so you kids can eat." Feeling rejected by his father, Kevin retreats to his room to brood. And Norma, predictably, intervenes on Kevin's behalf:

*Norma*: You gotta relax a little, Jack.

*Jack*: Dammit, Norma, don't tell me to relax. I mean what does he want to know. About the seven S–14 forms I've got to fill out every time I turn around? About the whining customers? About the incompetent jackasses in Shipping and Receiving?

*Norma*: Yeah. Yes, that's exactly what he wants to know. He wants to know more about you, Jack. I don't know why that's so hard for you to understand.

The intensity of this wife-husband interchange, of course, runs counter to the cheerful spousal collusion typical of most television comedy. Marriage, here, is not a merry adventure. In fact, as we discover, Jack partially blames his marriage and family responsibilities for his miserable existence.

Even so, to soothe Kevin's injured pride, Jack agrees to take him to work the next day. In a humorous sequence, Kevin meets the boring people who work in Jack's office, observes Jack handling a crisis involving the incompetence of a subordinate, and fantasizes about wielding the power and authority of a manager. But the highlight of Kevin's excursion into the world of corporate work comes when he accompanies his father on a coffee break. Away from the hectic atmosphere of the office, Kevin learns that when Jack was his age he wanted to be the captain of a ship:

*Jack*: Yeah. You know, one of those big ocean liners, or a freighter, or an oil tanker. Be out there in the ocean in the middle of the night . . . navigating by the stars. Of course, they use instruments for all that now, but I didn't know that. Yeah, I thought that'd be the greatest thing in the world.

*Kevin*: How come you didn't do it?

*Jack*: How come? Well, you know, one thing leads to another. Went off to college, met your mom, next summer I got a job on a loading dock here at Norcom. The rest is history.

*Kevin*: You'd have made a great ship's captain, dad.

*Jack*: Nah. Probably not. Probably get sea sick. You know, Kevin, you can't do every silly thing you want to in life. You have to make your choices. You have to try to be happy with them. . . .

The tranquil mood of this intimate moment is shattered when father and son return to the office. Jack's supervisor ambushes him there. And Kevin watches, in shock, as Jack suffers a humiliating chewing out.

As I hope this analysis demonstrates, this touching treatment of the father-son relationship also investigates what it means to be male in our society, the alienation of corporate life, the naive dreams of childhood, the sobering realities of adulthood, and the illusory character of freedom of choice. What is lost in this analysis is much of the historical texture of this story. Miniskirts, the military-industrial complex, the Vietnam War, the generation gap, the Washington Senators, and the "Buckle-Up-for-Safety" campaign are all invoked at various moments during this episode.

Admittedly, at one level *The Wonder Years* is an apologia that is often militant in its defense of middle-class life in the suburbs. This militancy is, in fact, even brought to the fore in the series itself. Consider, here, for instance, the closing narration of the pilot episode:

I think about the events of that day again and again . . . whenever some blowhard starts talking about the anonymity of the suburbs or the mindlessness of the TV generation. Because we know that inside each of those identical boxes with its Dodge parked out front and its white bread on the table and its TV set glowing blue in the falling dusk, there were characters and stories, there were families bound together in the pain and the struggle of love, there were moments that made us cry with laughter, and there were moments, like that one, of sorrow and wonder.

Yet, in telling the story of a middle-class family "bound together in the pain and the struggle of love," *The Wonder Years* also continually unmasks and explores central contradictions of the mainstream American experience. At times, these contradictions involve crises in the patriarchal order; at other times, they concern the alienation of corporate life; at still other times, they deal with the economic and social inequities of a stratified class system. Although the resolutions to most episodes generally confirm centrist American values—especially those associated with individualism—the show rarely offers complete closure. In other words, the force of the cultural contradictions represented on *The Wonder Years* tends to overwhelm the contrivances of the reassuring endings.

In fact, the contradictions often persist because, unlike in the conventional sitcom, the characters in *The Wonder Years* are allowed to change. For instance, after Kevin's excursion into the world of work in the episode analyzed above, the boy's relationship with his father enters a new stage. The final scene of the episode begins with Kevin watching through a window while Jack, once again, gazes at the stars through his telescope. As Kevin hesitantly steps out onto the back porch we hear the pensive narration of his adult voice: "That night, my father stood there looking up at the sky the way he always did. But suddenly I realized I wasn't afraid of him in quite the same way anymore. The funny thing is, I felt like I'd lost something." As the narration concludes, Jack sadly looks over, sees Kevin, and beckons for him to come join him. The episode then ends on a bittersweet note with Kevin peering through the telescope as his father tells him: "That's Polaris, the North Star. That's how the sailors used to find their way home."

At the close of the episode, then, Marlens and Black do not rescue the fictional father from the contradictions unmasked by the story. Jack Arnold is still very much a lost soul trapped by his job, his family responsibilities, and his place in the patriarchy.

## PRESERVING THE WINE OF AUTHORSHIP

Obviously, Marlens and Black have mastered the recombinant style that is much maligned by Gitlin (1985). However, we are not only unfair, but we are also irresponsible, when we depreciate the generic innovation of such perceptive cultural interpreters simply because it is popular—that is, because it appeals to modern-day "publicans and sinners" and it doesn't conform to an elitist definition of art.

Therefore, while I obviously agree with much of Bourdieu's stinging critiques (1984; 1986) of the ideology of charisma underlying traditional notions of authorship, I am not at all comfortable in completely writing off authorship as a dead issue. In acknowledging that all producers are inspired by self-interest, that they are intent on manufacturing a "product symbol [that] may spell mercantile success," we are still faced with the challenge of making distinctions between the good steward and the bad, between the friend and the panderer, between benefaction and exploitation. Although TV's creative artist is circumscribed by multitudinous forces—both intertextual and extratextual—we must continue to recognize that she still plays a significant, and sometimes decisive, role in the struggle for meaning. In discarding the old skin of traditional criticism, then, we must take care to preserve a portion of the wine of authorship—for to siphon out the community of creators from the blend of culture is to deny human beings any responsibility for history, and to surrender to the despair of some reductive form of psychological, economic, or technological determinism.

Of course, we can, and indeed should, reject such despair. If we consider *reality* to be a social construction and *thought* to be a public enterprise, then ideologies, and economies, and institutions, and technologies are all human products—and human intervention and struggle can still change history.[5] But in sharing responsibility for history, we must also recognize the need to hold people accountable for their contributions to maintaining or transforming the world. This chapter proposes that a dialogic view of authorship is both geared to the realities of contemporary cultural production and crucial to enforcing such artistic accountability.

## NOTES

The author thanks Brian Nienhaus for championing the work of Bourdieu. The author also expresses appreciation to Richard Campbell for reading and suggesting changes in earlier drafts of this essay.

1. Here, Jesus of Nazareth intended to translate a furious religious controversy into concrete terms that were both accessible and comprehensible to his followers. Because of the technological limitations of that period, wine was stored in animal skins before the fermentation process was complete. It was common knowledge that the inflexible leather of old skins could not withstand the internal pressures generated by this fermentation. The common folks listening to the parable realized that new wine required containers fashioned from fresh leather.

2. Newcomb and Alley also incorporate Sahlins's work into their view of television producers: "These creators are, as Sahlins suggests, true readers, true analysts of the cultures in which they live and work, the society in which they must seek and create an audience. They must be sensitive to many sorts of cultural change, technological as well as sociological, cognitive, or political" (1983, p. 32).

3. *The Wonder Years* and *Frank's Place* came in second and third behind the critic's favorite, *L.A. Law*. *"Slap" Maxwell* came in eighth, and *Molly Dodd* tenth.

4. As of this writing, the six existing episodes of the series have all been cowritten by Marlens and Black.

5. This conception of reality and thought is based on what Carey (1975) identifies as a "ritual view of communication."

## REFERENCES

Allen, R. (1987a). *The Guiding Light*: Soap opera as economic product and cultural document. In H. Newcomb, ed., *Television: The Critical View*, 4th ed. pp. 141–63. New York: Oxford University Press.

Allen, R., ed. (1987b). Talking about television. In R. Allen, ed., *Channels of discourse:*

*Television and contemporary criticism*, pp. 1–16. Chapel Hill: The University of North Carolina Press.

Allen, R., and D. Gomery. (1985). *Film history: Theory and practice*. New York: Alfred A. Knopf.

Anderson, C. (1987). Reflections on *Magnum, P.I.* In H. Newcomb, ed., *Television: The critical view*, 4th ed., pp. 112–25. New York: Oxford University Press.

Bakhtin, M. (1981). *The dialogic imagination: Four essays*. M. Holquist, ed., C. Emerson and M. Holquist, Trans. Austin: University of Texas Press.

Booth, W. (1987). The company we keep: Self-making in imaginative art, old and new. In H. Newcomb, ed., *Television: The critical view*, 4th ed., pp. 382–418. New York: Oxford University Press.

Bourdieu, P. (1984). *Distinction: The social critique of the judgment of taste*. Trans. by R. Nice. Cambridge: Harvard University Press.

———. (1986). The production of belief: Contribution to an economy of symbolic goods. Trans. by R. Nice. In R. Collins, J. Curran, N. Granham, P. Scannell, P. Schlesinger, and C. Sparks, eds., *Media, culture and society: A critical reader*, pp. 131–63. Beverly Hills: Sage Publications.

Carey, J. (1975). A cultural approach to communication. *Communication* 2: 1–22.

*Electronic Media* critics poll. (1988, May 2). *Electronic Media*, p. 18.

Feuer, J. (1987). The MTM Style. In H. Newcomb, ed., *Television: The critical view*, 4th ed. pp. 52–84. New York: Oxford University Press.

Fiske, J. (1987a). British cultural studies and television. In R. Allen, ed., *Channels of discourse: Television and contemporary criticism*, pp. 255–90. Chapel Hill: The University of North Carolina Press.

———. (1987b). *Television culture*. London: Metheun.

Gitlin, T. (1985). *Inside prime time*. New York: Pantheon Books.

Haithman, D. (1988, April 8). 'Wonder Years' Pays its Respects to '60s suburbia. *Los Angeles Times*, Part 6, pp. 1, 24.

Marc, D. (1984). *Demographic vistas: Television in American culture*. Philadelphia: University of Pennsylvania Press.

Miller, J. (1986). International roundup: The global picture. *Channels of Communications 1986 Field Guide*, pp. 16–18.

Newcomb, H. (1974). *TV: The most popular art*. New York: Anchor Books.

———. (1984). On the dialogic aspects of mass communications. *Critical Studies in Mass Communication*, 1, 1: 34–50.

———. (1987). Toward a television aesthetic. In H. Newcomb, ed., *Television: The critical view*, 4th ed. pp. 613–27. New York: Oxford University Press.

Newcomb, H., and R. Alley. (1983). *The producer's medium: Conversations with creators of American TV*. New York: Oxford University Press.

Reeves, J. (1988). Rewriting *Newhart*: A dialogic analysis. *Wide Angle*, 10, 1: 76–91.

Sahlins, M. (1976). *Culture and practical reason*. Chicago: University of Chicago Press.

Schwichtenberg, C. (1987). *The Love Boat*: The packaging and selling of love, heterosexual romance, and family. In H. Newcomb, ed., *Television: The critical view*, 4th ed., pp. 126–40. New York: Oxford University Press.

Sterling, C., and J. Kittross. *Stay tuned: A concise history of American broadcasting*. Belmont, California: Wadsworth Publishing Company.

Stevenson, R. (1985, October 20). The networks and advertisers try to recapture our attention. *New York Times*, Section F, p. 8.

# 12

# Television Production as Collective Action

*Cathy A. Sandeen and Ronald J. Compesi*

As a social phenomenon, television has been studied rather thoroughly in recent decades: the television audience, television content, and television's impact have all been major subjects of concern. Scholars typically pay considerably less attention to the television production organization and process, the way in which the television message—particularly television entertainment—is created.

A group of relatively recent studies has acknowledged the importance of understanding the television production process and organization. The question these studies typically ask is, "Who within the production organization is most responsible for the content of the final product?" Several different answers to this question have emerged.

Cantor (1971), in a study of prime-time drama and children's programs, has argued that the television producer is the most influential member of the television production team. Ravage (1978), in his study of twelve prime-time television directors, concluded that television producers and writers have more control than does the director. Stein (1979) argued that Hollywood television producers and writers influence the content of programs both consciously and unconsciously, and that the values that emerge in these shows are the result of their influence. Lynch (1973), Elliott (1979), Pekurny (1980), Ettema (1982), and Turow (1982) examined the production process and organization of various types of television programs, also focusing on the issue of control. The majority of existing production process research attempts, as Barbatsis (1981) argued it should, to identify "elements thought to predict or influence the creation and selection of program content," both "the independent variables of the production process and the relationship of these variables to the content that is produced or programmed" (p. 5). Because television is an extremely complex phenomenon, the value of isolating single causal or conditional factors is doubtful.

Although he focuses primarily on the production of the so-called "fine arts" (music, painting, and theater, for instance), Becker (1974, 1982) offers an alternative framework which can be applied to the study of television production organizations and processes. Becker (1974) argues that a work of art, in this chapter extended to include a television program, is the result of collective action and to understand the creative process one should "look for the network of people, however large or extended, whose collective activity made it possible for the event to occur as it did" (p. 775). Further, investigators should "look for networks whose cooperative activity recurs or has become routine and specify the conventions by which their constituent members coordinate their separate lines of action, "(p. 775)." The task of interpreting creative processes of any form involves identifying cooperating production personnel and the mechanisms which help govern routine behavior.

Although he did not apply his framework to television programs per se, Becker's emphasis on collective, cooperative recurring and routine activity in the production of art works makes his analytical scheme particularly applicable to television production. Television programs are seldom, if ever, created by one individual. Rather, television programs are made possible through the integration and coordination of a myriad of professional roles whose jobs are made more difficult due to the time constraints of the medium. Clearly, our understanding of the processes and organizations responsible for televised entertainment would benefit from focusing on cooperation and integration within production organizations rather than on who ultimately controls the process.

The purpose of this chapter is to examine the production organization and process of the current daytime serial, *The Young and the Restless* from the point of view of collective activity. Soap operas are produced one episode per day, five days a week, and thus embody the various commercial, technical, and stylistic components of most all television production—in an especially compressed form. The goal here is not to identify the independent variables which control the process and ultimately determine program content. Rather, this chapter is more interpretively based: to more fully understand how the artistic/craft cooperative operates in producing an episode of *The Young and the Restless*.[1] Questions this chapter will attempt to answer include: (1) What is the principal production network at *The Young and the Restless*? and (2) How do the members of this production network coordinate the numerous individual production decisions which contribute to a single episode of *The Young and the Restless*?

Basically, the production decisions at *The Young and the Restless* are coordinated by two broad mechanisms: (1) stylistic conventions and (2) organizational constraints. Each of these mechanisms is discussed in more detail following a brief description of the principal production network at *The Young and the Restless*.

## PRODUCTION NETWORK

Besides the technical crew (camera and audio operators, cue card holders, and so forth) who follow others' directions and have no individual creative input into the show, those members of the production organization at *The Young and the Restless* who make significant production decisions about the show include: the writer, producer, director, lighting director, art director, costume coordinator, music coordinator, and post-production director.

There are actually two classes of writers on the program. One is the headwriter who is responsible for writing the basic storyline and episode outlines and for establishing the characters. Basic storylines are prepared approximately one year before they will appear on the screen; these storylines are embellished into their final form roughly three months prior to production. Detailed show outlines for each individual episode are written two to three weeks prior to production.

The producer's responsibilities at *The Young and the Restless* are actually carried out by a group of people—the production staff—which includes the executive producer, associate producer, and other staff members. Together, they are responsible for coordinating all the financial, legal, and technical elements of the show. Responsibilities include administering the budget, ordering facilities, and dealing with network censors, labor unions, and talent agents. The program's associate producer described her duties: "I'm a trouble-shooter. I order all the facilities for the show from CBS. I handle the crews and the technical problems that arise with CBS. I administrate the budget."[2] Together, the producers oversee the entire production. As the executive producer explained:

We do very little as long as everybody else is doing what they're supposed to be doing. . . . We get very busy when the fabric we've created to produce the show falls apart. Our basic responsibility is putting together a unit of people and seeing that they do the best job they can. We're responsible for everyone who is involved in the show from the stage hands to actors. A producer has to know the technical side of the business: how to run a studio, the machines, the videotape equipment, edit, put a crew together, and how to work with actors and union rules (Gilbert, 1979, p. 170).

Although many of the producer's responsibilities are managerial and bureaucratic, the producers also take part in some of the aesthetic decisions about *The Young and the Restless*. The program's producer elaborated: "One of the main things is to be there and to help shape the show from the time we see it in runthrough 'til the time it airs. I'm like the third eye. I'm the third person up there, the guy who can sit in the back and be an unbiased observer and be the critic."

The director of *The Young and the Restless* is responsible for the overall visual treatment of the show. The director coordinates the technical aspects of the show, selecting the individual shots, and is responsible for getting the show onto videotape within the one-day time limit. But the director of *The Young and the Restless* is also responsible for deciding how to stage the scenes, how to move the cameras and performers, and is vital in influencing the interpretation and delivery of lines by the performers. One of the show's directors touched on the mix of technical and aesthetic skills in television directing: "You have to create at home and what little time you have before you get into the studio and then you have to become practical—an engineer—to put it on tape as fast as you can."

The lighting director is responsible for designing and executing the lighting for the show. The lighting director's responsibilities go beyond providing general illumination. As one of the show's two lighting directors explained, "the main function of a lighting director is to design a lighting condition or a lighting look for a show."

The art director is responsible for designing the sets for the show, including the elaborate permanent sets as well as the temporary sets used for only a few scenes. The art director described his duties at *The Young and the Restless*: "The definition of an art director is that he is responsible for all that visual look that's out of focus. . . . Here, for the most part, we build walls. And you just try to make it as interesting as possible."

The costume coordinator decides what costumes will be worn within the show. The costume coordinator is also responsible for building and maintaining wardrobes for the characters on *The Young and the Restless*. The costume coordinator elaborated: "A lot of it is being aware of the characters but also being aware of the actors and their personalities and their egos. What looks good on them and what doesn't look good on them. What's good for the character."

The music coordinator is responsible for integrating music into the show:

The primary function of the music coordinator is, of course, to supply the show with a certain amount of music, and that's divided into two parts actually. One part of which doesn't exist on a lot of other shows because they don't have live performances . . . which means there's additional work to do besides setting up the cues.

At *The Young and the Restless*, the music coordinator must not only select and play the background music within the show (called "cues"), but he or she must also clear the rights to the music performed live within the show. Sometimes the music coordinator also selects the songs to be performed live.

The post-production director supervises the editing of the show. Editing involves not only putting the individually recorded scenes together, but also editing in retakes or "pickups" of certain portions of scenes due to errors of some type. The post-production director described the job as " . . . putting pieces together as in a puzzle . . . what we are given is pieces of a puzzle and we will put them together and make them work until you see the final picture. . . . "

## STYLISTIC CONVENTIONS AT *THE YOUNG AND THE RESTLESS*

The various members of the production collective at *The Young and the Restless* coordinate their actions by following certain explicit and implicit rules. The first of these rules are stylistic conventions about how the program should look or sound.

Newcomb (1974) has observed that soap operas, on the whole, break many of the conventions established by prime-time entertainment shows. First, the narrative values of the serials are different. Stories and plot lines continue for weeks, months, or even years. Characters are not rigidly portrayed, but rather grow and change over time. Second, the production values of the soap opera are different from their prime-time counterparts. Soap operas, Newcomb points out, are far less slick and expensive looking (1974, p. 164).

Although soap opera characters, plots, and themes tend to be consistent across many, if not all, soap operas, each soap opera modifies certain production values or stylistic elements in some way to establish a unique identity. At *The Young and the Restless*, unique stylistic conventions include certain manipulations of lighting, sets and costumes, visualization, direction, and sound.

The lighting techniques used in *The Young and the Restless* contribute the most, perhaps, in setting the show apart from other soap operas. The lighting is very low-key and highly selective. Only the characters' faces and small portions of the set are lit. Even the lit portions of a scene contain a great deal of shadow. The effect is very dramatic and moody, almost ominous. The lighting director elaborated on the lighting techniques used in *The Young and the Restless*:

The lighting emphasis is on people. A lot of other daytime dramatic shows, soap operas, that you see, the people are often not ideally lit. On this particular show we strive for that more than anything else. We try to go for heavy modeling [facial shadows]. . . . We do not have to light the set.

The highly selective lighting adds an artistic dimension to the show. The producer admitted that "we always tell the lighting director to make it look like a Rembrandt."

Sets and costumes are another important and defining stylistic element on *The Young and the Restless*. Newcomb pointed out that in most all soap operas, "the people are elegantly but tastefully groomed . . . are the emblems of the upper middle class" (1974, p. 166). The costumes worn by the characters on *The Young and the Restless* follow this general soap opera convention, but are even more stylish and glamorous. The program's costume coordinator described the costuming philosophy of the show:

What we're striving for is to make the show bigger than life . . . a very chic, elegant type look. The look I want is almost like a classy Ross Hunter picture. . . . People really do look at soap operas to get away from their own problems, their own lifestyles. They don't necessarily want to see what they're living on the screen. They don't necessarily want to see their Sears and Roebuck shirtwaist dress on the screen. They want to see something better.

Sets, too, are treated differently on *The Young and the Restless* than on other soap operas. Because of the dramatic low-key lighting, not too much of the sets are visible on the screen. Set details are seldom emphasized. Nevertheless, the sets on *The Young and the Restless* attempt to incorporate a sense of three-dimensionality and depth on the two-dimensional screen. The art director explained:

We do have a lot of stage space so that some sets, the "Newman" set, for instance, is far bigger than any other of the sets that is just the living room . . . you can stand down at the end of the bar and look through the camera port and see forty-five to fifty feet through the bar, through the living room, through the solarium to the drop on the other side of the windows which, with the lens configuration, gives you a long, vast distance that your actors can walk and move and that adds, I think, to a richness on the show.

The element of visualization refers to the configuration and selection of individual shots within a show. Newcomb pointed out that in soap operas: "We are offered an almost unrelieved view of the faces of our characters. It is rare that more than three characters appear in a single shot, and in most cases we see only two characters. In these scenes it is also rare that we are offered more than a head-and-shoulders closeup" (1974, p. 168).

*The Young and the Restless* is most similar to the other soap operas in terms of its treatment of visualization. Most scenes contain two characters and facial close-ups are the most often used individual shot. However, the close-ups used in *The Young and the Restless* are not the usual head-and-shoulders close-ups noted by Newcomb. Instead, extreme facial close-ups, in which only a character's eyes are the main feature, are more common. The show's producer explained that "television is a close-up medium and we like to do those close-up shots so that the audience gets really involved."

The stylistic element, direction, moves beyond single shots to include broader visual concepts such as blocking, camera movement, and transitions.

Blocking refers to how the actors are positioned and how they are directed to move throughout the scene. Blocking, as well as camera movement, is usually determined by the director. Directors use these devices to add visual variety to a scene. The directors at *The Young and the Restless* consciously try to add more movement—and more unusual movement—into a scene than in most other soap operas.

In one confrontation scene between two characters, the director blocked the scene in an unusual way so that the female character repeatedly crossed in front of the male character. The director explained that he treated the scene this way in order " . . . to give her [the female character] her stage. I felt she was angry and I don't like a pacing pattern of somebody going back and forth or up and down stage so I tried to embellish it.''

Another component of the direction element is the use of transitions between scenes. The transitions shift the action in time and place. In *The Young and the Restless*, such transitions are virtually always achieved visually. The post-production director explained: ''You're almost editorializing a lot in transitions. Like a scene coming out of two characters that have a relationship, but they're in different places. You can tell a story by the transition you put between the two.''

Finally, the last stylistic element that is uniquely manipulated in *The Young and the Restless* is the element of sound. Sound here refers to any program audio, other than dialogue, including background music, live music, and sound effects.

Newcomb has pointed out that soap opera background music ''is one of the most obvious and parodied of soap opera devices'' (1974, p. 169). Instead of the old-fashioned melodramatic organ music so often parodied, the music heard beneath dialogue in *The Young and the Restless* is less obvious and better integrated into the program than in soap operas past. The subtle integration of background music is a deliberate goal of the show's music coordinator:

The principle, subtlety, that I feel so strongly about means that it [the music] enhances the mood, but you can't tell. It doesn't override the whole scene. Someone couldn't identify, wouldn't hear the music if they were trying to recall the scene. They would only feel the mood of the scene.

The various stylistic conventions which comprise the unique character of *The Young and the Restless* did not develop from the various production personnel who contribute to the show, but rather were articulated by the program's creator. The program's ''bible,'' a detailed description of characters, storylines, and production values, is written and distributed to all the production personnel involved prior to the program's production. The ''bible'' is referred to as a final authority over any production decision during the early stages of a soap opera production. However, the original ''bible'' is less important to the coordination of stylistic elements in *The Young and the Restless* since the show has been in production for over ten years. Stylistic conventions are no longer communicated as formally, but are communicated informally through certain organizational chains of command and patterns of behavior.

## ORGANIZATIONAL CONSTRAINTS

The primary organizational constraints within which the production personnel at *The Young and the Restless* make their individual production decisions involve a tension between autonomy and control. Due to the time constraints involved in producing an episode of *The Young and the Restless*, production tasks are divided among a large group of people. One person is not able to directly influence all production decisions. The coordination of individual decisions into a unified whole is accomplished by less direct means. The organization is structured so that rules are rigidly defined and decisions are monitored through an institutionalized chain of command.

Production personnel are afforded different degrees of autonomy to make decisions, but only as long as the production personnel behave within their rigidly defined roles. Part of their roles dictate that most decisions be verified with members higher up the production hierarchy. This hierarchical chain of command specifically allows for monitoring decisions. Production organization members know they must follow the stylistic conventions described in the previous sections. And they know organization members higher up the production hierarchy are greater authorities for such stylistic conventions.

Each of the primary production personnel at *The Young and the Restless*—the writer, producer, director, lighting director, art director, costume coordinator, and music coordinator—has a certain degree of autonomy in his or her job. However, the degree of autonomy is not the same for all these production personnel.

The subordinate directors—the lighting director, art director, costume coordinator, and music coordinator—are each responsible for a separate stylistic element in the show. Each of these subordinate directors is aware of the other stylistic elements in the show—the overall *The Young and the Restless* "look"—and consult with each other daily. The costume coordinator explained: "You have to work with the art director. You have to work with the lights. You know the whole situation that you work in is not a department here and a department there. There has to be an ensemble of that. You have to work together." In addition to consulting with each other, all the subordinate directors seek out and receive instruction and criticism from both the producer and director of the show.

The director of *The Young and the Restless* is the one person who stays with the production throughout the one-day production process. The director has the most control over coordinating the technical elements involved in the production and recording of the show. However, the director is also aware of the collective nature of the production:

The director has the final say. It has to be. You can't direct by committee. You can't have five people telling an actor how to play a scene. . . . I suppose in the end the director has the most control because he decides on the shot, he decides on how much of the set he's going to show, whether it's going to be a tight intimate scene. Overall, it's a team effort.

By making the various decisions about visualization and direction, the director is able to control not only the more technical elements involved with recording the show, but also important stylistic elements as well. However, the director's direct control over style is limited to the elements of visualization and direction. Although the director sometimes requests changes in the other stylistic elements within the show, for the most part, the director has little direct control over lighting, sets, costumes, and the sound in the show.

The extreme time restrictions involved in producing an episode of *The Young and the Restless* are a major factor in reducing the director's control over the show. The rapid production timetable forces the director to relinquish more of his or her stylistic control to other crew members and to limit stylistic input to what can be accomplished in the time allowed. The show's director commented:

When I first started in television [in the 1950s], I had eight days of rehearsal for an hour show. Not on this show. One full day was in the studio without cameras, just with the actors in the sets with props. Then you spent most of your time with the actors . . . [now] you have to direct by shorthand.

In addition, because the director is not involved in the post-production process, again mainly due to a lack of time, the director has no control over the transitions placed between scenes. The post-production director makes those decisions with the producer's approval. Further, due to the rigors of the director's job, several individual directors alternate directing duties at *The Young and the Restless*. Despite the input of different people who sit in the director's chair, the overall style of *The Young and the Restless* is maintained from episode to episode. The director, though essential to a successful production, does not have a significant amount of control over all the individual decisions that contribute to the show. At *The Young and the Restless*, the director is actually subordinate to the producers.

Though they aren't always present in the control room throughout the entire production day, the producers are directly involved with the production of each program episode. Unlike the directors who are not present for the episodes they do not direct, the producers are present for each and every episode and do have a significant amount of input into the show.

The art director admitted that he often consults with the producer about set designs. He claimed that it was not unusual to build and modify several models for a set before the final design was chosen by the producer. The costume coordinator claimed that he consulted with the associate producer about most costume decisions. The lighting director agreed that he consulted with the producers about lighting design "quite a bit."

Although she claims the background music used in the show is primarily her decision, the music coordinator described how the producers may influence the use of background music: "If it gets to be a scene that really drags down and bogs down in the middle, then quite often I'll be asked to use music to try and pick it up so that people don't go to sleep while they're watching you." The producer, she says, is the person who generally requests additional background music in these situations.

Thus, it seems clear that the producers have a significant amount of input into the stylistic conventions of lighting, sets and costumes, and sound in *The Young and the Restless*. They also have some influence, though perhaps not as much, over the elements of visualization and direction, ordinarily the realm of the director. According to one director, if there is a disagreement between him and the producer over a directorial decision, the producer's point of view prevails roughly 50 percent of the time.

Although the producers do have some influence over the elements of lighting, sets and costumes, visualization, direction and sound, their influence is less active than *reactive*. The producers rarely initiate stylistic decisions. Rather, they react to the stylistic decisions by other production personnel. The producers' role is to ensure that the other production personnel follow the established stylistic conventions of the show. The producers have stylistic control in the form of veto power.

The producers do influence the style of *The Young and the Restless* in a number of ways, but actually, many of the producers' duties are managerial, more concerned with technical and financial matters than with aesthetic ones. In the case of *The Young and the Restless*, the producers' primary responsibilities are to handle the business details of the production company: hiring the crews, securing the production facilities, and administering the budget. Overall, the producers are there to ensure that the production operation runs smoothly, and on time.

In addition, the influence of an individual producer at *The Young and the Restless* is further diffused because more than one person is responsible for producing the show. Cantor (1980) pointed out that the producer of most prime-time television programs "is a salaried employee working for a program supplier, [and] he or she does not have complete control" (p. 84). This is true as well for the producers of *The Young and the Restless*. The producers do have veto power over the lighting director, the art director, the costume coordinator, and the music coordinator, and even at times the director. But the producer merely defends and maintains the stylistic conventions established by another member of the production collective. And the producers are accountable to that member as well: the headwriter.

Unlike feature films where the director usually establishes and maintains stylistic conventions, and unlike prime-time filmed television programs where the producer often fill this role, at *The Young and the Restless* the headwriter has the ultimate authority over stylistic decisions. The headwriter/creator of the program established the stylistic contentions in the first place and organized the production hierarchy in such a way as to maintain control over the elements.

Virtually every stylistic decision made at *The Young and the Restless* begins and ends with the script. One of the most obvious features throughout the production process of *The Young and the Restless* is the blue three-ring binder everyone carries which holds the script for the day. Descriptions of sets, costumes, and even direction (when to use a close-up, for instance) are written into the script. But besides influencing stylistic decisions through script descriptions, the writer also makes direct requests through the producer.

The production collective members seem acutely aware of the writer's influence. With reference to the degree of autonomy in his job, the costume coordinator claimed he was free to make his own decisions, "unless the script, unless the writer in Chicago calls for a definite thing." The art director conceded that ultimately all set "descriptions come from Chicago." One director commented on the status of the script in relation to his directorial duties: "It's the actor's face up there and it's the author's words and you're just trying to find the best way to tell the story with those two major elements."

The high degree of influence over the production of *The Young and the Restless* exercised by the headwriter is seldom equaled in other types of television programs where the producer, director, and even the actors frequently rewrite portions of the script. Besides the inability to alter existing scripts, the production personnel are rarely able to make suggestions to the writer. The show's director commented: "That's impossible on this show because the writers are in Chicago and we never see them—maybe once a year. And they're in the middle of writing something two weeks hence." At *The Young and the Restless*, there is very little, if any, variation from the written script.

The control wielded by the writer of *The Young and the Restless* is especially noteworthy because the writer works in Chicago, over 2,000 miles away from Hollywood where the show is produced. The headwriter's strong influence is the result of two factors. First, there is little, if any, time available to make suggestions to the writer or to make major changes in the script. (There is barely enough time to produce the script as written.) Second, the headwriter of *The Young and the Restless* is the cocreator of the show. The headwriter established the show's style and has overseen the production of the show since its inception. It is primarily this position of *continuous* familiarity and control which enables the headwriter to influence *The Young and the Restless* so overwhelmingly. The headwriter not only has control over story development and casting, but also sees that the stylistic conventions he established for the show are maintained. The headwriter does this directly through scripted descriptions and indirectly through his daily communication with the producer of the show. The headwriter's success with *The Young and the Restless* in terms of ratings, ensures that his position of power will be maintained.

## DISCUSSION

The production of *The Young and the Restless* involves the coordination of a myriad of different roles and functions. The lighting director, costume coordinator, art director, music coordinator, director, producers, and headwriter make numerous production decisions each day that affect the final production product. Unlike feature film productions and some prime-time television productions, *The*

*Young and the Restless* is produced under very severe time constraints. In film and prime-time television production, consistency and quality are maintained by the direct input and attention of one individual. At *The Young and the Restless* production decisions are delegated to many production personnel. These production personnel have a moderate level of autonomy in their jobs. There is no time for one individual to directly contribute to and oversee each and every minute production decision.

Nevertheless, at *The Young and the Restless* two interrelated coordinating mechanisms help to integrate the separate activities of the various production personnel. The two primary coordinating mechanisms are stylistic conventions and organizational constraints.

Stylistic conventions are rules about the ultimate look or sound of the program. These stylistic conventions are formally enunciated by the program's creator in the show's "bible" prior to the production of the show. Over time, these conventions become internalized by the production personnel involved in the program. The conventions are defended and maintained by those higher up on the production hierarchy—especially the show's producers. Stylistic conventions are an important part of the "social knowledge" of the production organization members. The production organization members recognize these conventions as "the right way to do their job."

Stylistic conventions are enforced by organizational constraints (particularly specialization and chains of command) built into the structure of *The Young and the Restless* organization. Decisions made at the lower end of the production hierarchy (subordinate directors) are monitored and occasionally vetoed by members higher up the production hierarchy (producer and headwriter). A behavioral mechanism, a full-dress rehearsal before every taping session, ensures that all production decisions can be monitored by the producer. Dress rehearsal is followed by a "notes" session, during which changes are incorporated into the production. The goal of *The Young and the Restless* organization is to properly interpret the headwriter's script and to maintain consistency with the headwriter's established style for the show. The producer fulfills a liaison role between the headwriter and other production personnel. The daily communication between the headwriter and producer is a means by which to accomplish "proper interpretation."

The veto of production decisions has a direct effect on the final product of *The Young and the Restless* organization. But the threat of veto has a much more subtle effect as well. Lower level production personnel, in an effort to avoid having their decisions challenged, pay careful attention to the implicit and explicit stylistic conventions. Lower level production personnel try to make decisions that will be consonant with the existing set of conventions. Suggestions and criticism from higher up the production hierarchy are less frequent once the stylistic conventions are internalized and routinely followed by all production personnel. At *The Young and the Restless*, stylistic conventions have been established to coordinate separate production decisions into a unified coherent style for the entire program. Organizational constraints have been established to ensure that these stylistic conventions are adhered to.

For the sake of brevity, only two coordinating mechanisms—stylistic conventions and organizational constraints—were discussed in this chapter. Additional coordinating mechanisms no doubt operate in *The Young and the Restless* organization. Further examination might include the issues of business/corporate constraints or conventions, regulatory constraints or conventions, and audience-based mechanisms (such as ratings and other feedback). Nevertheless, the stylistic and organizational mechanisms discussed here increase our understanding of the collective activity involved in the production of an episode of *The Young and the Restless*.

Although the coordinating mechanisms described here have been related specifically to the production process and organization of *The Young and the Restless*, they may be applicable to other production organizations as well. An extremely fruitful future research endeavor would be to identify several more general coordinating mechanisms which apply to a broader range of different types of television programs.

In any event, this discussion illustrates the utility of using an interpretively based perspective from which to study television production. Studying *The Young and the Restless* from the usual positivist perspective would most likely lead to the conclusion that the headwriter of the program exhibited the most control over program content. Although this is no doubt the case, such a knowledge claim does not really tell us much about how this control is manifested. Looking at television production from the perspective of collective activity—looking for cooperative links—permits a richer understanding of not only how television production "gets done" at *The Young and the Restless*, but also permits a better understanding of how television production "gets done" in general.

## NOTES

1. The examples used in this chapter were collected during a one-week observation of the production of the daytime serial, *The Young and the Restless*, June 1980.

2. Unless otherwise specified, all direct quotations from production personnel at *The Young and the Restless* are taken from transcripts of tape-recorded interviews conducted during the observation period.

## REFERENCES

Barbatsis, G. S. 1981. Television theory development: The contribution of production research. Paper presented at the annual meeting of the Speech Communication Association, Anaheim, CA.

Becker, H. S. 1974. Art as collective action. *American Sociological Review* 39: 767–76.

———. 1982. *Art worlds*. Berkeley, CA: University of California Press.

Cantor, M. G. 1971. *The Hollywood TV producer: His work and his audience*. New York: Basic Books.

——. 1980. *Primetime television: Content and control*. Beverly Hills, CA: Sage.

Elliott, P. 1979. *The making of a television series*. Beverly Hills, CA: Sage.

Ettema, J. S. 1982. The organizational context of creativity: A case study from public television. In J. S. Ettema and D. C. Whitney, eds., *Individuals in mass media organizations*. Beverly Hills, CA: Sage.

Gilbert, A. 1979. *All my afternoons*. New York: A & W Visual Library.

Lynch, J. E. 1973. Seven days with "All in the Family": Case study of the taped TV drama. *Journal of Broadcasting* 17: 259–74.

Newcomb, H. 1974. *TV: The most popular art*. Garden City, NY: Anchor Press.

Pekurny, R. 1980. The production process and environment of NBC's "Saturday Night Live." *Journal of Broadcasting* 24: 91–99.

Ravage, J. W. 1978. *Television: The director's viewpoint*. Boulder, CO: Westview Press.

Stein, B. 1979. *The view from Sunset Boulevard*. New York: Basic Books.

Turow, J. 1982. Unconventional programs on commercial television: An organizational perspective. In J. S. Ettema and D. C. Whitney, eds., *Individuals in mass media organizations*. Beverly Hills, CA: Sage.

# 13

# Authorship and Point-of-View Issues in Music Video

*Gary Burns*

Among all the arts, music video raises some of the most interesting issues in the analysis of authorship. For the most part, music video is a form in which authorship ambiguity prevails. By this I mean that it is often very difficult to tell "whose" video one is watching. This is important because one of the best ways to understand the arts is to examine works grouped according to who created them—the plays of Shakespeare, the films of Bergman, etc. Although auteurism certainly has its deficiencies,[1] it nonetheless seems that one leaves out something very important if, in discussing a music video clip or group of clips, one does not devote some attention to who created the clip(s).

The problem is that each clip is a collaborative effort, but ordinarily the viewer learns the identity only of the recording artist and record company.[2] This is "whose" work the video is, according to the music industry gatekeepers.

In keeping with music video's economic purpose to sell records and promote musicians' careers, graphics identify the song, album, and band. If the song is from a movie, it becomes necessary to name the movie also[3] (although not the director, even though the video often includes footage from the film). Naming the record company serves, it would seem, as a form of institutional advertising. "Behind-the-scenes" personnel (as well as video performers other than the recording artist) remain anonymous, since identifying them would not, in most cases, cause increased record sales.

But is music video really a "musician's medium"? Based on available evidence, which is skimpy, the answer is no. Generally speaking, musicians do not know how to make videos. This may eventually change, just as many musicians broadened their domain to include songwriting and record producing beginning in the 1960s. But for the time being, the situation in music video seems to be that most musicians (and, of course, their managers and other handlers) merely cultivate some visual or conceptual image, which often (but not always) will have some bearing on the content of their videos—just as a film star will try to maintain a certain image by appearing in some films and not others.

But film, according to conventional wisdom, is a "director's medium," not an "actor's medium." A film star's decision whether to appear in a film is based on the film's script—and very few movie stars write their own screenplays (film is not a "writer's medium" either). Actors interested in gaining more creative control over their films generally gravitate toward directing (e.g., Clint Eastwood). Similarly, screenwriters often become directors, either because they are tired of the abuse (as they see it) their scripts receive at the hands of other directors, or because directing was what they wanted to do in the first place.

By contrast, relatively few musicians seem to have much interest in their videos beyond a general concern with image and, naturally, intimate involvement with the recording that provides the soundtrack for the video. Some musicians (e.g., Joe Jackson, Bob Seger) resisted video in the early 1980s when MTV was becoming a major marketing outlet for the music industry in the United States.[4] Even though making videos is now almost obligatory in order to achieve and maintain stardom, some musicians still resent the necessity of spending their time on an essentially nonmusical activity that they do not enjoy or understand. Similarly, the band Journey reportedly turned away from video in 1986 in order to avoid "[putting] themselves at the mercy of some video director who's going to put a concept to their songs that could be very short-lived while the songs could be timeless."[5]

In addition, video heightens the music industry's tendency to market individual singers rather than whole bands. Thus many videos that ostensibly promote bands contain little footage of any band member other than the singer. The prevailing view of television as a "close-up medium" discourages group shots, while any attempt to tell a story generally requires a protagonist—almost always the singer. Video can, in a sense, redefine a band as a lead singer plus backup musicians. In doing so, it also redefines authorship of the *record* in favor of the singer, at the expense of the rest of the band.

Still, the case for the musician as video auteur is weak.[6] The best one can do in building such a case is to note certain exceptions to the general trend. Kevin Godley and Lol Creme, for example, are former members of 10cc who became successful video directors. Devo member Gerald Casale has codirected Devo videos. Tony Basil, David Byrne, Eurythmics, and Thomas Dolby are other recording artists who have directed videos. Certain musicians consistently appear in interesting videos (Duran Duran, Peter Gabriel, David Bowie) and seem to be both cinematically astute and highly involved in the creation of their videos. Some musicians have worked often enough with specific collaborators or in a certain style that their videos seem to constitute a "body of work" (more so to the extent that the sound recordings on which the videos are based display some coherence). Possible examples include Madonna and Michael Jackson.

Since every video springs from a record, it is tempting to follow music industry logic and conclude that the recording artist is author of the video by virtue of being author of the sound recording. There are problems with this reasoning, in connection with both the sound recording and the video.

Arguably, a song's author is the songwriter, and a recording's author is the record producer. These people would then have some claim to the authorship of the video as well—but neither is named on screen (and credit on the record is given only in fine print).

Correlatively, whoever "writes" the video should receive some consideration as an author. Here another problem arises in that music video "writing" consists of prescribing images to accompany a soundtrack that someone else has written. The format for video writing is usually a storyboard or treatment. Who does this writing? Often not a writer in the usual sense, but the director, possibly assisted by a graphic artist in the case of a storyboard.[7]

Thus the case for the director as music video author is strong. It is the music video director who has principal control of everything that is added to the preexisting recorded sound text. The video production industry (as a separate entity from the music industry) treats the director as author. Some video directors have gained relative notoriety (e.g., Julien Temple) and have graduated to feature films, where the director is even more clearly established as the author.[8] Some of the earliest serious studies of music video included reviews of work by specific directors.[9]

One of the main problems in viewing music video as an art form, either actual or potential, is that it is a mystery who directed which video. Without knowing who directed what, it is likewise impossible to engage such questions as who makes the best videos, and why. Industry insiders know who directed what, but for anyone else the information is hard to come by. The trade journal *Film & Video* (formerly called *Film & Video Production* and before that, *Optic Music*) is a reliable source for music video production credits, but this journal is expensive to subscribe to, not readily available on newsstands or in libraries, especially inaccessible in back issues, and largely unknown to the researchers and critics who might find it useful.[10]

The problems attendant to authorship research in any of the electronic media are particularly troublesome in music video research. Assuming one reaches some decision as to "whose" medium music video is, and sets out to research the videos of a specific "author," the first problem is to find out what videos the author has made. This can be difficult even when the "author" is a recording artist. Useful reference works exist,[11] but published sources will in most cases provide an incomplete list. Compiling a list of the videos of a particular director is even more problematic.

Assuming one manages to list a recording artist's or director's entire video output, the next problem is how to get access to all the videos in order to study them. Some videos are available on videocassette for purchase or rental, but most are not (and those that are, are usually grouped according to recording artist, not director). Some videos can be taped from MTV or other channels, but only a fraction of the videos produced ever make it onto these channels. The time at which a video will be played on MTV is not announced in *TV Guide*, and seldom promoted in advance on the network itself. Taping at the right time is mostly a matter of luck. Old videos other than major hits are seldom if ever shown. Comprehensive studies of specific video authors, if and when they occur, will probably have to rely on the cooperation of musicians, directors, and record companies—who may or may not be willing or able to give it.

The logistical problems associated with authorship studies of music video make it unlikely that many such studies will take place. Even if they do, the researchers who undertake them will be writing for an audience that has even less access to the videos in question. For these reasons, studies of music video will probably continue to be based on whatever videos the researcher happens to have seen. Thus there will be many studies of individual videos (especially those most readily available—i.e., the recent and the often-shown), occasional genre studies, and many philosophical discussions about the general nature of music video.

Even though these studies will seldom focus on the collected video works of somebody-or-other, still, concern with authorship, as well as with related matters such as narrative attribution, point of view, and star images, will be necessary in order to understand, even in a rudimentary way, how some of the more complicated videos do their work. To demonstrate this, I would like to discuss briefly one of the more interesting videos released in the past few years.

*Don't Come Around Here No More* is a rather notorious video that accompanied the 1985 hit record by Tom Petty and the Heartbreakers. The song was written by Tom Petty and David A Stewart. The recording was produced by Tom Petty, David A. Stewart, and Jimmy Iovine. The video was directed by Jeff Stein. An article in the trade journal *On Location* describes the production of the video (and attributes the concept primarily to Stein), and at least two academic articles and one book contain critical analysis of the video.[12]

The video opens with a woman in her twenties, but dressed to look much younger, wandering through a field of giant mushrooms. We soon realize she is Alice in Wonderland. She climbs a stairway of mushrooms and accepts something to eat (apparently a bite of mushroom) from David Stewart, who sits atop the tallest mushroom, smoking a hookah (like the caterpillar in the Alice stories). The mushroom Alice ingests causes her to fall backward down the stairway. Apparently the rest of the video is her hallucination, suggesting that the mushroom contained some sort of drug. The Alice in Wonderland motif continues, with Tom Petty, dressed as the Mad Hatter, lip-syncing lyrics that express his negative feelings toward the woman. A nightmarish tea party takes place, concluding with Alice turning into a cake that is eaten by Petty and his party guests (played by the Heartbreakers and backup singers).

The video raises several issues pertaining to authorship and related subjects. The source "author" is Lewis Carroll (along with John Tenniel, the illustrator who drew the pictures most often used in Alice in Wonderland books), but much of the action in the video (the cannibalism, for example) has no basis in either *Alice's Adventures in Wonderland* or *Through the Looking-Glass*. Carroll's principal "contribution" is to provide a prestigious literary context in which bizarre events are somewhat believable and acceptable.[13]

A less obvious source serving a similar function is the song "White Rabbit," written by Grace Slick and recorded by Jefferson Airplane. This song, a big hit in 1967, combined an Alice motif with explicit drug imagery, partially substituting pills for mushrooms and retaining the "hookah-smoking caterpillar" from Carroll. The Slick lyric "Go ask Alice" became the title of a 1972 TV movie about a drug-abusing high school student. *Don't Come Around Here No More* thus draws its drug implications more from Slick (as reinforced by the TV movie) than from Carroll's stories, which, despite Alice eating and drinking numerous substances with curious results, suggest dreaming (rather than drugs) as the ultimate cause of Alice's strange visions.

Of course, Lewis Carroll and Grace Slick are not the creators of *Don't Come Around Here No More*, but their ideas are visible on the screen, albeit refracted by Tom Petty, MCA Records, and numerous unnamed collaborators. One of these unnamed people is David Stewart. Stewart's presence and role are interesting for several reasons.

First, Stewart is the coauthor of the song, and he played sitar on the recording. Therefore both the song and record are partially "his." Despite this, the conventions of music video do not in any way "require" his presence on the screen. The fact that he is visible suggests (whether accurately or not) that he had a significant role in creating the video. Just how significant is an empirical question, but this issue is actually less interesting than that of how the viewer might use assumptions about Stewart's possible authorship in interpreting the video.

At one extreme, a viewer with no knowledge about David Stewart might assume that the person on top of the mushroom is an actor of no particular importance. At the other extreme, a viewer might recognize Stewart, know that he helped write the song, know that he played sitar on the record, know that he is Annie Lennox's partner in Eurythmics, and know that Lennox has an androgynous or feminist image. A viewer who knows all these things is likely to consider Stewart an important collaborator on the video and may ask two questions that make the video's interpretation even more difficult then before: First, how does this video, which includes the devouring of a woman, square with Lennox's/Eurythmics' androgynous/feminist image?[14] Second, what is the significance of the fact that it is Stewart, portraying an apparent drug user and supplier, who gives Alice the substance that causes her hallucination?

Ultimately, Stewart serves, like Carroll and Slick, as a legitimizer. Some viewers will recognize him as a Eurythmic and a pioneer in music video. Few, if any, will have a preconceived, negative view of him as antifeminist. His presence invokes, for the "competent" viewer, the memory of other texts— Eurythmics' records and videos. These, together with Carroll's stories and "White Rabbit," bask in each other's hip aura and envelop *Don't Come Around Here No More* in subliminal ethos.

This type of ethos occurs in many videos and governs not only the video per se but also the supposedly subjective visions contained in many of them. These include dreams, hallucinations, fantasies, mediated images, and other forms. As I have argued elsewhere, there are formalistic reasons for the widespread use of these devices in music video.[15] Formalism aside, the suggestion of subjectivity introduces the question, "whose subjectivity?" This is sometimes a more troublesome question than one might expect.

In *Don't Come Around Here No More*, the hallucination is apparently Alice's. But since it is Stewart the performer who gives her the mushroom that sends her reeling, there is some implication that what we see is what he wants to happen to her. This leads back to questions about Stewart the author's attitude toward women.

Similarly, the hallucination (and possibly our view of Stewart as well) must be somehow attributable to Tom Petty, whose name is attached to the video. To some extent, presumably a great extent, Alice sees what Petty wants her to see. This is plain not only from the fact that Petty made the video, but also from certain cinematic techniques suggesting that Alice, and therefore the audience also, is seeing through the Mad Hatter's eyes. Numerous match cut subjective camera shots of Alice and Petty looking at each other imply a metaphorical, and therefore psychological, identity of the two individuals.

A similar effect results when Alice sees, in a subjective camera shot, a live video image of herself in Petty's magical eyeglasses. Alice, along with the audience, sees herself as Petty sees her. Similarly, Alice later peers into a baby carriage and sees herself inside it, as half baby, half pig.[16] We see through her eyes in this shot, and apparently through Petty's in the next, which is a shot of Alice, recoiling in shock at what she has seen and looking beseechingly at the camera/viewer/Petty. The video implies that the repulsive image in the baby carriage is what Petty wants her to see.

Students who watch the video with me usually have trouble making sense of its layers of possible attribution. Many students think the video is "sick," but do not know exactly why. When I point out Petty's cannibalism, which many students do not initially recognize as such, the students often defend the video (even though it is "sick"), on two grounds.

First, the video does not really show cannibalism. The characters eat cake, not actual human flesh (and the visual emphasis is on the cake being carved, not on the eating).[17] By this reasoning, eating Alice is no more objectionable than a magician's trick of sawing a woman in half. The literal triumphs over the symbolic, in a manner opposite that of Holy Communion. Alice's depiction as cake is "humorous" and possibly ironic, especially to the extent that the viewer buys into the aforementioned hip ethos.[18] This conclusion vindicates and even congratulates the authors, whoever they are.

Second, the bad things that happen to Alice are, after all, her own hallucination. She does not really turn into a cake—it is only a bad dream. Many students seem quite willing to let it go at that.

At this surface level of interpretation, authorship is effaced and accountability is nonexistent. The misogynistic meaning of the video's storyline is easily overlooked because the video's violence is symbolically displaced and presented as Alice's mental creation.

Looking at it this way, as many students do, Alice, even though she is only a character, is in effect the author. Petty lip-syncs the lyrics and is somewhat analogous to a narrator or storyteller, only the lyrics do not tell a story. The story is supplied by the visuals and attributed to Alice the hallucinator. If Alice suffers, it is her own fault. If we accept this premise, we are in effect blaming the victim of the cannibalism. Misogyny becomes a figment of the female's imagination, and Petty and Stewart can be seen as innocent bystanders.

To relate these matters to more traditional authorship concerns would require something I am not prepared to undertake—a comprehensive review of the videos (and other work) of Tom Petty, director Jeff Stein, and possibly others. Based on the few videos I am familiar with by Petty and Stein, it seems that Stein is the individual whose "personal stamp" most shapes *Don't Come Around Here No More*.[19] This is supported by the article in *On Location* and by a similar article in *New York* magazine about Stein's direction of *My New Boyfriend*, based on the Carly Simon recording. The *New York* article reports that "The National Coalition on Television Violence denounced [*Don't Come Around Here No More*] as 'sexually sadistic'—which Stein takes as a compliment: 'Why settle for bringing back paisley,' he says of the pseudo-psychedelic clip, 'when you can bring back *cannibalism*?' "[20] Cannibalism is also implied in *My New Boyfriend* as a man is boiled alive in a large pot in a "humorous" parody of jungle movies.[21]

In addition, Stein directed *You Might Think*, from a record by the Cars. This prize-winning video, like *Don't Come Around Here No More*, is more misogynistic than most and features a man terrorizing a woman.[22]

An interesting problem arises here if we return to the issue of accountability. A viewer who perceives and objects to misogyny in *Don't Come Around Here No More* and *You Might Think* will most likely "blame" Tom Petty and the Cars, rather than Jeff Stein—since it is not common knowledge that Stein directed both videos. If it is true that Stein is the best candidate for "author" of both videos, it means that Petty and the Cars are, to an extent, carriers of Stein's message, which, in each case, goes far beyond any misogynistic meaning inherent in the lyrics, music, and recording.

Herbert Gans has argued that popular culture audiences are generally more interested in performers than in writers (whereas with high culture audiences, the opposite is true).[23] Possibly these contrasting patterns of interest would arise spontaneously from audiences, but it is nonetheless true that the mass culture industries generally encourage their audiences to ignore authorship. In music video, this occurs through the on-screen identification of performers but not writers, producers, and directors; through use of cinematic techniques that provide ambiguous information about narrative attribution; and through the performer-centered style of presentation that dominates MTV and other major distributors of music video. (On MTV, VJs and the network itself are identified frequently; writers, directors, programmers, and other major behind-the-scenes "authors" of the MTV format are seldom if ever identified.)

Music video is here to stay, whether one likes it or not. Although the novelty has largely worn off, the economic and aesthetic effects of music video remain highly visible and controversial. Critical scrutiny of the people who create videos is overdue, not only for the sake of aesthetic understanding, but also so that people outside the industry may intelligently debate the issue, who is making admirable videos, who is not, and according to whose standards.

## NOTES

1. For critical perspectives on the auteur approach in film studies, see *Theories of Authorship: A Reader*, ed. John Caughie (London: Routledge & Kegan Paul, in association with the British Film Institute, 1981). See also the last chapter of Kaja Silverman, *The Acoustic Mirror: The Female Voice in Psychoanalysis and Cinema* (Bloomington: Indiana University Press, 1988), pp. 187–234.

2. The now-defunct program *Night Flight*, on the USA network, often identified the director. Most other networks, including MTV, do not. Directorial and other credits usually do appear on videocassette compilations of music videos.

3. See Becky Sue Epstein, "Music Video—The Hot New Way to Sell Hot New Movies," *Boxoffice*, July 1984, pp. 12–13, 16–17.

4. See Christopher Connelly, "Why Joe Jackson Said No to Rock Video," *Rolling Stone*, August 30, 1984, p. 32; and Steven Levy, "Ad Nauseam: How MTV Sells Out Rock & Roll," *Rolling Stone*, December 8, 1983, pp. 30–37, 74–79, esp. p. 79.

5. Herbie Herbert, manager of Journey, quoted in Anthony DeCurtis, "Stars Reject Videos," *Rolling Stone*, June 5, 1986, p. 11.

6. For a contrasting view, see Lisa A. Lewis, "Form and Female Authorship in Music Video," *Communication* 9 (1987), 355–77. For a brief discussion of related issues, see David Tafler, "The Economics of Renewal: Music Video and the Future of Alternative Filmmaking," *Afterimage*, September 1986, pp. 10–11; and Sally Stockbridge, "Whose Videos?" *Cinema Papers*, November 1985, pp. 30–32.

7. For a description of how the process usually works, see Michael Shore, *The Rolling Stone Book of Rock Video* (New York: Quill, 1984), pp. 147–81.

8. There has also been traffic in the opposite direction (John Landis, Brian De Palma, Francis Ford Coppola) and to and from the directing of TV commercials (Bob Giraldi, Tim Newman). See Richard Grenier, "Rock Videos Drawing Film Stars and Directors," *New York Times*, August 26, 1985, p. C14.

9. Shore, *The Rolling Stone Book of Rock Video*, pp. 114–46; Arlene Zeichner, "Video Auteurs," *Film Comment*, July-August 1983, pp. 42–45; Arlene Zeichner, "Encyclo-Video," *Film Comment*, July-August 1983, pp. 46–47; and Elliot Schulman, profile of Bob Giraldi, *Film Comment*, July-August 1983, p. 48.

10. It is available from Optic Music, Inc., 8170 Beverly Blvd., Suite 208, Los Angeles, CA 90048–4513. *Billboard* also publishes video credits, but they are less complete than those in *Film & Video*.

11. *Film & Video* magazine; Shore, *The Rolling Stone Book of Rock Video*; Michael Shore, *Music Video: A Consumer's Guide*, ed. Patricia Romanowski (New York: Ballantine Books, 1987); John Chu and Elliot Cafritz, *The Music Video Guide* (New York: McGraw-Hill Book Company, 1986); and *Who's Who in Rock Video*, executive editor Maxim Jakubowski, text by John Tobler (London: Zomba Books, 1983).

12. "Mad Hatter 'Comes Around' for Petty," *On Location*, May 1985, pp. 192–93; Gary Burns, "Dreams and Mediation in Music Video," *Wide Angle*, 10, no. 2 (1988), 41–61; Marsha Kinder, "Phallic Film and the Boob Tube: The Power of Gender Identification in Cinema, Television, and Music Video," *One Two Three Four*, no. 5 (Spring 1987), 33–49; and E. Ann Kaplan, *Rocking Around the Clock: Music Television, Postmodernism, and Consumer Culture* (New York: Methuen, 1987), pp. 141–42. Kaplan's book also deals interestingly with certain authorship issues in an analysis of the Madonna video *Material Girl*, pp. 116–27.

13. An additional source is artist M. C. Escher, whose distorted perspectives influenced the set design. See "Mad Hatter 'Comes Around' for Petty."

14. On Eurythmics' image, see Frank W. Oglesbee, "Eurythmics: An Alternative to Sexism in Music Videos," *Popular Music and Society*, 11, no. 2 (1987), 53–64.

15. Burns, "Dreams and Mediation in Music Video."

16. A similar episode occurs in *Alice's Adventures in Wonderland*, except that the baby is male and is held by Alice in her arms—and there is no implication of Alice seeing herself as a baby or pig.

17. A somewhat similar occurrence takes place near the end of *Through the Looking-Glass*, when Alice slices into a pudding, whereupon the pudding says, "What impertinence! I wonder how you'd like it, if I were to cut a slice out of *you*, you creature!" The incident ends there.

18. Humorous or ironic intent is often used as a justification for sleazy content in rock music and videos. For a sarcastic refutation of this excuse, see S. A. Urgente, "Simple, Modest, Manly, True," *One Two Three Four*, no. 6 (Summer 1988), 80–81.

19. Stein's other work as director includes the feature film *The Kids Are Alright* (starring the Who), the video documentaries *Pack Up the Plantation Live!* (starring Tom Petty), and *30th Anniversary Rock and Roll Tribute* (starring Chuck Berry and Bo Diddley), and videos to accompany the following records (as reported in available issues of *Film & Video, Film & Video Production*, and *Optic Music*):

Gregg Allman: "Can't Keep Runnin' "

Gregg Allman Band: "I'm No Angel"

Breakfast Club: "Kiss and Tell," "Right on Track"

Cars: "Tonight She Comes"

Gene Loves Jezebel: "Desire"

Daryl Hall and John Oates: "Out of Touch," "Method of Modern Love"

Heart: "These Dreams"

Billy Idol: "Rebel Yell"

Jacksons: "Torture"

Little Steven: "Out of the Darkness"

Robbie Nevil: "Wot's It to You"

Tom Petty and the Heartbreakers: "Rebels," "So You Want to Be a Rock 'n' Roll Star," "Make It Better"

Quiet Riot, "The Wild and the Young"

Vinnie Vincent Invasion: "Boyz Are Gonna Rock"

John Waite: "These Times Are Hard for Lovers"

plus the Cars and Carly Simon videos mentioned later in the text.

20. Eric Pooley, "The Video That Devoured Menemsha," *New York*, August 26, 1985, pp. 56–60, quote on p. 58, emphasis in original.

21. Ibid., pp. 59–60.

22. Interestingly, this video was reportedly the subject of an authorship dispute between Stein and the video production company Charlex, which wanted to share director's "credit" with Stein. The arbiter of this dispute was Elektra Records, which ruled in favor of Charlex. Thus record companies have considerable power in determining how music video authorship is defined and negotiated. See ibid., p. 59.

23. Herbert J. Gans, "Popular Culture in America: Social Problem in a Mass Society or Social Asset in a Pluralist Society?" in *Social Problems: A Modern Approach*, ed. Howard S. Becker (New York: John Wiley & Sons, 1966), pp. 549–620, esp. pp. 584 ff. I am greatly simplifying Gans's argument and categories, which he develops over several pages.

# 14

# The Comic and Artistic Vision of Lorne Michaels and the Production of Unconventional Television

*George M. Plasketes*

When former network executive/programming pioneer Pat Weaver was honored at the 1983 Emmy Awards ceremony, he emphasized the need for television to "return to 'pure television' and innovative programming—and lots of it." Weaver insisted that comedy particularly should be more spontaneous and return to its roots in live TV. Although few individuals in television's history have pursued alternative formats for the comedy show, occasionally someone emerges with a fresh, artistic approach to the medium and a unique, personal comic vision. Among the examples of innovators were Ernie Kovacs with his visual bag of tricks, Uncle Miltie's "good clean dirt," Sid Caesar's *Your Show of Shows*, and Steve Allen during TV's infancy in the 1950s; Tom and Dick Smothers' controversial comedy and George Schlatter's rapid-fire editing kaleidoscope, *Rowan and Martin's Laugh-In*, during the 1960s. Recently the contributions have been primarily after-hour, north of the border imports—the Canadian *SCTV Network* and Toronto native Lorne Michaels's creations *Saturday Night Live* and *The New Show*. These shows used both unconventional themes and forms as they probed attitudes and involved audiences in unpredictability.

But the line between "unconventional" and "innovative" is unclear. Both terms are used interchangeably when discussing new products. A definition of innovation common among sociologists of organizations is "the implementation of a new idea, product, or service."[1] With other Western societies, our culture usually glamorizes the innovative, unconventional, daring, and nontraditional. The almost daily claims of "unique," "special," and "new and improved" have become cultural catchphrases. Because "new" has so many meanings, literature on innovation often suggests the value of differentiating between the development of novel products along a continuum. At one end are the "conventional innovations''—products recognized as essentially derivative of those currently available. On the other end lie products which are strong departures from accepted approaches; these are the "unconventional innovations.''[2]

Within television, as with the other popular arts industries, several conditions and circumstances foster or hinder the inception, development, distribution, and success or failure of an unconventional product.[3] Many of these factors form a complex web of relationships—individual, sociocultural, historical, and organizational—and are relevant when examining authorship within contrasting environments of television's late-night fringe hours and prime time. One case that offers perspective within such a context involves comic architect Lorne Michaels. By examining Michaels's late-night triumph *Saturday Night Live* and his ill-fated 1984 prime-time effort, *The New Show*, the results shed light on the television creator, meaning in unconventional programming, and the creative, comic, and production processes.

## *SATURDAY NIGHT LIVE:* FRINGE BENEFITS

The date could not have been more appropriate: April 1, 1975. For years, Lorne Michaels had traversed the Canadian-American border, "paying dues" writing, directing, producing, and sometimes performing for CBC-TV and Radio, Woody Allen, Joan Rivers, *The Beautiful Phyllis Diller Show, Laugh-In*, Flip Wilson, and three Lily Tomlin specials. Finally he got the opportunity to put his personal artistic vision into television. On April Fool's Day Michaels signed a contract with NBC to develop a late-night comedy show. His creation eventually became a "TV institution" and had a significant impact on both comedy and television. That show—"Live! From New York"—was *Saturday Night Live (SNL)*.

Early in 1975, NBC President Herb Schlosser hoped to develop a series of pilots which might flower into a regular series for Saturday nights. *The Best of Carson* reruns that filled the 11:30 PM to 1 AM slot on Saturdays were stale, and the overexposure was weakening Johnny's regular weeknight show. Schlosser was looking for a show that might convince young people that television was worth watching on Saturday night. He wanted ratings, not a revolution.

Michaels felt he knew the ingredients for such a show, although he was not sure of the exact combination. He was interested in a production that was "frank and intelligent, for young urban adults.''[4] He also saw the show as an opportunity to mix a number of ideas, experiences, and values of his generation, a territory television had only mildly touched. Although the show he conceived included traditional elements of the comedy-variety show (a repertory company, musical guests, blackout sketches), Michaels sought a different style wherein writers would speak loudly and carry the performer's schtick. He envisioned a live, experimental show that combined various comedy styles with a sneak-into-the-studio look. In this free-for-all writers could express themselves unbound from the usual rituals of television production. The music would be that which was not being performed on TV. The show might also include a satirical news segment, like the BBC's *That Was the Week That Was*, as well as commercial parodies, short takes by young filmmakers, and a different host each week.

"I envisioned this show in which all these individual styles were gotten across as clearly as possible with me clearing the network and technological barricades," said Michaels. He began by negotiating with NBC for things he considered necessities. First, he did not want to do a pilot because he felt if NBC saw the show beforehand, they would say, "You can't do that on television." Nor did he want to provide a tape every week to be reviewed by the Broadcast Standards Department. Michaels was not looking for a total takeover, but for a "pirate operation." The first demand was partially accomplished simply by meeting the second requirement—the show was to be live. To Michaels, only a live format allowed for discovery and pure communication between writers, performers, and audience. The electricity of "anything can happen" was crucial and also represented an ideal countercultural situation. If, by chance, the show went "too far" and rattled the TV establishment, NBC could do nothing because there was no editing, only live TV. Finally, because of the risk involved and the unconventional nature of the show, Michaels wanted more development time and a period to cultivate an audience. He wanted a commitment for twenty shows, but settled for eighteen and six months development time.

A network's granting the demands of relatively young and unproven Michaels might seem unusual. Several factors, however, beyond Michaels's artistic vision worked in his favor and allowed him more freedom than might normally be permitted.

Most obviously Michaels was dealing with late-night television, not prime time, where the stakes and demands were much higher. The late-night weekend slot allowed for more freedom, not only in development time, but with content and the inherent risks of doing a live show. Late-night was also a suitable training ground for young talents. Steve Allen, Jack Paar, and others served apprenticeships there before graduating to prime-time slots.

Also significantly Michaels was working with NBC, not ABC or CBS. The other networks might have been more cautious about granting his freedom. NBC had always been a champion of late-night programming. Because of the success of Allen, Paar, and *The Tonight Show* since 1962 with Carson, NBC was firmly established in TV's fringe hours. When ABC and CBS surfaced in the after hours in 1969, their challengers, Dick Cavett and Merv Griffin, were no match for the mighty Carson.

As leader of the late-night pack, NBC could afford to take a risk and they had much to gain by developing Michaels's project. Replacing Carson's *Best of* reruns might strengthen his weeknight foothold. In addition, this approach allowed NBC to expand into Saturday's late-night period opposite movies on other networks. NBC had made its initial thrust into weekend late-night programming with *The Midnight Special*, a rock-variety package hosted by Wolfman Jack, which followed Carson on Friday nights.[5]

While NBC might have been the late-night leader, it continually lagged in the overall network ratings. The union of an unestablished producer with a network experiencing problems favors the development of an unconventional show.[6] NBC recognized that the show had enormous possibilities as well as many pitfalls. No live entertainment program had appeared on the network for nearly a decade. Nonetheless, executives believed Michaels was likely to draw the youthful audience they were targeting. He was not engaged in any other on-going production and was free to focus all his energies into nurturing the *SNL* project.

Michaels's relative anonymity could have easily worked against him. He did not have a "track record" that established him as a "safe" producer. By choosing people whom they consider, in some sense, "safe" producers of entertainment, the networks foster a rather severe limit on the range of experimentation they will accept even in their unconventional shows. The accepted rationale is simply that few people have the experience and know-how required to coordinate television and all its complications. Despite these strikes against Michaels, NBC was receptive to his ideas from the start. He recalled during a personal interview:

I wanted the show to be devoid of definition . . . not a comedy show, political show, or musical show. The mandate was to keep pushing it and finding new areas where it belonged in. I talked to NBC a lot about the show discovering itself on the air and that with comedy shows it was necessary to see what to emphasize, where the hit was. I think the brass at NBC were real open to it. Television executives are not morons. They are generally bright people who are caught in an economic approach.

Among the NBC executives, Dick Ebersol emerged as supporter for Michaels and his ideas. Michaels felt fortunate to have encountered an executive who shared his attitudes toward programming, including humor, resistance to TV's formulas, and an obsession with spontaneity. In large organizations like the networks, new executives may be likely to push for an unconventional show. Ebersol was relatively new as Vice-President of Late-Night Programming at NBC. He came to NBC via ABC, where he worked under the sports-minded wing of Roone Arledge. Ebersol is also younger than Michaels, which may explain in part his openness to the project. In addition, a young executive may be more willing to back an unconventional show with hopes of upward mobility in the corporate hierarchy because of the program's success. Ebersol's association with *SNL* did, in fact, gain him advances.[7]

## TALKIN 'BOUT MY GENERATION

An old show business adage, particularly among comedians, is "It's all in the timing." To link cause and effect in attempting to gauge whether a show will "hit" is difficult. Nonetheless, timing was another factor in Michaels favor, not only within television, but from a cultural and countercultural perspective as well.

To a certain degree, *SNL* is indebted to *Laugh-In* and *Monty Python's Flying Circus*, a hit in 1975 on PBS. Both shows featured a free association mixture of comic stylings. Their national successes may have paved the way for Michaels and contributed to an open-mindedness on the part of Schlosser and NBC.

Feeling that 30-year-olds were left out of television, Michaels wanted a show for and by the TV generation. This was also the demographic ideal of NBC— the young and urban. NBC knew from endless surveys that a huge audience— the 25 to 40-year olds—did not watch prime time and tended to stay at home on weekends. As one late *SNL* cast member put it, these people were even more likely to stay at home "if they had good dope contacts and a show to get high before, during, and after its airing; as high as the show's actors clearly are."[8]

Michaels saw *SNL* as being rooted distinctly in persistent 1960s values which reflected a life-style never aired on TV before. In February 1976, Michaels commented:

*Mary Tyler Moore* and *Rhoda* are the most up to date shows on the air now, but they are liberated Fifties. Until now, people have run TV the same way they ran radio. Our show is the first done by and for a generation that came of age in the Sixties.[9]

Michaels understood this generation because he was a part of it, even though as a Canadian he was somewhat of an outsider. Sharing the values and experiences of the time, he wanted to present that culture on TV. The remains of the counterculture desperately needed something to unite its increased fragmentation by the mid–1970s. Michaels hoped that *SNL*'s comedy, music, and consciousness could perform a role similar to the one that music had fulfilled earlier. Depending on its presentation, comedy, like music, was capable of analyzing, commenting upon, and even making sense of the dominant social order. Just as the music was liberating, Michaels's vision of *SNL* might serve the same purpose by offering alternative views of the culture and its institutions.

*SNL*'s challenge to the standard view was a direct result of Michaels, the cast, and the writers' shared comic sensibilities, which were shaped by the experience of growing up in the 1960s. Their humor was a reaction against the piety of the times. It was direct, honest, personal, irreverent, sexual, anarchistic, and iconoclastic. Even the name of the repertory group, "The Not Ready for Prime-Time Players," reflected the rebellious overtones and resistance to conventional TV. The very first show was also an indication that *SNL* resembled the counterculture in the 1970s. The undertones surfaced in a commercial parody which featured activist Jerry Rubin selling sixties' graffiti wallpaper, an exclusive offer, available only on TV's late-night fringe. No prime-time sponsors or even K-Tel could boast such a line of products.

But Michaels did not create the show as a reactionary vehicle carrying radical messages. Realizing that "times were a-changin' " he had larger artistic aims for his project. In light of the self-reflexive quality of television, Michaels felt the values that his generation had been most influenced by should be included in their humorous attacks. To Michaels, laughing at themselves was "different than Bob Hope laughing at us."

A large segment of Michaels's audience did not fall into the more structured demographic categories of shows like *Mary Tyler Moore, Rhoda*, or *Carol Burnett*. "We wanted to communicate that it's OK to live a life that isn't portrayed on *The Bionic Woman*," said Michaels. "No matter what a sketch was about, we wanted to be there to say you're not crazy if you don't feel you fit in." Michaels was content not fitting in, particularly in TV's mainstream. Being on in prime time was not an issue, at least not initially.[10] What mattered to Michaels was that *SNL* "went to the people that wanted us."

*SNL* represented the first attempt since *Laugh-In* designed for the under-30 generation of television-tube babies. The small screen was programmed almost exclusively for grown-ups as Mary Richards and the WJM staff, Carol Burnett, and others were courting chuckles from adults. *SNL* was a grab for mainstream media power by the new generation that grew up on TV, and then "outgrew" it. Critic Tom Shales offered this perspective in the *Washington Post*, November 8, 1975:

NBC's *Saturday Night* can boast the freshest satire on commercial TV, but the show is more than that. It is probably the first network series produced by and for the television generation—those late-war and post-war babies who were the first to have TV as a sitter. They loved it in the '50s, hated it in the '60s, and now they are trying to take it over in the '70s.

Thus, the Baby Boomers had their own *Show of Shows*, or as John Belushi put it, a show for "everybody who is sick of the other things on TV."[11] Michaels characterized *SNL* as a show that played upon the love/hate relationship with popular culture and made television itself the program. In his view, this approach brought back a young audience that had turned cynical toward the medium.

Michaels produced *SNL* for five seasons, exploring directions and boundaries for television and comedy until the show had, in his view, "dwindled to an institution." As *SNL* developed some of the decade's most important comic writers and performers, their humor defined the comedy of the period. To Michaels, his late-night show in itself was a triumph when compared to the rest of television. "When you're trained in the other TV system, it is such exhilaration the simple fact that *Saturday Night Live* existed," said Michaels, "It was a technological miracle because we didn't slip back into being television."

## TV COMEDY IN THE 1980S: NO LAUGHING MATTER

When Michaels left *SNL* in 1980, he explained, "I'd just like to take some time off, watch TV again, get angry about what I'm seeing, and then start thinking about a new show." For someone who took comedy as seriously as Michaels, television offered much to focus on. The entire comedy genre was in the midst of a low cycle. From the comedy-variety shows on the late-night fringe to prime-time's sitcoms, programming was no laughing matter.

For five seasons under Michaels' direction, *SNL* made NBC's peacock proud, not to mention, blush on occasion. The show provided an innovative brand of comedy, developed young talent, and delivered awards and high ratings. NBC soon discovered how dramatically different things were without Michaels and his merry bank of late-night lampooners, most of whom had defected to film. Perhaps in their tunnel vision to the Nielsens, or out of misunderstanding of the longevity of comedy or the significance of a certain producer, NBC allowed the "*SNL* P.M. (Post-Michaels) Era" to begin. What they failed to realize was that the original innovative concept could only work for a relatively short period before it became a cliche of itself, which audiences would grow weary of. Broadcast history reveals that those comedy programs recognized as innovative in their time had relatively short lives, with few lasting longer than five seasons. *Your Show of Shows* ran for four years (1950–54); Ernie Kovacs' gags appeared for two years on two different networks (1952–53 on CBS and 1956 on NBC); the Smothers Brothers' four seasons included stops at all three networks (1967–69 on CBS, 1970 on ABC, and 1975 with NBC); and *Laugh-In* totalled five seasons (1968–73). Even in his five-year tenure, Michaels wondered if he was making the mistake most comics make by "staying on too long."

The innovative work is valued not only for its vision, but for its sheer difference. The two are vitally intertwined in what Walter Benjamin refers to as "aura" of a work of art.[12] That sharp and startling artistic perception embodied in an experimental or innovative form runs counter to the norm, the accepted, the confirming, and conforming. By 1980, *SNL*'s aura had diminished. What began as experimental television had become formula, one primary reason for Michaels leaving the show. After five seasons, few directions remained to explore. Nonetheless, without changing the name to protect the innocent, NBC insisted on milking *SNL* further. The resulting "sequels"—*SNL II, III*, and *IV*, were a comedy of errors, mere ghosts of Michaels's version that slavishly reused his form, but failed to recreate and capture the feel, consciousness, and environment.

Certainly, *SNL* was a tough act to follow; but the "Next Generation" on *SNL* totally misread the secret of the original show's appeal. With each season, the show drifted farther away from its concept and cornerstones.[13] Ingredients and standards from Michaels's original recipe (an ensemble, spontaneity, intelligent writing, and experimentation) were replaced by a star system (Eddie Murphy and Joe Piscopo) and established comics (Billy Crystal), emphasis on make-up, gimmicks like wrestling, and writing that assaulted audiences by determinedly going for the "cheap" and "sure" laughs with sex and drug jokes. The preference for the risqué rather than the risky violated another Michaels principle—no fear of failure. While exploring various boundaries of comedy and television to see where they led or how far they could be extended, Michaels and his troupe were willing to "miss the mark" rather than compromise their artistic mission.

"The problem with the sequels," wrote Ron Rosenbaum, "is that they are *too* ready for prime-time and succeed in capturing the spirit of the Not Ready for Prime-Time Players about as well as the Monkees did the Beatles."[14] Even with the second coming of Michaels as executive producer in the show's eleventh season, the inspired irreverence, talent, and consciousness *SNL* pioneered in the 1970s with such impact was missing.

Perhaps most significant is the point that *SNL* should have ended with Michaels in 1980 and the reincarnations should have never existed. The *SNL* Post-Michaels Era was a result of too many individuals not realizing when it was time to let a good thing die. Too often, *SNL IV*'s Harry Shearer's analogy comparing *SNL* to the "lumbering beast with bullets in every part of its body except the one that can kill it"[15] best described the staggering status of the installments until a notable revival under Michaels most recently (1986–89).

While the *SNL* sequels failed to capture the original *SNL* audience and spirit, a number of other clones, pseudo-spinoffs, and "AM versions"[16] fared just as poorly. Using one show's success as blueprint for others is commonplace in television programming. While inspiring imitations may have been a compliment to Michaels, these shows did little to move television comedy in new directions. Comedy-variety send-ups in the 1980s included ABC's West Coast interpretation of *SNL*, *Friday's*, "Live from Los Angeles"; the short-lived pilot, *Big City Comedy*; and humor magazines, *Road Show* and Dick Clark's *All Kindsa Stuff*. Even the ageless teenager Clark resorted to sex and drug jokes as a hook for his installment. Rosenbaum summed up this series of programs the networks were airing:

In their frenzied search to capture an audience, the networks must conceive us as sex and drug freaks who respond with Pavlovian salivations at every lewd or lude reference; all of these programs have lost sight of the real legacy of *SNL*—a special kind of social history with a comic consciousness that lay in some unexplained territory between Sid Caesar and Firesign Theater.

Emerging as an exception to the gloomy late-night comedy landscape was the even later-night *SCTV Network*, originating from neither Coast, but from "Melonville." The Second Citizens managed to work in the same vein the original *SNL* exploited so well—making fun of television itself. *SCTV*'s versatile ensemble integrated precise impressions with original characterizations as they took the sporadic TV-parody approach one step further by creating the total TV-satire mechanism, presenting an entire "programming day" and its operations from sermonette to sign-off. It may have been an appropriate programming move had NBC flip-flopped *SCTV* with *SNL*, moving the show from beyond the fringe into *SNL*'s 11:30 PM slot.

## THE NEW SHOW: NOT READY FOR PRIME-TIME?

Television comedy's sad state not only plagued the comedy-variety shows of the fringe hours, but prime-time programming as well. By 1984, for the first time in 30 years, no half-hour situation comedies appeared in the top ten rated shows. Only five years earlier, in 1978–79, nine of the top ten shows were comedies. And ten years earlier, viewers were enjoying what Fred Silverman called "The Second Golden Age of Comedy." Saturday nights alone were a gallery of comic masterpieces with *All In The Family, M*A*S*H*, and *The Mary Tyler Moore, Bob Newhart*, and *Carol Burnett* shows. While the 1980s may have been a low cycle for the comedy genre, similar to ones westerns and variety shows faced years earlier, the industry struggled to endure the comedy depression.[17] *Buffalo Bill* producer Dennis Klein's view was not optimistic:

It's as though you can't have an agreed upon laugh anymore. It's like all the conventions of comedy were destroyed, the rules swept away, and there's nothing to take their place. So you look around and all you see is either tired sentimentality or spoofs, this vulture-like feeding off each other because no one has anything to say.[18]

Michaels was among those who believed the old molds had to be broken and the comedy genre needed redefinition and redirection. Comedies from the previous decade broke the molds on issues they focused on and offered personal, socially relevant points of view. The revolution culminated with *SNL*. Ironically, Michaels's creation was a primary force contributing to TV comedy's problems. The late-night lampooners set a standard and made things pariticularly tough on comedy programs because much of what *SNL* did was to satirize the sitcoms set in sanitized, safe family environments with precocious kids cracking jokes and happy endings with a moral. The more self-reflexive television became with shows like *SNL* and *SCTV*, the more difficult the standards became for comedy.

To Michaels, the 1980s situation was not much different than years earlier. Too few comedy creators were willing to make any commitment to programming other than spinoffs, bloopers, and formulas. Michaels also realized that each season viewers grew more sophisticated as they logged thousands of hours in front of their TV sets. They were familiar with comedy's structures, pace, and conventions. It was difficult not to be predictable to audiences as the "aha" occurred to them much earlier in a program. At the same time, competition for viewers and ratings intensified among networks, cable, and independent stations. Networks found it increasingly difficult to justify any experimentation and granted producers little creative autonomy. With hopes of instilling some originality, laughs, and vitality back into TV's comedy, Michaels decided to return to the small screen after a three-year hiatus. "I still want to be on the cutting edge of high risk comedy," said Michaels. "I don't see anybody else fighting for that on television."

This time the circumstances were different and presented an even larger challenge to Michaels and his new creative mission. He was no longer producing for low-key, late-night television, but was about to face the hour of reckoning—prime time.[19]

Michaels emerged with a comedy-variety-musical series for NBC's Friday 10 PM slot. The title for his return show was as modest and unassuming as *SNL*; Michaels's new show was called appropriately, *The New Show (TNS)*. Unlike his live original, Michaels's 1980s' invention was taped before a studio audience on the day prior to its telecast. In addition, Michaels was no longer producing for a loose-limbed ninety minutes, but for a stricter sixty. The public also had bigger expectations for Michaels than ten years earlier. With a success behind him, viewers, critics, and NBC all had high expectations for another innovative show.

NBC may have been the focus of network viewers' laughs and not simply because it frequently occupied the ratings basement. Cellar-dweller status notwithstanding, NBC's lighter action-adventure shows like *The "A" Team, Knight Rider*, and *Riptide* were working rather well at the time. The success of dramas laced with comic elements made it even more difficult for comedies to break into schedules. Audiences also liked the *Candid Camera* peeks at celebrities embarrassing themselves provided by NBC's comedy-reality hybrids along the bloopers, bleeps, blunders, and practical jokes axis. While other networks were hesitant about any new comedy undertakings, NBC was resurrecting Flip Wilson to host another schlockumentary offspring, *People Are Funny*.[20] A more interesting development was former Monkee Michael Nesmith's *TV Parts*, a music video/comedy which wed slapstick gags and parodies with pop-music tracks, while drawing heavily on video imagery and editing techniques. NBC had confidence in Michaels, but at the same time was apprehensive about the early-TV comedy-variety format he planned to use and about how prime time viewers might respond. Could Michaels popularize a 1950s program design in 1984 or was he committing telecide? NBC's apparent willingness to experiment got Michaels a guarantee of thirteen installments of *TNS*. Noting that it took *SNL* almost that many episodes to gel and find itself, Michaels admitted concern over whether NBC would be equally patient in the high stakes, quick-to-cancel video climate of prime time.

The problems, however, did not deter Michaels from holding to his usual approach to producing television. Despite the different circumstances, the familiar Michaels style emerged. *TNS* featured an ensemble, although considerably smaller than *SNL*'s satirical seven. *TNS* "regulars" included *Get Smart* cocreator and popular *SNL* host, Buck Henry; chameleon-like impressionist Dave Thomas from *SCTV*; and Canadian comedienne, Valri Bromfield. Michaels once again targeted his generation by drawing heavily on performers who appealed to the older 25- to 40-year-old segment of the audience. Guest hosts included late-night alums Gilda Radner, Laraine Newman, and *SCTV*'s John Candy and Catherine O'Hara; *Big Chill*ers Jeff Goldblum and Kevin Kline; and old Michaels standbys and stand-ups Steve Martin, Candice Bergen, Penny Marshall, and Paul

Simon. Most *TNS* writers, including head writer Jim Downey, were veterans of the original *SNL*.

The live, exploratory feel as well as the simultaneous homage and critique of entertainment were at work in *TNS*. The inspiration was less anarchistic than that of *SNL*, but instead attempted to capture the domestic spirit of the 1950s variety shows like *Your Show of Shows* and *The Colgate Comedy Hour*. This appreciation of early TV forms was apparent as soon as the opening titles appeared for *TNS*. The graphics danced with domestic emblems of the 1950s (toasters, blenders, and kidney-shaped swimming pools), as well as catchphrases like "smoother" and "modern." The aluminum foil from a TV dinner unwraps into a bold "New." Soon to follow, a flashlight spotlights polaroid-like snapshots of the regulars and special guests as a voice-over announces them over an orchestrated musical score. Formally, the sets, staging, and lighting also combined to create the distinct 1950s feel. The dance numbers and presentations of the musical guests in particular removed viewers from the jump-cut editing and pastels of 1980s TV and took them nostalgically to its earlier years, perhaps rekindling images of *Ed Sullivan Show* performances.

The humor of *TNS* also reflected a changed perspective. To a degree, cultural changes, age itself, and prime time contributed to the softened edges of Michaels's 1984 model. A decade had passed since *SNL*'s premiere. Michaels and his circle of writers and performers were more absorbed into the cultural mainstream. Their view was now much more tolerant and mature than it had been, settling in a middle ground somewhere between *SNL* and *Family Ties*. While certain elements of *TNS* remained welded to the faded premise of *SNL*, the show's humor was dependent upon concepts that courted chuckles of recognition rather than nervous laughter or guffaws. "Time Truck," for example, added peculiar twists to the science fiction/cartoon concept of time traveling. The special effects of a Handi-van swirling and spinning down the halls of time evoked images of mid-1960s TV travelers Tony Newman (James Darren) and Doug Phillips (Robert Golbert) in a similar vertigo in Irwin Allen's creation, *The Time Tunnel*. Whether long sketches like the Orwellian parody, "1984," the playful "Food Repairman," the political "Campaign Trail of Blood," or television targets such as "The Meunsters," a *Dallas* takeoff about a wealthy Wisconsin cheese family or "Walter Cronkite's World of Bloopers," the humor was comparatively benign. The "softening" and ten-year difference between *SNL* and *TNS* were most obvious in the staples of the two shows. Over a decade, *SNL*'s satirical news segment "Weekend Update" evolved into "Weekend Tonight," *TNS*'s restatement of entertainment-magazine shows. Dave Thomas and Buck Henry played the cheery, gee-whiz hosts of an "infotainment" show infatuated with celebrityhood, swirling graphics, and inane charts like "Top Grossing Dives and Hellholes," "Top Five Snarled 8-Track Tapes Found on Roadsides in America," and "Most Common Causes of Injury during Spring Break."

Hovering near last place in the ratings, *TNS* found itself on television's death row waiting for NBC's executioner. Michaels's show became a comic casualty before its full thirteen-week trial. After eleven weeks—nine shows plus two compilations, *The New Improved Show* (week 7) and *The New Show With Extra Added Comedy* (week 11)—NBC bought out the final two installments of the show's contract and designated *TNS*, "The No Show." *TNS*'s failure was a strong contrast to *SNL*'s success. Many factors that contributed to *SNL*'s achievement did not work for Michaels in 1984. The result was a critical and popular disappointment. Was Michaels being punished for committing original sin; or had he simply charted his own course for disaster? Or was *TNS* really as bad as everyone claimed? *TNS*'s dismal showing and demise can partly be attributed to choices Michaels made as the show's producer; but the failure must also be placed in perspective within the structures, demands, and operations of the television industry. This context indicates that while Michaels's new show may not have been quite "ready for prime-time," likewise, prime time was not ready for *TNS*.

*TNS* may have been cursed before it reached the air. Tied to the credibility Michaels earned with his triumph on *SNL* were inevitable expectations and comparisons. NBC's promos for Michaels's encore announcing: "*SNL* creator returns," and "from the producer of the original *SNL*" parallel those annual bold cries from the music industry proclaiming another artist as "the new Bob Dylan." Such hype usually spells failure since few individuals or shows survive such high expectations and the hopes bound to them. NBC had no reason to expect that Michaels could not perform similar comedy miracles with a prime time program. Audiences, too, anticipated *TNS* being a force that might redefine and redirect TV comedy in the 1980s the same way *SNL* had done the previous decade. Even most critics could not avoid comparing *TNS* and *SNL*, claiming there was little "new" about the show.

Most of Michaels's stylistic traits did carry over from *SNL* to *TNS*. No matter in which direction an artist works, he or she holds onto certain techniques, standards, or ploys that emerge as characteristic of his or her work. A closer examination reveals that *TNS*'s domestic flavor, concept, and humor were distinct from *SNL*'s underground quality and sharper satire. With *TNS*, Michaels chose to dig deeper, straddling the fine line between tribute and imitation, and to elevate the roots of TV's early variety shows rather than breed *SNL* verbatim. Ironically, his obsession with generating new ideas and forms cost him with *TNS*. By attempting to take *SNL* one step further and to alter, shape, and modify its structure into a new format, Michaels may have been trying to "perfect perfection." Although it would have violated his personal standards, using *SNL*'s blueprint probably would have been a safer, and more successful, choice.[21]

Using multiple guest hosts rather than one was also a departure from previous formats. While this initially seemed to be a twist that might add a dimension of flexibility, having two or more guest hosts disrupted the show's focus and continuity. The lengthy sketches also affected the show's structure. While the concepts themselves were interesting, clever, and original, their execution resulted in long, drawn out routines which affected the pacing. Comedy shows working at the time were the faster paced humor magazines like *Bloopers*. To the

Flashdance-MTV-video arcade consuming younger audience, extended blackout sketches were not suitable. Viewers' short atttention spans practically demanded that material be instantly funny. Subtle relationships, connections, and references were not prized; viewers required fast food for thought and a joke every few seconds. But Michaels and his writers were from the joke-a-second school of comedy writing. They preferred to deal in accurate parodies, fresh points of view, and subtleties rather than the obvious.

A comedy series commonly needs time to develop and often weeks of on-air fumbling before things crystallize and the show finds its identity. Prime-time's climate was considerably different from late-night in this respect as it did not allow for the "picked at the moment of perfection" approach to programming. Michaels's track record did not necessarily guarantee him more freedom or leverage in negotiating for a number of episodes as he had done with *SNL*. All programs were given thirteen weeks to "prove they belong" and unconventional shows were no exception to the rule.[22] Because of the high stakes and increased competition for viewers, networks could not afford to take risks or grant producers the luxury of longer development time waiting for a concept to find its mark. In NBC's case, while it might have been the late-night leader, the network was lagging in the prime-time sweepstakes. This, of course, did not make the situation any easier for Michaels or *TNS*.[23]

The nature of *TNS*, the audience, and timing never seemed to synchronize. *TNS* did not have the same underground quality of *SNL* and the timing was not appropriate in the mid-1980s. While the writers and performers had matured, so had the audience. The show's pace and humor did not draw in the younger audience and the structure required that viewers recognize conventions from early television. The older audience was prepared for an *SNL* imitation rather than a 1950s tribute. Prime time audiences are also uncomfortable with trial or error and any show that appears unsure of itself.[24] *TNS* may have confused, disoriented, and demanded too much of its viewers. While prime time audiences cried out for new approaches to comedy programming in the 1980s, the failure of unconventional shows such as *Buffalo Bill, Police Squad*, and *TNS* indicated audiences were more comfortable with safe formats than they realized. Old or young, underground or domestic, 1950s or 1980s, *TNS* never cultivated an audience large enough to justify its continuance.

Michaels would have liked more development time but was well aware of the various demands of prime time television. Despite its problems and the production and programming constraints, *TNS* still managed to appear more original than most 1980s comedy programs and Michaels, as a creator, did not substantially compromise his artistic vision.

## TELEVISION AUTHORSHIP: BOAT ROCKERS AND THE SEVEN Cs

The evolution of *SNL* and *TNS* reveal the contrasting environments of television's late-night fringe and prime time and how they affected Lorne Michaels, as well as the creative, comic, and production processes. While the wellspring of unconventionally creative ideas is likely to be an individual, the encouragement of such ideas, their development and implementation are likely to be linked to and nourished by the social, historical, cultural, and organizational contexts in which those individuals exist.

Michaels's case supports the premise that there is potential for personal design or authorship and innovation in an industry that often conventionalizes, inhibits, and ultimately destroys artistic vision. Whether enjoying the fringe benefits of TV's late-night workshop or struggling with the demands of prime time, Michaels's artistic personality emerged in his approach to the comedy-variety format.

The concept of authorship—one individual expressing his or her personal world view and style—is often viewed as a hopelessly romantic notion that ignores history and the material circumstances of production. Still, despite the validity of many of the criticisms of traditional authorship studies, it seems almost impossible to do away with the sense of "signature"—that there truly is an individual creative presence somehow behind the screen, speaking to us through settings, characters, events, and images.

Horace Newcomb and Robert Alley, in *The Producer's Medium*, argue that there is potential for the unique and personal within television.

The creative producer is well aware of the strengths and weaknesses of the tradition and is able to make his own expression distinct within it. Or the producer may be known as the true innovator, one who takes the traditions in new directions or creates new forms that are closely identified with his work alone.[25]

Perhaps the television auteur should not be viewed so much as an author, but as the creative and controlling force—that individual who chooses to exercise control within the collaborative effort. He is not the solitary artist creating, but the interpretive artist who steers the project, and knows his or her artistic goals and what must be done to realize them. In Richard Corliss's description, that individual is "less an architect than a foreman, less a painter than an illustrator, less a composer than a conductor." He or she is the person who must first surround himself with an organization capable of understanding and expressing a similar vision, style, and consciousness. He or she must then be able to simultaneously immerse and detach himself from the work. In doing this, it assures that the original artistic goals will not be lost sight of through the various stages of the production process. Perhaps John Cawelti's definition of auteur is most useful in a television context: "A creator within a framework of conventional structures and commercial imperatives who nonetheless stamps the conventional with his own artistic personality."[26]

At times the act of creating replaces the importance of the object created. Success and failure often do not reveal as much as the process involved and the role of the individual who is the creative and controlling force behind the production. Michaels is one of those individuals who chooses to pursue alternative forms of presentations. In the process, he has shown a degree of courage in his willingness to experiment, explore, and ultimately pay the price many innovators must pay—failure. Call these creators boat-rockers, nonconformists, risk takers, visionaries, innovators, artists, or auteurs, but the clichéd lament is that television could use more of them. As Phil Donahue once said, "These people are the best people for television. They get things done, don't get sucked in, and retain a little piece of their souls." On his journey from the fringe to prime time and back, Michaels has rocked the boat amidst television's Seven Cs—constraint, coping, control, collaboration, commercialism, conformity, and controversy. From the individual creator's point of view, two more Cs—courage and caring— quietly emerge as perhaps the most significant qualities. Individuals must have the courage and also care enough to try to make television something different.

In attempting to put into perspective the impact and success of *SNL* within the vast realm of the television industry and its history, Michaels said "they moved television ahead a quarter of an inch." At times an individual and one show might seem small and insignificant in relation to the industry and its heritage. Yet, individual contributions, no matter how small they appear, are significant. In the final analysis, the individual is a force who can make a difference and have an impact in television. It is his or her small steps, even if they are only a quarater of an inch, that eventually lead to greater strides.

## NOTES

1. As cited by Joseph Turow, "Unconventional Programs on Commercial Television, An Organizational Perspective," in J. S. Ettema and D. C. Whitney, eds., *Individuals in Mass Media Organizations: Creativity and Constraint* (Beverly Hills: Sage, 1982), p. 107.

2. Ibid., p. 108.

3. Turow has formulated six hypotheses about the genesis of unconventional television programs based on literature on innovation. Ibid., p. 110.

4. Unless otherwise indicated, quotes from Lorne Michaels within the text are from personal interviews conducted by the author with Michaels in New York City, 20 November 1984 and 11 April 1985.

5. See David Marc's insightful discussion in *Demographic Vistas* (Philadelphia: University of Pennsylvania Press, 1984), p. 149.

6. Turow, "Unconventional Programs on Commercial Television," p. 108.

7. Several of Michaels's associates suggested during informal interviews with the author that Ebersol's "ego problems" eventually led to strains in his relationship with Michaels. Much of this stemmed from Ebersol's attempt to take credit for being cocreator of *SNL*.

8. Quoted in Tom Burke, "NBC's Saturday Night" *Rolling Stone*, 15 July 1976, p. 36.

9. Michaels quoted in "Flakiest Night of the Week," *Time*, 2 February 1976, p. 72.

10. In 1979, two *Best of SNL* compilations aired in—of all places—prime time. They were so successful that 13 one-hour installments were added.

11. Belushi quoted in John Blumenthal and Lindsay Marcotta, "Playboy Interview: "NBC's *Saturday Night*," *Playboy*, May 1977, p. 88.

12. Walter Benjamin, "The Work of Art in the Age of Mechanical Reproduction," *Illuminations* (New York: Knopf, 1968).

13. *SNL* may have reached its low point in its initial season after Michaels's departure (1980–81) when new cast member, Charles Rocket, uttered the ultimate four-letter-word, something the censors feared since Michaels's first show in 1975. *SNL II* was produced by a former Michaels assistant, Jean Doumanian. Dick Ebersol came down from the executive ranks to take over production in 1981 until 1983.

14. Ron Rosenbaum, "*Saturday Night Dead*, TV's New Formula: Sex + Drugs$^{nth}$ = Bore," *Rolling Stone*, 19 February 1981, p. 12.

15. Shearer quoted in Tome Greene, "A Comic Escape from *SNL*," *USA Today*, 1 August 1985, p. 3D.

16. David Marc, *Demographic Vistas: Television in American Culture* (Philadelphia: University of Pennsylvania Press, 1984), p. 158.

17. Richard Turner, in "The Grave Condition of TV Comedy," *TV Guide*, 21 July 1984, pp. 5–8, provides discussion of TV comedy's problems in the early 1980s. See also Ben Brown, "TV Sitcoms Sad State of Affairs," *USA Today*, 7 March 1984, pp. 1–2D.

18. As cited in Turner, "The Grave Condition of TV Comedy," p. 8.

19. *The New Show* was not Michaels's first appearance in prime time as a writer-producer. In addition to the *Best of SNL* compilations in 1979, Michaels's credits include: *The Beach Boys Special* (NBC, 1976), an Emmy Award-winning *Paul Simon Special* (NBC, 1977), and a Beatles documentary parody, *The Rutles All You Need is Cash* (NBC, 1978). With these specials, Michaels further demonstrated that his abilities were particularly well-suited for the comedy-variety-musical format. Perhaps more than any of his productions, *The Paul Simon Special* might best serve as a shining example of Michaels's artistic personality, philosophy, and approach to creating for televison. For a more extensive discussion of these shows and Michaels's career, see author's Ph.D. diss., "Creativity and the Cutting Edge: The Comic and Artistic Vision of Lorne Michaels and the Production of Unconventional Television," Bowling Green State University, 1985.

20. In 1983, CBS, the number one network, added only one comedy—*After MASH*—in its fall schedule and only three the following year. ABC placed one, plus a spinoff, *Three's a Crowd*. Marc frequently uses the term "schlockumentary" in his text to describe the comedy/reality hybrids. See *Demographic Vistas*, p. 192.

21. *The New Show* began to find its mark by what would be its next-to-last show in the tenth week. By then the sketches appeared tighter, there was one musical guest (The Pretenders) and only one guest host (Teri Garr). The show also had the rhythm and flow Michaels liked. Ironically, this installment came closest to resembling *SNL*.

22. Michaels tried to avoid critical comparisons to *SNL* by bringing his younger performers along gradually ("by the seventh or eighth show.") He admitted that he miscalculated and should have pushed them to the fore as early as possible. "I guess out of cockiness or whatever, I thought I'd have longer to build it," said Michaels. "But in prime-time you have to be a hit by your first show, or you're off the air. We weren't."

23. *The New Show*'s Friday 10 PM slot (opposite *Matt Houston* on ABC and CBS stalwart *Falcon Crest*) also contributed to the show's demise. The time period is a graveyard for most series, particularly one that is new or unconventional. Had *TNS* shown more promise or been granted more developmental time, perhaps a different slot would

have benefited the show. Wednesday night in particular has traditionally been a popular night for variety shows.

24. The more structured one-hour, taped format (rather than ninety minutes live) did not significantly affect *TNS*. Michaels's philosophy remained the same—"comedy minds don't work ahead, they work under the gun." However, days before the premiere, there was still doubt as to what exactly the show was to be. In a personal letter (dated 3 January 1984, three days prior to *TNS*'s premiere) *TNS* videotape editor John Fortenberry wrote to me: "I cannot begin to describe the confusion. I haven't been home in two days and probably won't for another two. . . . " During a later interview with Fortenberry in New York (19 November 1984), he felt the failure of the show in part could be attributed to Michaels's "picked at the moment of perfection" approach. "What Lorne tried to do was get the best of both live and taped TV," said Fortenberry. "Unfortunately, the result was that we got the worst of both in the process."

25. Horace Newcomb and Robert S. Alley, *The Producer's Medium, Conversations with Creators of American TV* (New York: Oxford, 1983), p. xiii.

26. John Cawelti, "An Aesthetic of Popular Culture," *Journal of Popular Culture* 2, Fall 1971, p. 264.

# Selected Bibliography

Alvarado, Manuel, and Edward Buscombe. *Hazell: The Making of a Television Series*. London: The British Film Institute, 1978.

Becker, Howard. *Art Worlds*. Berkeley, CA: The University of California Press, 1982.

Cantor, Muriel. *The Hollywood TV Producer: His Work and His Audience*. New York: Basic Books, 1971.

Caughie, John, ed. *Theories of Authorship: A Reader*. London: Routledge and Kegan Paul, 1981.

Elliott, Philip. *The Making of a Television Series*. London: Constable, 1972.

Ellis, John. *Visible Fictions—Cinema: Television: Video*. London: Routledge and Kegan Paul, 1981.

Feuer, Jane, Paul Kerr, and Tise Vahimagi, eds. *MTM—"Quality Television."* London: The British Film Institute, 1984.

Gitlin, Todd. *Inside Prime Time*. New York: Pantheon, 1983.

Levinson, Richard, and William Link. *Off Camera*. New York: New American Library, 1986.

Marc, David. *Demographic Vistas*. Philadelphia: The University of Pennsylvania Press, 1984.

———. "TV Auteurism," in *American Film*. November 1981, pp. 52–81.

Newcomb, Horace, and Robert Alley. *The Producer's Medium*. New York: Oxford University Press, 1983.

Perry, Jeb. *Universal Television: The Studio and Its Programs, 1950–1980*. Metuchen, NJ: The Scarecrow Press, 1983.

Ravage, John. *Television: The Director's Viewpoint*. Boulder, CO: Westview Press, 1978.

Sarris, Andrew. *The American Cinema: Directors and Directions 1929–1968*. New York: E. P. Dutton, 1968.

Thompson, Robert J. *Adventures on Prime Time: The Television Programs of Stephen J. Cannell*. New York: Praeger, 1990.

Tulloch, John, and Manuel Alvarado. *Dr. Who: The Unfolding Text*. New York: St. Martin's Press, 1978.

Wicking, Christopher, and Tise Vahimagi. *The American Vein: Directors and Directions in Television*. New York: E. P. Dutton, 1979.

Wooley, Lynn, Robert Malsbary, and Robert G. Strange, Jr. *Warner Brothers Television*. Jefferson, NC: McFarland and Co., 1985.

# Index

# About the Editors and Contributors

GARY BURNS is an associate professor of Communication Studies at Northern Illinois University.

ROBERT J. THOMPSON is an associate professor of Communication Studies at The State University of New York at Cortland.

CHRISTOPHER ANDERSON is an assistant professor in Telecommunications at Indiana University.

DAVID BARKER is in the Department of Radio-Television-Film at Texas Christian University.

SUSAN BOYD-BOWMAN is a lecturer in film and television at the University of Bristol.

RICHARD CAMPBELL is an assistant professor of Communication at the University of Michigan.

RONALD J. COMPESI is professor and chair of the Department of Broadcast Communication Arts at San Francisco State University.

DAVID MARC is at the Annenberg School of Communications at the University of Southern California.

JOE MOOREHOUSE is in the Department of Communication at the University of Michigan.

HORACE M. NEWCOMB is a professor of Radio-Television-Film at the University of Texas at Austin.

GEORGE M. PLASKETES is an assistant professor of Communication at Auburn University.

JIMMIE L. REEVES is an assistant professor of Communication at the University of Michigan.

CATHY A. SANDEEN is in the Department of Broadcast Communication Arts at San Francisco State University.

THOMAS SCHATZ is a professor of Radio-Television-Film at the University of Texas at Austin.

JONATHAN DAVID TANKEL is an associate professor in the R.H. Park School of Communications at Ithaca College.

BERNARD TIMBERG is an assistant professor in the Department of Theater Arts and Speech at Rutgers University in Newark.

TONY WILLIAMS is an assistant professor in the Department of Cinema and Photography at Southern Illinois University.